AF898123

Prior Praise for Michael Wildes' *Safe Haven in America*

I thank Michael Wildes for his counsel in reviewing my own path to the American Dream, for his knowledge and professional dedication, not to mention his warmth and concern. He has shown himself to be a scholar in this field.

~ *Melania Trump, First Lady of the United States*

Only once does the Hebrew Bible command us to love our neighbor. Yet thirty-six times, it commands us to love the stranger. A neighbor is one we love because he or she is like us. A stranger is one we are taught to love precisely because he or she is not like us. Throughout this fascinating book, Michael shows his love for the "stranger" and his passion for opening the doors of America to the world.

~ *Rabbi Lord Jonathan Sacks, Chief Rabbi, United Kingdom*

I appreciate Leon Wildes and his son Michael from when they handled my friend John Lennon's green card, right up to Michael's handling of my very own visa. Their legend as champions of international immigration is well-deserved.

~ *Pele, soccer legend/icon*

Praise for *From Origin to Opportunity*

During some of the hardest times of my life, when hope felt far away, Michael Wildes stood beside me and my family. His kindness and determination made it possible for us to start a new life in safety. From Origin to Opportunity *is filled with the same heart and humanity I have seen in him firsthand, and it reminds me that there are still people in this world who will fight for what's right, no matter what the cost.*

~ *Mohammad Gulab, protagonist in* Lone Survivor *film, saved U.S. Navy SEAL*

In my darkest hour, after surviving captivity and unimaginable loss, Michael Wildes extended his hand to help me rebuild my life with dignity. He guided me with compassion and gave me the strength to carry my story forward so that others might hear the truth and hold on to hope. From Origin to Opportunity *reflects the same humanity and courage that he showed me. It is a book about the evolution of immigration law, yes, but it is also about the people who stand with us when everything else has been taken away.*

~ Andrei Kozlov, Russian-Israeli former hostage

Michael Wildes has a gift for making something very complex and difficult feel human and approachable. When I needed help, he was there with warmth and remarkable skill. I see that same spirit reflected in From Origin to Opportunity. *It's a brilliant reminder that immigration is not only about law, but also about dreams . . . and finding a place to belong.*

~ Boy George, musician/performer

Michael Wildes embodies what it means to serve, with vision and an extraordinary commitment to people. As mayor of Englewood for five terms, he has worked tirelessly to strengthen his community for many years. From Origin to Opportunity *reflects the same dedication I've seen in his public service: a belief that every individual deserves dignity and a chance at a brighter future.*

~ Phil Murphy, New Jersey Governor 2018–2026

From Origin to Opportunity

UNLOCKING U.S. IMMIGRATION LAW

MICHAEL WILDES

FOREWORD BY GERALDO RIVERA

INTRODUCTION BY JOSHUA WILDES

AMERICANBARASSOCIATION

Cover design by Elizabeth Kulak/ABA Design

Printed in the United States of America.

30 29 28 27 26   5 4 3 2 1

ISBN 978-1-63905-696-5

A catalog record for this book is available from the Library of Congress.

For my grandparents Hilde and Max Schoenwalter and Sarah and Harry Wildes, who came to America through Ellis Island carrying little more than determination and dreams for future generations.

For my parents, Ruth and Leon Wildes, whose love, guidance, and example shaped my life in countless ways.

For my wife, Amy, my partner in every sense of the word.

For our children and their spouses—Raquel and Aryeh, Josh and Vicky, Lauren Ruth and Joseph, and Jaclyn and Jake—and for our grandchildren, Abigail Bailey, Evie Rose, Romi Adar, Charlie Irving, Jordan Abraham, Leila Ruthie, Lielle Nova, Livia Hannah, Sadie Lennon, and Reyna Charlotte—may you always cherish the extraordinary legacy of those who came before you.

Filming of author on Ellis Island (Fox News, 2021)

Wildes family 2026

CONTENTS

FOREWORD

For decades, I've been on the front lines, chasing stories, confronting truths, and igniting important conversations at the dinner table. And few issues have roused more debate, controversy, and raw emotion than immigration. It's the story of America. A nation of immigrants, built by waves of dreamers, innovators, and those seeking a better path.

Who can come to America? Who can stay? The policies that dictate the answers to those simple questions, and the motivations behind them, can take erratic turns spurred by politics and public opinion. The consequences are life altering.

In this deeply divided moment, we need clear-eyed, principled voices who not only understand the law but also grasp the human heart of the matter. Now, my good friend Michael Wildes—a man who comprehends the labyrinthine world of immigration law better than anyone I know—has penned a vital work. This isn't just a dry legal text. This is a deep dive into the fabric of who we are, seen through the lens of those who seek to join us.

From the desperate faces at the border to the vibrant communities that new arrivals build, I've heard the arguments, the fears, the hopes. It's never simple. There are no easy answers. But what Michael does, brilliantly, in this book is to lay out the complexities, to explain the legal frameworks, and most importantly, to remind us of the human stories at the heart of it all. I've known Michael for years—as a trusted legal mind, a long-serving mayor, and the son of Leon Wildes, the legendary immigration attorney who fought the Nixon administration to defend John Lennon and Yoko Ono from politically motivated and unjust deportation. Immigration is in his blood, not only professionally but also morally.

Michael practices justice. He's fought for the rights of the vulnerable, navigated the treacherous waters of bureaucracy to help bring tremendous talent to benefit America, and stood up for what's right, time and again. His insights are born not just from legal precedent, but from countless hours spent with real people, facing real challenges, who aspire to be a part of what makes our nation so great.

With empathy and expertise, he has represented everyone from global celebrities and business leaders to refugees fleeing war and persecution. His clients are as diverse as America itself. Yet he brings to each case, regardless of status, the same conviction: that every individual deserves dignity, due process, and a fair chance at the American dream.

In these pages, you'll find clarity amidst the chaos. You'll gain a deeper understanding of the laws that govern who comes here, how they come, and what their journey entails. But more than that, you'll be challenged to think and, perhaps, to reevaluate your own perspectives on an issue that defines our past, shapes our present, and will undoubtedly determine our future.

This book is a call to conscience. Michael takes us beyond courtrooms and policy debates and into the real lives of immigrants, showing us the system's potential and its profound shortcomings. He does not shy away from the hard truths, nor does he offer easy answers.

Whether you are a student, an advocate, an immigrant, or just seeking to better understand this constant and complex issue in our world, this book is essential reading for anyone who wants to move beyond the soundbites and the political rhetoric. It's for those who truly want to understand the intricate dance between law, humanity, and the impact our words, actions, and ethics have on the real lives of Americans and those who aspire to be.

—Geraldo Rivera, Manhattan, New York

Photo taken at Leon Wildes' bookwarming for *John Lennon vs. the U.S.A.* at Cardozo Law School. Geraldo first interviewed Leon during the historic John Lennon case and has been a valued friend and supporter of the firm ever since.

(Photo courtesy of the Wildes family archive.)

PREFACE

In 2018, the American Bar Association published my first book, *Safe Haven in America*. For me, it was an opportunity to share the extraordinary stories of my clients, from defecting KGB agents to victims of international kidnapping cases. For those individuals involved, and countless others in similar circumstances, these narratives served as a poignant illustration of the serious flaws that continue to impede the success of our immigration system. They also set the stage for my latest work, *From Origin to Opportunity*, in which I seek to unravel the hows and whys of the problems impacting those on all sides of the immigration debate, and find the common ground necessary to begin solving them.

To understand how we got here, we must travel back in time to the birth of immigration law in this country. *From Origin to Opportunity* provides a deep exploration of immigration law, tracing its evolution from inception to the present day. Beginning with the earliest immigration laws of the 1700s, with their highly exclusionary and racist provisions, the history of immigration law has profoundly shaped the politics, ideologies, and demographics of our nation. Fortunately, as our society's perspectives on human rights have evolved, so too have our immigration policies. Whether we have appropriately kept pace is an ongoing study this text will examine. Continuing that evolution is a challenge that will fall upon future policymakers to uphold.

We are living in a time marked by political divisions, terrorist threats, and continued racial injustice, yet when we take a step back and consider the entirety of immigration law history, it becomes evident that significant progress has been made in our approach to creating policies and laws, particularly over the past century. Much of our progress in recent years seems to follow a "two-steps-forward, one-step-back" trajectory, but it instills hope, nonetheless. There is, however, much work to be done, which will only compound over time if not properly addressed.

Immigration laws have always been shaped by public opinion, but that opinion has changed dramatically over the past 100 years. This shift in opinion was most pronounced in the period following the Holocaust. With its horrific revelation of systematic genocide and human rights abuses, the Holocaust had a powerful effect on many Americans and their view of social justice issues, particularly in the context of immigration. The Holocaust served as a grim example of the consequences of isolationism and indifference to global affairs.

The United States began to understand that it needed to play a more active role in preventing such atrocities and promoting international human rights, which ultimately led to a move away from isolationism. The realization that global security and morality were interconnected played a pivotal role in shaping the nation's post-war foreign policy, and in the developing identity of America as an icon of liberty and inclusivity within the global community.

This era also brought forth a surge of activism across multiple fronts—battling racial injustice, combating anti-Semitism, championing women's rights, and advocating for the rights of individuals escaping violence and persecution in their home countries. Americans, who had been insulated from much of the war's devastation, were deeply moved by the stories and images of displaced individuals. In response, many took action by advocating for the admission of Holocaust survivors as refugees, though it would take a few years for any significant action to occur.

In 1948, the United States passed the Displaced Persons Act of 1948,[1] which aimed to address the needs of refugees and survivors of the Holocaust, among others displaced by war, persecution, or other severe factors. This act represented a significant effort to provide humanitarian assistance to those in need, despite shortcomings which demonstrated the continued challenges of addressing a crisis of such magnitude.

Primarily focused on admission to the United States, the act failed to address the broader issues of rehabilitation and repatriation for Jewish refugees, or to acknowledge the particular horrors and trauma they had experienced. Despite these serious flaws, the establishment of the Displaced Persons Act was a major turning point in the nation's immigration policies.

In many ways, the act marked a significant departure from restrictive immigration policies, reflecting the growing recognition of the United States's role in addressing global humanitarian crises. By prioritizing people affected by the devastation of World War II and similar circumstances, the Displaced Persons Act signaled a shift toward a more compassionate and responsive approach, even if limited in scope.

This legislation also laid the groundwork for future policies that would address refugee crises and human rights issues on a broader scale.

1. Pub. L. No. 80-774, 62 Stat. 1009 (June 25, 1948).

It highlighted the moral and ethical imperative of offering refuge to those fleeing persecution, a concept that would later influence the development of asylum laws and refugee resettlement programs in the United States. Although imperfect, the act served as a precursor to more comprehensive measures, such as the Refugee Act of 1980,[2] which formally aligned U.S. immigration policies with international standards.

The Holocaust further led to a growing acknowledgment of the need for anti-discrimination and hate crime policy initiatives. The United Nations' Universal Declaration of Human Rights, while not a law itself, established a global framework for protecting individuals from discrimination and hate, and this sentiment was codified in legislation such as the U.S. Civil Rights Act of 1964.[3] In the years leading up to the Holocaust and in the years following, organizations like the Anti-Defamation League and the Southern Poverty Law Center were founded to combat bigotry, racism, and discrimination. Human rights organizations such as Amnesty International were created to advocate for the rights of individuals worldwide. These organizations played a critical role in shaping public opinion about social justice, sparking calls for the reevaluation of immigration policies in the United States. The overwhelming sense was that the country needed to be more compassionate and open to those fleeing violence and persecution in their home countries.

In this way, the post-Holocaust period helped birth the Civil Rights Movement in the United States. The fight for racial equality and against segregation was, in many ways, an extension of the broader conversation about justice. Activists like Rosa Parks and Martin Luther King Jr. put their lives on the line to fight for civil rights, and the movement's influence on American society reverberated well beyond racial issues.

When we compare the inclusive policies that came out of the Civil Rights Movement to the extreme "free white persons" provisions of the Naturalization Act of 1790,[4] it's easy to see how far we've come in amending our definitions of concepts such as "liberty and justice for all." But, as with many aspects of life, the most insidious problems usually reside in the subtleties. Just as "subtle racism" is often harder to identify and combat than blatantly racist acts, so too are the problems within our current immigration system.

2. Pub. L. No. 96-212, 94 Stat. 102 (Mar. 17, 1980).

3. Pub. L. No. 88-352, 78 Stat. 241 (July 2, 1964).

4. U.S. Congress, An Act to Establish an Uniform Rule of Naturalization, 1st Cong., 2nd sess. (Mar. 26, 1790), in Statutes at Large, vol. 1, 103.

These subliminal factors can be difficult even for historians and legal scholars to track. When it comes to the broader public, these "less sexy" aspects of the immigration debate often go unnoticed. As we have acknowledged the role of public opinion on immigration policy, we have to consider what gaps in policy are coming to pass as a result of this growing information gap.

For instance, the lengthy and complex bureaucratic processes within the immigration system disproportionately affect marginalized communities, making it much harder for them to navigate the system and attain legal status. Those with the least access to the knowledge and resources to navigate these complex systems are often the ones who need them the most. And inconsistent enforcement practices can lead to racial profiling and unjust deportations, which may not always make headlines, but have profound, life-altering effects on individuals and families.

These problems stem from a variety of sources. Visa quotas and categories can unintentionally favor immigrants from certain countries while placing undue burdens on others. Employment-based immigration systems can perpetuate wage disparities and exploitation, particularly in industries that rely on immigrant labor. These major problems within the immigration system often go unnoticed by the broader public, but contribute to systemic inequalities and injustices that persist in today's society. Worst of all is when these complex issues are packaged as political propaganda, ignoring their real-world impact in favor of eliciting an emotional response for campaign or publicity purposes. Recognizing and addressing these nuanced issues in an honest context is an essential step toward creating a more equitable and inclusive immigration system.

I wrote *From Origin to Opportunity* with law students and new lawyers in mind, but anyone interested in the inner workings of immigration law and the quest for a more equitable and efficient system should find value in its pages. My mission is to provide a comprehensive study of immigration law, exploring its historical context, the motivations underlying its policies, and the consequences of those policies. By acknowledging the legitimate concerns and apprehensions fueling the immigration debate, while also recognizing the immeasurable contributions of immigrants, I hope to foster a balanced dialogue and facilitate constructive solutions.

This book serves as a resource for individuals on all sides of the immigration debate, extending insights, legal knowledge, and historical context to cultivate a more holistic understanding of this age-old issue. It places a significant emphasis on the history of immigration law, as a comprehensive resolution of systemic problems necessitates an understanding of their roots and our subsequent responses throughout history. After all, we know what happens when we fail to learn from history.

For those advocating stricter immigration policies, their concerns revolve around national security, economic competition, and the preservation of cultural cohesion. Conversely, proponents of more open and compassionate immigration policies emphasize the contributions of immigrants to the nation's prosperity, underlining that the United States is fundamentally a nation forged by immigrants. It is imperative to acknowledge that both sides make valid points, and even so exist only as a broad dichotomy within countless layers of highly complex policy and opinion.

My goal is to explore both perspectives and identify opportunities for cooperative and constructive growth. Together, we will explore strategies for improving the laws, regulations, and policies that govern the lives of countless individuals who have aspired to, and continue to aspire to, lead better lives in America, all while ensuring the prosperity, security, and overall well-being of our nation.

To truly make this book come to life, several chapters close with an interview featuring one of my clients. Whether it's Martha's heart-wrenching story of losing her husband in the Jersey City terrorist attacks, after he saved the lives of countless others, or the suffering Eric Dai has endured since becoming a national hero, their stories vividly depict the extremes of the immigrant experience. Sadly, these "extremes" are shockingly common.

These personal accounts, showcasing how an individual's life can be wholly contingent on an administrative or bureaucratic decision, serve as the most compelling means to illustrate the urgent need for a comprehensive overhaul of our immigration system. These are real-world manifestations of the immigration system of the United States of America.

Developments Under the Second Trump Administration

The changes that were taking place while this book was in preparation unfolded at an extraordinarily accelerated pace, and I would be remiss not to address these significant and unprecedented developments. When I began this project, the country was still under the Biden administration. As I completed the final chapters in late 2025, the second Trump administration had moved aggressively to reshape U.S. immigration law and enforcement—primarily through executive action and budgetary policy rather than comprehensive legislation.

Rather than sifting through each section of the manuscript attempting to integrate developments that continue to shift on an almost daily basis, I chose to expand on Chapter 3, "Immigration Today," adding a section devoted solely to the recent developments under the second Trump administration. This approach preserves the historical integrity of the book as originally written, grounded in hundreds of hours of research spanning more than 250 years of immigration history. While President Trump may indeed be rewriting immigration policy, that does not mean he gets to rewrite this book. His actions over the past ten months warrant their own section—not only so readers can fully grasp the ease with which policy can affect people's lives almost overnight, but also to give voice to the hundreds of thousands of individuals directly affected by these dramatic shifts, many in devastating ways.

Having been in this field as long as I have, I know that while this moment is extraordinarily challenging and will undoubtedly cause lasting, and in some cases irreparable, harm to countless individuals and families, it is still a moment that will pass. It deserves its own chapter, but it does not, in my view, belong interwoven into the historical arc that precedes it in a way that blurs or reshapes the history already told.

We remain a nation of compassion, tolerance, and opportunity—a country that has long welcomed people from every race, religion, and country of origin. This dark period has cast a long shadow, but storms do pass, and I believe we will emerge stronger for having weathered it.

INTRODUCTION

On January 2, 2025, I had the privilege and honor of swearing in my father, Michael Wildes, for his fifth term as mayor of Englewood, New Jersey. Standing beside him, I couldn't help but think of the remarkable individuals who had done the same in years past—governors, dignitaries, even Kweku Mandela, the grandson of Nelson Mandela. To join that legacy, not as a politician or public figure, but simply as a son, was one of the most humbling moments of my life. It was a reminder that behind every title he holds, my father remains grounded not only in his fierce devotion to justice, but also in his commitment to his family.

I was still in high school when I first sat in on one of my father's lectures. He was teaching business immigration law at the Benjamin N. Cardozo School of Law—the same school where he had once met my mother, where I would later enroll as a student, and where, year after year, his students walked away not only with a clearer understanding of visa categories and court decisions, but also with a deeper sense of what it means to advocate for someone's right to belong.

That day, watching him speak with such conviction, I felt a sense of awe I hadn't fully understood as a child. To me, he had always just been Dad—the one who came home late from council meetings, who answered every call no matter where he was or whom he was with, who insisted we make room at our Sabbath table for those with nowhere else to go. But in that classroom, I saw what so many others had long recognized: that Michael Wildes was not just a lawyer or a public servant. He was—and still is—a bridge between people and possibility.

My father inherited this work from his father, Leon Wildes, whose name still echoes in immigration law classrooms and courtrooms across the country. The same firm my grandfather founded—now led by my father and where I am fortunate to work—was built on a simple but powerful idea: that America should live up to its promise, and that lawyers have a duty to hold that promise accountable. My grandfather gave voice to that mission in landmark cases, most famously when he represented John Lennon.

My father has carried it forward, advocating for refugees, whistleblowers, children separated from their parents, and some of the most recognizable names in the world. But what has always struck me most is that he treats every client—famous or not—with the same dignity, patience, and passion.

His career has encompassed public service and federal law enforcement, immigration advocacy and elected office. As a young man, he served as an NYPD auxiliary police officer, walking the streets of New York in full uniform for nearly ten years, including during high school and college. Later, as a Special Assistant U.S. Attorney in Brooklyn, he worked on cases tied to national security and testified before Congress in support of anti-terrorism legislation. His voice carried weight then, as it does now—not because it was loud, but because it was grounded in integrity and awareness.

When he entered local politics in Englewood, New Jersey—first as a city councilman, then as a two-term mayor, and now once again as mayor—he brought that same spirit of advocacy to public life. His constituents knew they had a leader who wouldn't just shake hands but would roll up his sleeves. He showed up for the community not just at press conferences, but in emergency rooms, courtrooms, and council chambers—wherever his presence could make a difference.

Growing up, I saw firsthand both the toll and the reward of this work. I watched my father stay up late drafting legal briefs while juggling the demands of city politics. I remember the nights when police stood guard outside our home after threats from terrorist organizations—threats that came as he worked to help someone escape them. I saw him, licensed to carry a firearm, travel across the country to guide families through the darkest moments of their lives—walking beside them with steady hands, an open heart, and the trust of serious law enforcement agents. And through it all, I saw how deeply he believed in the law—not as a tool of power, but as a pathway to fairness.

I'll never forget the time when my younger sister, Jaclyn, then just a little girl, said to my father as he walked through the door after work, "Daddy, take your shoes off." Puzzled, he asked her why. She answered, "Because if you don't have shoes on, you can't run for mayor again—and other people need you so much when you're mayor." It was one of those moments that said so much in so few words. Even at her young age, she understood the sacrifices our family made—and she just wanted a little more time with her dad. That memory stays with me as a reminder that true public service often carries unseen costs.

I spent many years at the firm in various roles before joining the Department of Justice after law school. When I returned in 2021 as an attorney, it felt like stepping into something sacred. Not because the firm bears our family's name, but because it carries our family's values. My father never pressured me to follow in his footsteps. Instead, he showed me the meaning of the work through his actions—through his devotion to his clients, his reverence for his father, and his belief that the law is at its best when used in service of others.

This book, *From Origin to Opportunity*, is more than a historical account. It is a guidebook for future lawyers, a call to conscience for policymakers, and a reminder to all of us that immigration is not just policy—it's people. My father traces the evolution of immigration law not only through statutes and case law, but also through the lived experiences of those who dreamed of a better life—and those who helped make that dream a reality.

I am proud to stand beside him—not only as his son, but also as his colleague. And I am deeply grateful that he has poured a lifetime of wisdom, experience, and heart into these pages.

To those just beginning their journey in immigration law—you are needed. The road ahead is not easy, but it is deeply worthy. And you could not ask for a better guide than Michael Wildes, a legend I am proud to call Dad.

—Joshua Wildes, Manhattan, New York, August 2025

Three generations of the Wildes family—Leon, Michael, and Joshua Wildes—photographed at the family's law offices at 515 Madison Avenue, where the firm has remained since Leon Wildes founded it in 1960. The photo was taken shortly after Joshua joined the practice.

CHAPTER 1

The Genesis of Immigration Law

As the 19th century dawned, the nation was still in its infancy, but its growing pains were dramatically shaping the contours of immigration law. The evolution of immigration law in this country has been characterized by an interplay of opportunities, discriminatory practices, and changing perspectives on who is "other," and who is allowed to become an American.

The earliest immigration policies in the United States were characterized by a focus on certain European immigrants. This preference for those from Europe owed much to the demographics of the country's initial settlers, predominantly of European descent. The laws greatly reflected an inclination to continue this trend and facilitate the arrival of more immigrants from the same continent first and foremost, although with preferences for and against those of certain nations, religions, or other factors.

The Naturalization Act of 1790,[1] among the earliest federal immigration laws, played a pivotal role in setting the tone for the nation's immigration policies. It established the criteria for acquiring U.S. citizenship, allowing only "free white persons" to become naturalized citizens, a reflection of the deeply rooted biases of the time, excluding non-white immigrants from the path to citizenship. While such extreme racial bias is deeply troubling to us today, it was very much in line with the prevailing attitudes of the late 18th century, as the country grappled with complex issues surrounding race, slavery, and societal hierarchies. It leads us to wonder if some common consensus of today's society might be similarly eschewed by future generations.

1. U.S. Congress, An Act to Establish an Uniform Rule of Naturalization, 1st Cong., 2nd sess. (Mar. 26, 1790), in Statutes at Large, vol. 1, 103.

Beyond considerations of race, early immigration policies were imbued with substantial economic motivations. Immigrants were viewed as invaluable contributors to the young nation's growth and development. They filled labor gaps across sectors, including agriculture, mining, and construction, and played an important role in propelling the westward expansion. For most Americans, the correlation between immigrants and the nation's flourishing economy was abundantly clear, but for many of those immigrants and their families, their place in American society as more than economic tools was far more ambiguous.

The waves of European immigration that followed the 19th century were further influenced by various push-and-pull factors, including political instability, economic hardships, and the promise of better opportunities in America. This led to a significant influx of immigrants from countries such as Ireland, Italy, and Germany, which had not been major players in the initial waves of immigration from which the bulk of the American population had grown.

Influence of Social, Economic, and Political Factors

The development of immigration law has always been intimately connected to the social, economic, and political circumstances of the day. During the late 18th century and the 19th century, the United States underwent a profound economic transformation from its early days as an agrarian society to becoming an industrial powerhouse. This shift, known as the "Industrial Revolution," was characterized by the rapid growth of urban centers, the development of manufacturing, and the expansion of railroads. Immigrants were not just seen as a valuable source of labor, but as an indispensable driving force behind the country's economic growth.

As the United States expanded westward, there was a pressing need for a more comprehensive approach to immigration. The doctrine of "Manifest Destiny," which encapsulated the belief in American expansion from coast to coast, spurred a massive westward migration. In the mid-19th century, this westward expansion brought with it a surge of pioneers, miners, and settlers. The tracks of the transcontinental railways and the floors of countless factories and mines, absorbing unimaginable amounts of blood, sweat, and tears, bore witness to the indomitable spirit and invaluable contributions of immigrant laborers. The country's borders expanded, and immigration patterns shifted, demanding new immigration policies to manage the influx of newcomers.

These "newcomers" were primarily comprised of Chinese immigrants, who worked under grueling conditions on the Central Pacific Railroad; Irish immigrants, many of whom fled famine and economic hardship in their homeland; and German immigrants, who often took up work in farming, skilled trades, and factories. Mexican laborers also played a significant role, especially in regions that had recently become part of the United States following the Mexican-American War. And free African Americans migrated westward in search of new opportunities.

Several major historical events also deeply influenced our nation's immigration policies. U.S. involvement in both World War I and World War II had a particularly significant impact. During these global conflicts, immigration restrictions were temporarily relaxed to address labor shortages. In World War I, this was exemplified by the Immigration Act of 1917, which allowed for the entry of workers from Mexico and other countries to meet wartime labor needs. In World War II, the Bracero Program, initiated in 1942, facilitated the temporary employment of millions of Mexican agricultural laborers to support the war effort.

These wartime labor programs underscored the instrumental role immigrants played in bolstering the U.S. workforce during times of crisis, but the laws surrounding them were filled with restrictive, nativist policies, and they left the door wide open for exploitation and mistreatment of immigrant communities. This incongruous treatment contingent on times of need would become a common theme throughout the development of U.S. immigration policy.

In this section, you will be introduced to some of history's most influential immigration policies, from the Naturalization Act of 1790, and its notably exclusionary provisions, to the contemporary constructs of the Diversity Visa Program (a.k.a. the visa lottery). These earlier policies are not mere antiquities of legislation—they are reflections of the ideas, beliefs, and values that have shaped and reshaped the American identity. To grasp the full scope of their impact is to comprehend the undercurrents that have carried the United States through its unfolding narrative.

The Naturalization Act of 1790

The Naturalization Act of 1790 was one of the earliest laws passed by the U.S. Congress to establish rules and procedures for the naturalization of immigrants. It was the first federal law that provided guidelines for the process of granting U.S. citizenship.

The act's defining criterion for naturalization was the requirement that applicants be "free white persons." This racial prerequisite restricted citizenship to individuals of European descent, excluding those from other racial backgrounds. It explicitly excluded Native Americans, enslaved African Americans, and other non-white populations from the naturalization process. The act's racist policies reflected the attitudes of the late 18th century when slavery was widespread, and Native American communities faced forced removal from their ancestral lands.

The 1790 act stipulated a minimum residency of two years in the United States before an immigrant could apply for citizenship. This requirement, though seemingly liberal in retrospect, formed a precedent against which subsequent naturalization laws would be measured. Furthermore, immigrants seeking citizenship under the act were required to take an oath of allegiance to the United States. This oath, laden with significance, compelled them to renounce any previous allegiances to foreign rulers or nations, emphasizing the importance of loyalty to the newly formed American government.

The law was later replaced by the Naturalization Act of 1795,[2] which extended the residency requirement to five years and introduced other changes to the naturalization process. These changes included both administrative and procedural updates aimed at reinforcing the seriousness of citizenship and ensuring that applicants were adequately integrated into American society. Administratively, the 1795 act required immigrants to file a "declaration of intent" at least three years prior to their application for citizenship, signaling their commitment to becoming U.S. citizens. Procedurally, it mandated that applicants provide evidence of good moral character, typically through affidavits from witnesses, adding an additional layer of scrutiny to the process. These measures reflected a growing concern with

2. Naturalization Act of January 29, 1795, ch. 20, 1 Stat. 414.

national identity and security in the early years of the Republic while laying the groundwork for future refinements in U.S. naturalization laws.

The subsequent Naturalization Act of 1802[3] further refined the process by standardizing the requirements for citizenship and simplifying some of the administrative procedures. In addition to reinforcing the five-year residency requirement and maintaining the need for a "declaration of intent," it also introduced a system of registration for arriving immigrants, aiming to create a record of those who intended to seek citizenship.

These early laws set the stage for the development of U.S. immigration and naturalization policies by establishing core principles such as residency requirements, allegiance to the nation, and moral character assessments. They also reflected the nation's balancing act between maintaining an inclusive pathway to citizenship and safeguarding its political and social stability.

Over time, the United States would grapple with complex issues surrounding race, immigration, and the ever-cherished status of citizenship. These struggles would ultimately pave the path toward the development of more inclusive and non-discriminatory policies. But, as with many major societal transformations, its relative progress would rise and fall over time based on the surrounding circumstances of the day.

The Chinese Exclusion Act of 1882

Our nation's immigration policies were also heavily influenced by the dominant political ideologies of the time. An illustrative chapter in this saga unfolds with the Chinese Exclusion Act of 1882,[4] which prohibited Chinese laborers from entering the United States. It was in many ways a response to the economic concerns of American workers who feared job competition from Chinese immigrants, who had come to the United States in significant numbers during the mid-1800s. These apprehensions were mixed with deeply ingrained racial prejudices that were widespread during that era. Chinese laborers played an integral role in the construction of the Transcontinental Railroad, which helped shape the physical and economic landscape of the American west, and were also pioneers of collective labor actions for

3. Naturalization Act of April 14, 1802, ch. 28, 2 Stat. 153.
4. Ch. 126, 22 Stat. 58 (May 6, 1882).

wage equity and workplace conditions. Nonetheless, when the job at hand was completed, their reward was not open arms with recognition of their contributions to American society, but rather the label of a scapegoat singled out by an official government act.

Rather than considering contributions to America, the issue of Chinese opium dens in the United States became the hot topic, billowed by the deep-seated racism and xenophobia of the time. Opium dens became a focal point of American hostility toward the Chinese. While opium use was certainly not limited to Chinese immigrants, they were disproportionately targeted due to the prevailing racial prejudices of the time. Authorities conducted raids on Chinese opium dens while often turning a blind eye to non-Chinese opium users. Anti-Chinese propaganda and media depicted Chinese immigrants as morally corrupt, associating them with the opium trade and portraying them as a threat to the social fabric of the nation.

While opium dens existed in many different communities, the singling out of Chinese immigrants in the context of opium use was a reflection of broader racial prejudices and the scapegoating of a particular immigrant group. The Chinese Exclusion Act, initially a ten-year ban on Chinese immigration, was repeatedly extended until it was only repealed in 1943 as a gesture of goodwill toward China during World War II.

These historical events serve as an important reminder of the potent influence of racism on the development of immigration policies and the treatment of immigrant communities during this period. But one cannot help but draw parallels with the present day, where equally divisive ideologies persist, resulting in the stigmatization and marginalization of contemporary immigrant communities, including those from the Middle East and Mexico, for example.

For the sake of an easy comparative analysis, let's consider the nation's current concerns about immigration from Mexico and other Central American nations and how they compare to the anxieties that surrounded Chinese immigration during the late 19th and early 20th centuries.

- The Chinese Exclusion Act was a significant historical precedent for targeted exclusionary immigration policies, which in fact sought to restrict or remove immigrant populations who had previously been welcomed or even actively sought for the economic well-being and growth of America. Similarly, policies affecting immigrants from

Mexico and Central America have long been contentious, with measures like the Bracero Program (1942–1964) and the more recent immigration restrictions being prominent examples.

- The Chinese Exclusion Act emerged partly as a response to economic concerns from American workers who feared job competition from Chinese laborers. This mirrors concerns about economic competition and job displacement that have been associated with immigration from Mexico and Central America, while ignoring the benefits reaped from those same laborers.
- Chinese immigrants were often portrayed as morally corrupt and involved in criminal activities. The opium trade and other misunderstood elements within the community were used to generalize all Chinese immigrants as criminals. Mexican immigrants often face a similar stereotype of being criminals, which can be perpetuated through concerns about immigration status and a focus on border security. Furthermore, certain political narratives have associated Mexican immigrants with widespread drug trafficking and sexual violence. "Somebody's doing the raping" is a simple phrase but had profound effects on the perception of the Mexican and broader immigrant population within the context of American politics.
- Chinese immigrants faced significant violence and discrimination during the era of the Chinese Exclusion Act, including incidents such as the Rock Springs Massacre. Immigrants from Mexico and Central America have been subjected to extreme discrimination, violence, and family separations in contemporary contexts, particularly with regard to heightened immigration enforcement and border policies. In recent years, discriminatory practices have included racial profiling, harsh detention conditions, forced relocation, intentional family separation, and the criminalization of undocumented migrants.
- Both historical and contemporary policies have had profound effects on immigrant communities. The Chinese Exclusion Act left a lasting impact on Chinese Americans that continues to be felt today. The act not only curtailed immigration but also institutionalized racial discrimination, creating an environment of hostility and exclusion that shaped societal attitudes for generations. It separated families, as many Chinese immigrants were unable

> to bring their spouses or children to the United States, leading to fragmented communities. The stigma associated with the act contributed to enduring stereotypes about Chinese Americans as perpetual foreigners, a narrative that still affects how they are perceived and treated in society. Furthermore, the legacy of the Chinese Exclusion Act is evident in ongoing challenges, such as underrepresentation in political and civic spaces and incidents of anti-Asian hate, which surged during the COVID-19 pandemic. Similarly, current immigration policies significantly affect Mexican and Central American communities, with implications for family dynamics, labor markets, and community cohesion.

In both historical and contemporary contexts, the criminalization of immigrants has been a recurring theme. Today, media portrayal also plays a significant role in shaping public perception. Understanding why these stereotypes exist and how they came to be can provide valuable insights into the persistence of negative narratives and the broader context of immigration in the United States. These harmful stereotypes have long been used to justify anti-immigrant policies even though they fail to accurately represent the diverse and complex reality of immigrant communities.

Immigration Act of 1917

The Immigration Act of 1917[5] ushered in a new era in American immigration policy, one where the contours of global labor migration were redrawn. As part of this legislation, the first iteration of the Mexican Contract Labor Program—often regarded as a precursor to the later Bracero Program—was established. This program aimed to address persistent labor shortages by permitting Mexican nationals to work in the United States on a temporary basis in various industries, including agriculture, mining, and the railroad sector. Mexican workers under this program were typically recruited for seasonal or short-term employment, and their contracts specified the terms and conditions of their employment.

The program was a response to the demand for labor during World War I and the economic needs of the United States. It allowed Mexican laborers

5. Pub. L. No. 64-301, 39 Stat. 874 (Feb. 5, 1917).

to enter the United States legally for work, often in jobs that were considered low-skill or manual labor. While it provided economic opportunities for Mexican workers, the program was rife with criticism and allegations of labor exploitation, in many ways reliving the experience of the Chinese mere decades prior.

Their work was backbreaking, yet they were frequently paid meager wages that barely sufficed to support themselves and their families. They endured grueling workdays, often exceeding 10 to 12 hours in harsh conditions, particularly in agriculture and railroad construction. Workers in agricultural fields were required to harvest crops under scorching sun, with little access to water or breaks, while railroad laborers performed dangerous tasks involving heavy machinery and explosives with minimal safety precautions. Despite the demanding nature of their work, wages were exceedingly low—many workers earned as little as $1 to $1.50 per day, far below the prevailing wages for similar work performed by non-Mexican laborers. These wages were often insufficient to cover basic necessities, leaving families in a cycle of poverty.

Additionally, the contracts, which ostensibly existed to protect workers' rights, were in actuality used as tools of coercion and control. Workers, unfamiliar with the American legal system and often unable to speak or read English fluently, were vulnerable to exploitation. Employers often manipulated the terms, withholding wages or threatening deportation to ensure compliance. For instance, it was common for employers to confiscate workers' identification documents and permits, effectively trapping them in exploitative conditions. Workers who resisted or demanded better conditions were frequently dismissed and reported to immigration authorities, creating a climate of fear and vulnerability, with no representation or recourse for the very immigrants who had been recruited to fill a pressing need for the American people.

One particularly disturbing example of the injustices faced by Mexican laborers can be found in the Bisbee Deportation of 1917.[6] Over a thousand striking miners, including many Mexicans, were forcibly removed from the town of Bisbee, Arizona. They were transported 200 miles in cattle cars to the deserts of Hermanas, New Mexico, where they were left without food, water, money, or transportation. All because they dared to demand better

6. James Tracie, *The Bisbee Deportation*, 35 J. of the Southwest 4 (1993), at 457–84.

working conditions and fair treatment within the scope of a program where their labor would benefit America.

While the Immigration Act of 1917 allowed for Mexican contract labor, it also imposed restrictions and quotas on immigration from other parts of the world, particularly from countries in Southern and Eastern Europe. The act, also known as the Literacy Act or the Asiatic Barred Zone Act, was passed by Congress and signed into law by President Woodrow Wilson on February 5, 1917. In addition to the Mexican Contract Labor Program, it introduced several key provisions that had a notable impact on immigration to the United States during the early 20th century.

One of the central provisions of the 1917 act was the introduction of a literacy test for prospective immigrants aged 16 and older. This required immigrants to demonstrate basic literacy skills in their native language or a designated foreign language. The test was intended to limit immigration from Southern and Eastern European countries and increase immigration from Western and Northern European nations, once again underscoring the limited definition of the already exclusionary "free white men" who were favored by the law. Countries targeted by the literacy test often faced economic hardships, political instability, and social inequality, conditions that limited access to quality education, making it more challenging for potential immigrants to pass the literacy test. The test was part of a broader set of policies aimed at shaping the composition of the immigrant population, favoring those from Western and Northern Europe while excluding or discouraging immigration from other regions.

The act also created an "Asiatic Barred Zone," which extended an existing ban on immigration from certain Asian countries. The zone included most of Asia, the Pacific Islands, and parts of the Middle East. Immigrants from these areas were largely prohibited from entering the United States. It further expanded the categories of inadmissible individuals by excluding various groups, including those with physical or mental disabilities, individuals with contagious diseases, and other groups deemed undesirable.

Another notable feature of the 1917 act was that it imposed a head tax of $8 on immigrants to fund the administrative costs of processing them. It was the first time a fee had been required for immigration to the United States. This head tax served multiple purposes, both practical and ideological. One of its primary objectives was to provide a dedicated source of revenue to cover the administrative costs associated with processing and accommodating immigrants.

However, the tax also acted as a means of economic screening. The idea was that potential immigrants who could afford to pay the fee were more likely to have financial stability and could contribute to the U.S. economy. In this way, the head tax was used as a crude mechanism to select for immigrants who were perceived as more self-sufficient and less likely to become dependent on public assistance. It also underscored a growing desire for greater regulation and control over the flow of immigrants into the country. This sentiment was part of a broader shift in immigration policy at the time, reflecting a desire to shape the nation's demographics, foster assimilation, and respond to prevailing social and economic concerns.

To indicate baby steps in the direction of progress, it should be noted that—for all its faults—the Immigration Act of 1917 did include some provisions related to family reunification. It allowed for the admission of wives, unmarried children under 18, and parents of U.S. citizens if they were financially capable of supporting their family members.

The Immigration Act of 1917 was part of a series of immigration restrictions in the early 20th century and set the stage for more comprehensive restrictions in the 1920s with the National Origins Quota System of 1924, which imposed strict national origins quotas. These measures reflected the nativist sentiments and concerns about immigrants from certain regions that were prevalent during that era.

National Origins Quota System of 1924

Another defining moment in U.S. immigration history was the enactment of the National Origins Quota System, also known as the Johnson-Reed Act,[7] in 1924. This legislation was a response to shifts in the labor market and various other factors. It aimed to further curtail immigration from specific countries and regions, primarily those in Eastern and Southern Europe, by imposing quotas.

7. Immigration Act of 1924 (Johnson-Reed Act), Pub. L. No. 68-139, 43 Stat. 153 (May 26, 1924).

The National Origins Quota System of 1924 represents another dark chapter in U.S. immigration history. While economic factors played a role, the political climate was equally significant. Legislation was influenced by a desire to protect American workers from perceived job competition with immigrants, who were believed to be willing to work for lower wages. Further, the political environment of the time was marked by heightened nativism and concerns about overpopulation in major cities, such as New York and Chicago. There was a widespread belief that too many immigrants were overcrowding urban areas, exacerbating social and economic issues. In the context of our progress in American immigration policy and racial consciousness as a whole, this was a period of regression, where fear and bias led to discrimination and scapegoating that would hamper both liberty and prosperity in America.

The 1920s witnessed the rise of anti-immigrant sentiment and the reemergence of the Ku Klux Klan (KKK), which had been dormant since the late 19th century, reflecting broader societal anxieties. The KKK expanded its agenda to include not only racial but also anti-immigrant and anti-Catholic sentiments. By the mid-1920s, the group boasted millions of members, making it a significant political and social force. They actively campaigned for stricter immigration policies, with a particular focus on limiting immigration from Southern and Eastern European countries, as well as advocating for exclusionary measures targeting people of non-Protestant faiths, especially Catholics.

The KKK's influence extended beyond its membership numbers. It effectively propagated xenophobic and prejudiced rhetoric, framing its anti-immigrant stance in terms that stirred up fear and animosity. They depicted immigrants, especially those from Southern and Eastern Europe, as undesirable elements who threatened the nation's stability and prosperity. This rhetoric not only fueled public apprehension, but also influenced policymakers who sought to align with the sentiment of their constituents.

The KKK's influence, combined with the anxieties about immigration and overcrowding, greatly contributed to the passage of the National Origins Quota Act. Their role in the resurgence of anti-immigrant sentiment during the 1920s illustrates how extremist groups and discriminatory ideologies can shape the trajectory of a nation's immigration policies.

The National Origins Quota System also imposed almost complete restrictions on immigration from Asia. As a result, immigration to the

United States saw a sharp decline. Chinese immigrants had already faced severe restrictions, including the Chinese Exclusion Act of 1882, which virtually banned immigration from China. The 1924 act extended this exclusionary approach to encompass other Asian countries, particularly Japan and the Philippines, from which many immigrants had previously come to the United States.

The consequences were dire for Asian immigrants. It drastically reduced their numbers, effectively halting immigration from Asia to the United States for many years. The act perpetuated harmful stereotypes and xenophobic attitudes toward Asians, leading to decades of discriminatory immigration policies.

The quota system also had a significant impact on immigration from Italy. The number of immigrants from Italy in the 1920s was less than a third of what it had been in the previous decade. During this era, economic opportunities in Italy began to improve, reducing the need to emigrate in the first place, and the anti-immigrant sentiment in the United States influenced Italians who wanted to emigrate to seek opportunities elsewhere.

U.S. Response to Jewish Immigrants Before, During, and After the Holocaust

The late 19th and early 20th centuries saw a significant wave of Jewish immigration to the United States, primarily from Eastern Europe. Jewish immigrants were driven by a mix of push-and-pull factors. They were escaping religious persecution, particularly in the Russian Empire, as well as economic hardship. Religious freedom and economic opportunities in America brought the promise of a better life.

However, the situation quickly changed with the implementation of the Johnson-Reed Act.[8] This new legislation established strict quotas on the number of immigrants from specific countries and regions. Eastern and Southern European countries, from which many Jewish immigrants hailed, were severely restricted. This not only had a profound impact on the Jewish population seeking refuge, but also exemplified a broader sentiment of nativism that was prevalent during that era.

---

8. *Id.*

As the Nazis came to power in Germany and intensified anti-Semitic policies, a refugee crisis emerged. Many Jews desperately sought refuge in the United States, but the immigration restrictions of the time created significant barriers. The U.S. consulate in Germany imposed stringent visa requirements, making it challenging for Jewish applicants to meet the criteria. Further compounding the issue, the U.S. State Department, under Secretary of State Cordell Hull, often delayed issuing visas. The bureaucracy was slow to process visa applications, which had dire consequences for those attempting to escape persecution.

Despite increasing awareness of the Holocaust and the dire situation faced by Jews in Nazi-occupied Europe, the U.S. government did not take significant action to rescue Jewish refugees. There were multiple factors contributing to this inaction. Concerns about national security during World War II, isolationist sentiments that prevailed before U.S. entry into the war, and, notably, anti-Semitic biases within government circles played a role in shaping this response. Many individuals and organizations attempted to facilitate Jewish immigration, but their efforts often encountered bureaucratic obstacles and resistance.

The U.S. belief in maintaining distance from the world's entanglements firmly blocked proactive intervention on behalf of Jewish refugees in their darkest hour. Yet perhaps the most chilling influence was the presence of anti-Semitic biases within the U.S. government. These biases cast a pall over the decision making of the time, insidiously shaping the response—or lack thereof—to the unfolding catastrophe. One prominent example was the State Department, where officials like Breckinridge Long, Assistant Secretary of State, actively worked to obstruct immigration by Jews fleeing Nazi persecution. Long instructed consular officials to delay the processing of visa applications through bureaucratic red tape, resulting in thousands of lives being lost because refugees could not secure timely entry to the United States.

Even in moments of heightened awareness, anti-Semitism influenced the framing of policy debates. For example, during the 1943 Bermuda Conference—ostensibly convened to address the refugee crisis—the discussions yielded no actionable plans to rescue Jews, partly because of fears that increasing Jewish immigration might provoke backlash or disrupt domestic stability. This pervasive bias, coupled with security concerns and isolationism, contributed to a response that, at best, was passive and, at worst, complicit in the tragedy.

In the aftermath of World War II, the Displaced Persons Act of 1948[9] was enacted. This legislation allowed the entry of 200,000 displaced persons into the United States, including Holocaust survivors. Many Jewish survivors benefited from this policy, but it was criticized for its limited scope. The act was seen as insufficient, barely scratching the surface of the monumental refugee crisis that had unfolded in Europe.

While the United States did eventually admit Holocaust survivors and refugees, the response was often limited by immigration quotas, which retained their restrictive contours until the 1950s. As a result, a substantial number of those seeking refuge were unable to secure entry into the country. The response to Jewish immigration before, during, and immediately after the Holocaust was marked by a mix of compassion, fear and xenophobia, and bureaucratic obstacles. It is a complicated and often tragic chapter in U.S. immigration and refugee policy.

In the years following the Holocaust, public opinion in the United States began to experience a kind of "moral awakening." The Holocaust served as a dark illustration of how unchecked prejudice, racism, and discrimination can lead to horrific acts, including genocide. Many Americans began to question the prevailing racial segregation and inequality in their own country, with the atrocities of the Holocaust putting the United States in a somewhat awkward position on the world stage.

The United States had fought against fascism and the Nazi regime in Europe, yet racial segregation and discrimination were rampant at home. The contrast between the nation's professed commitment to freedom and democracy and the reality of racial segregation was increasingly difficult to justify, both domestically and internationally. My own city of Englewood, New Jersey, was home to a number of members of the Tuskegee Airmen, a legendary black fighter squadron in the U.S. Army. Despite their heroics in World War II, fighting for freedom and liberty abroad, they were segregated even in military service, and returned to a home where they still faced discrimination and disrespect, a counterintuitive shame our nation will always bear.

While the Holocaust did not directly cause the Civil Rights Movement that would occur some 20 years later, it did have a significant impact on the nation's moral and political climate, and it contributed to a greater sense of the need for legislation to protect civil rights. The Holocaust and the post-war

9. Pub. L. No. 80-774, 62 Stat. 1009 (June 25, 1948).

Nuremberg Trials, which prosecuted war crimes, helped foster international awareness and condemnation of racial discrimination and human rights abuses. This increased international scrutiny encouraged the United States to address its own racial injustices. This atmosphere of change and growing social awareness laid the groundwork for the passage of key civil rights laws, such as the Civil Rights Act of 1964[10] and the Voting Rights Act of 1965.[11]

The Civil Rights Movement drew from this evolving landscape, as it sought to dismantle institutionalized racism and achieve greater civil rights and equality for African Americans. The horrors of the Holocaust inspired some Jewish activists, many of whom saw parallels between the persecution of Jews in Europe and the struggles of African Americans for civil rights, to join the Civil Rights Movement.

The Bracero Program: A Double-Edged Sword

The Bracero Program, which was established during World War II, stands as both another testament to the contributions of Mexican immigrants and another example of the challenges of temporary labor programs. Similar to the Mexican Contract Labor program instituted in 1917, there were benefits to both the American economy and Mexican immigrants, but there were also serious drawbacks and controversies.

While the Bracero Program provided Mexican nationals with a legal means to secure employment in the United States and earn wages that were substantially higher than what they could earn in Mexico, workers were not granted permanent residency or a path to citizenship. This created yet another precarious situation in which laborers were essential to the American economy during the program, but could not secure their future in the United States. It was also marred by reports of labor exploitation, just like its 1917 predecessor.

Many braceros faced subpar working conditions, inadequate housing, and, in some cases, unethical treatment by employers. Additionally, the Bracero Program was controversial for its impact on U.S. labor. The availability of inexpensive bracero labor was criticized for potentially depressing wages

10. Pub. L. No. 88-352, 78 Stat. 241 (July 2, 1964).
11. Pub. L. No. 89-110, 79 Stat. 437 (Aug. 6, 1965).

and working conditions for domestic farmworkers. These concerns echo those of earlier temporary labor programs for Mexican immigrants and, sadly, are quite similar to the concerns surrounding Mexican laborers to this day.

Comparing the 1917 Mexican Contract Labor Program and the Bracero Program side by side provides a compelling case study in the evolving landscape of U.S. immigration law from its inception to the present day. On the surface, these two programs exhibit striking similarities: both were established to address temporary labor needs, lacked provisions for permanent residency, featured poor working conditions, and raised concerns about immigrant workers competing for U.S. jobs. However, taking a step back reveals subtle but significant distinctions within the broader narrative. Another example of baby steps in the right direction.

During the Bracero Program, while issues of exploitation and mistreatment of Mexican workers persisted, the legislation incorporated notable provisions for wage guarantees, housing, and healthcare. These measures, though imperfect, marked an advancement in safeguarding the rights and well-being of laborers.

In its nascent stages, the 1917 program operated with relatively little public awareness or organized activism. In contrast, the Bracero Program garnered heightened public scrutiny, with labor and civil rights organizations, as well as unions, fervently advocating for the rights of bracero workers. This increased awareness and activism, resulting in meaningful changes in labor conditions and protections.

The legacy of these programs also diverged. The Mexican Contract Labor Program gradually faded away after World War I, leaving limited lasting impact. The Bracero Program, however, persisted for nearly two decades and contributed to the shaping of subsequent immigration and labor policies, particularly as they pertained to guest worker programs and labor rights.

The Red Scare and the McCarran-Walter Act of 1952

The post-World War II era was marked by the Red Scare, a period of intense anti-communist sentiment and the fear of Soviet infiltration in the United States. This climate led to significant restrictions on immigrants perceived as potential threats to national security. The McCarran-Walter Act of 1952,[12] for instance, imposed strict ideological and political criteria for immigration, barring entry to individuals who were members of or affiliated with communist organizations. These restrictions were part of a broader effort to protect against perceived internal threats and underscored the influence of geopolitical tensions on immigration policy. The U.S. government was deeply concerned about communist infiltration and espionage, which extended to fears of potential subversion through immigration.

The McCarran-Walter Act provided broad discretion to the Attorney General to exclude or deport individuals deemed to be members of or affiliated with communist organizations. This discretion often led to deportations and denials of entry based on vague or tenuous associations with left-leaning groups. In high-profile events like the Hollywood Blacklist, individuals in the entertainment industry were accused of communist affiliations and subsequently blacklisted from employment.

The Hollywood Blacklist specifically targeted individuals in the entertainment industry who were suspected of having communist or leftist sympathies. This included screenwriters, actors, directors, and other professionals working in the film and television industry. The fear was that their political beliefs or associations might lead to the spread of communist propaganda through the powerful medium of film.

In 1947, ten screenwriters and directors, dubbed "The Hollywood Ten," refused to cooperate with an investigation conducted by the House Un-American Activities Committee (HUAC), a congressional committee, into communist influence in Hollywood. They cited First Amendment rights and the principle of not self-incriminating. As a result, they were found in contempt of Congress and sentenced to prison. This had a chilling effect on creativity and free expression in Hollywood. Many writers and artists self-censored to avoid suspicion, leading to a decline in artistic quality and diversity of ideas in films and television.

The McCarran-Walter Act's ideological and political criteria significantly affected immigration patterns. It severely impacted individuals with any perceived left-leaning or communist sympathies and had far-reaching consequences, limiting the entry of immigrants from countries and regions that were perceived as having communist influence. By granting the federal government

12. Immigration and Nationality Act of 1952 (McCarran-Walter Act), Pub. L. No. 82-414, 66 Stat. 163 (June 27, 1952).

more power than ever before to detain and prosecute suspected subversives based on intangibles such as suspected ideology, a precedent was also set for increased manipulation of immigration practices for political purposes.

Interestingly, however, this highly exclusionary act did include a few positive aspects. It established provisions for refugees and asylees, seemingly recognizing the need to provide a safe haven for those fleeing persecution. This marked a positive shift in immigration policy, though these specific provisions were often underutilized. The act also allowed for the granting of visas to individuals from countries behind the Iron Curtain as part of U.S. diplomatic efforts to encourage defection and information sharing, perhaps itself serving as an asterisk aside the intended definition of "persecution."

Furthermore, the McCarran-Walter Act abolished the racial restrictions on naturalization and removed the formal bans on Asian immigration, appearing to move the U.S. immigration system toward greater inclusivity (at least as it pertained to race). But its practical application proved less progressive.

While it eliminated explicit racial exclusions, the act still maintained immigration quotas and restrictions that had a differential impact on immigration based on the quota allocations from different nations. Some Asian nations retained very limited quotas, making it challenging for individuals from these countries to immigrate to the United States.

The era of the Red Scare and the McCarran-Walter Act is another poignant example of how geopolitical events and domestic concerns can significantly shape immigration policies. It underlines the importance of safeguarding civil liberties, protecting against discrimination based on political beliefs, and ensuring that immigration policies are just, fair, and aligned with democratic values. Despite the end of the Cold War, applicants for U.S. citizenship are still required to disclose whether they have ever been members of the Communist Party or any other totalitarian organization. While the question is often waived in cases where membership was involuntary or occurred in a non-hostile context, its inclusion still evokes controversy.

Immigration and Nationality Act of 1965

The passage of the Immigration and Nationality Act of 1965,[13] commonly referred to as the Hart-Celler Act, represents a watershed moment in U.S.

13. Immigration and Nationality Act Amendments of 1965 (Hart-Celler Act), Pub. L. No. 89-236, 79 Stat. 911 (Oct. 3, 1965).

immigration policy. This landmark legislation caused a profound shift in the country's approach to immigration, setting the stage for a more inclusive and compassionate system. It abolished the national origins quotas that had been in place since the 1920s, which had severely limited immigration from certain countries and favored Western and Northern European immigrants. Instead, the emphasis was redirected toward family reunification and skills-based immigration, leading to more diverse immigrant flows from Asia, Latin America, and other regions. But what brought about this monumental shift toward a more diverse and inclusive era of immigration to the United States?

The 1960s was a period of significant social and political change in the United States. The Civil Rights Movement was gaining momentum, challenging systemic discrimination and racial segregation. The juxtaposition of ongoing civil rights activism with immigration policies that favored certain racial and ethnic groups was increasingly untenable. There was a growing consensus that the nation's immigration system needed to align with principles of equality and justice.

Advocacy groups and individuals had long called for the elimination of the national origins quotas that had been in place since the 1920s. These quotas were viewed as discriminatory and out of step with the nation's evolving values. Their rigid restrictions on immigration from specific countries had led to a skewed and imbalanced immigrant population.

The Hart-Celler Act reframed the objectives of the U.S. immigration system. It dismantled the national origins quotas, thereby ending the discriminatory preference for immigrants from Western and Northern European countries. Instead, the act emphasized two key principles: family reunification and skills-based immigration.

The new law gave priority to family reunification, enabling U.S. citizens and lawful permanent residents to sponsor their relatives for immigration. This family-based system recognized the importance of keeping families together and promoted compassionate immigration policies. This has become one of the central tenets of American immigration policy, though not without controversy. At times vilified in the media or politics with terms such as "chain migration" or "anchor babies" used to demean the practice, family reunification and, as an offshoot, even the right to naturalization by birth, have come under attack. Only time will tell how our nation will proceed with these important policies, with the outcome sure to have an indelible impact on our future.

Interestingly, the 1965 act broached another topic under current debate. It also introduced a skills-based immigration system, offering opportunities to individuals with specific talents and expertise. It was designed to attract highly skilled workers and professionals who could contribute to the nation's growth and development. Current disagreements at the highest levels of our federal government have focused on immigration policy for workers in advanced technology, science, and engineering sectors who might be denied entry due to nationality, but are desired for either government or private sector employment in their fields.

The Immigration and Nationality Act of 1965 had an immediate and profound effect on immigration patterns. It marked the beginning of a more diverse and inclusive era, with greater numbers of immigrants beginning to arrive from Asia, Latin America, and Africa. This massive change led to a more equitable distribution of visas and facilitated a more varied immigrant population.

Refugee Act of 1980

The Refugee Act of 1980[14] represented a major shift in the United States' approach to dealing with refugees. For starters, the act defined a refugee as someone who is unable or unwilling to return to their home country because of a "well-founded fear of persecution" based on their race, religion, nationality, political opinion, or membership in a particular social group.

It further established a formal procedure for admitting refugees into the United States, authorizing the President to determine the annual refugee admissions ceiling and establishing a formula for distributing these admissions among regions and countries. This was intended to make the process more structured and less reliant on ad hoc decisions.

In an effort to help reunite families that had been separated due to conflict and persecution, the act prioritized the admission of refugees who were family members of individuals already granted asylum or refugee status in the United States. It allowed NGOs to participate in the resettlement process and provided funding for various services to assist refugees in their

14. Pub. L. No. 96-212, 94 Stat. 102 (Mar. 17, 1980).

resettlement, including language training, employment services, and cultural orientation.

The Refugee Act of 1980 led to more systematic and regulated procedures for the admission and resettlement of refugees in the United States and endorsed a more humanitarian approach to refugee issues, reflecting a commitment to assisting those fleeing persecution and violence. The passage of this act solidified the legal framework for the refugee admissions process and continues to influence U.S. refugee policy to this day.

The stories of those who flee their homes seeking safety, refuge, and a chance at a better life often elicit mixed reactions from nations, the United States included. Despite significant challenges in the way the United States handles contemporary refugee crises, there is a noticeable trend of progress. To illustrate this progress, we can compare the nation's handling of two major refugee crises of the 20th and 21st centuries: Jewish refugees during the Holocaust and the Syrian refugee crisis.

While both crises witnessed problematic U.S. responses, the approach to the Syrian refugee crisis was undeniably more compassionate. To begin, the United States displayed a willingness to admit a significant number of Syrian refugees early on, surpassing 15,000 admissions in 2016. This demonstrated a commitment to providing a safe haven for those escaping a devastating civil war. Furthermore, the United States actively contributed substantial humanitarian aid to support Syrian refugees and host communities in neighboring countries. This aid played a critical role in alleviating the suffering of displaced individuals.

Conversely, during the Holocaust, the United States implemented stringent immigration quotas, favoring immigrants from Western and Northern Europe. These quotas imposed severe limitations on the number of Jewish refugees permitted entry to the United States. One of the most tragic episodes of this period was the United States turning away the *MS St. Louis* in 1939, a ship carrying more than 900 Jewish refugees. Forced to return to Europe, many passengers later perished in Nazi concentration camps. Three years after the Holocaust, the Displaced Persons Act of 1948 authorized entry for 200,000 displaced persons, including many Holocaust survivors. But for many, this relief came far too late.

Both responses present difficult narratives. However, they undeniably underscore the evolution in the U.S. approach to addressing refugee crises, from the Holocaust to the present day. The lessons learned from these experiences highlight the importance of empathy, humanitarianism, and the need for flexible immigration policies that adapt to evolving global crises.

Immigration Reform and Control Act of 1986 (IRCA)

The Immigration Reform and Control Act of 1986 (IRCA)[15] aimed to address the issues of unauthorized immigration and employment, including undocumented workers. It was signed into law by President Ronald Reagan on November 6, 1986.

One of the most significant aspects of the IRCA was its provision for granting amnesty to certain undocumented immigrants who had been residing in the United States continuously since before January 1, 1982. The move intended to bring these individuals out of the shadows, allowing them to live and work legally in the country by applying for temporary legal status and, after meeting additional requirements, to eventually apply for permanent residency. It was a major step toward addressing the status of undocumented immigrants already in the United States, with the significant acknowledgment that deportation was not the only option.

The IRCA also attempted to reduce unauthorized immigration by introducing employer sanctions that made it unlawful for employers to knowingly hire or continue to employ undocumented workers. Employers were required to verify the employment eligibility of their workers by completing the Employment Eligibility Verification Form I-9. This led to the Basic Pilot Program (now known as E-Verify), which is still in use today.

Despite these measures, many employers continued to hire undocumented workers with little consequence, and the law inadvertently created a black market for false identification and other documents, including false Social Security cards and green cards, as people sought to meet the requirements for amnesty.

According to the Social Security Administration (SSA), about 75 percent of unauthorized workers today are using fraudulent Social Security numbers. It should be noted, however, that the SSA also estimates that earnings by unauthorized immigrants create a net positive effect on the overall

15. Pub. L. No. 99-603, 100 Stat. 3359 (Nov. 6, 1986).

financial status of the Social Security program, contributing billions to the program's cash flow each year without the eventual payback to a legitimate SSA recipient. As annual filings reveal fake Social Security numbers each year, those workers must be removed. While some will come back year after year with a new fake identity, SSA funds are automatically deducted from their paychecks, similar to any funds withheld for federal or state taxes for which they cannot receive rebates, or other medical, retirement, or programs from which they will never be able to receive benefits.

Another feature of the IRCA was that it allocated resources for increased border enforcement measures, including the hiring of additional border patrol agents, the construction of barriers in high-traffic areas, and enhanced surveillance. Border agents are tasked with detecting and apprehending individuals attempting to cross the border without proper documentation or bypassing border checkpoints. Enhanced surveillance technologies and equipment, including cameras, sensors, and monitoring systems, provided real-time intelligence on border activities and enabled agents to respond more effectively to illegal border crossings.

Although the IRCA's amnesty provisions provided a path to legal status for millions of undocumented immigrants, the law did not address the root causes of illegal immigration, such as economic disparities, political instability, and inadequate legal avenues for migration. As a result, the number of undocumented immigrants in the United States began to rise again in the years following the IRCA's implementation. Moreover, the family reunification program failed to account for varying circumstances between family members, and actually had the unintended consequence of separating some families. Some family members who were ineligible for amnesty faced deportation, while others qualified for legal status, creating a fragmented dynamic within households. For instance, under the IRCA, only those who could prove continuous residence in the United States prior to January 1, 1982, were eligible for legalization. Family members who arrived later, including children or spouses, often found themselves excluded from the process. This discrepancy led to heartbreaking situations where parents gained legal status while their children remained undocumented or were deported. Measures such as a waiver of residency length requirement in family reunification cases could have resolved these issues, but the practical application never matched up to the lofty goals of this philosophy. Additionally, the heightened enforcement measures introduced alongside the IRCA, such as increased border security and employer sanctions, further exacerbated these separations by making it more difficult for undocumented family members to join or remain with their loved ones at all.

While the Immigration Reform and Control Act of 1986 contained several positive elements and was a big step in addressing immigration issues, it ultimately did not provide a long-lasting solution to the myriad challenges of immigration in the United States. The issues surrounding unauthorized immigration and pathways to legal status for undocumented individuals remain challenging and politically sensitive today, with the core aspects of family reunification and border security constantly at the forefront of public debate.

Immigration Act of 1990

The Immigration Act of 1990[16] represented another notable change in U.S. immigration policy, moving toward a more compassionate and comprehensive approach that prioritized family unity and recognized the contributions of immigrants. It was signed into law by President George H.W. Bush on November 29, 1990.

The act was marked by a pronounced shift in priorities. It placed family reunification front and center, acknowledging the importance of maintaining and nurturing family ties across borders. It also increased opportunities for employment-based immigration, skilled workers, and diversity in the immigration population. While this may sound similar in its stated scope to the Immigration and Nationality Act of 1965, the Immigration Act of 1990 took a far more dynamic approach to immigration, leading to a greater degree of effectiveness in meeting those goals. It exemplified an evolving perspective that not only prioritized the unity of families, but also actively sought out individuals capable of enriching the U.S. economy with their contributions. The reasons behind this shift in perspective were wide-ranging:

- The U.S. economy had been experiencing significant growth during the latter half of the 20th century, and Americans recognized that immigrants had played an important role in fueling this expansion.

16. Pub. L. No. 101-649, 104 Stat. 4978 (Nov. 29, 1990).

- The increasing interconnection of economies and rapid advancements in technology were changing the way labor markets operated, and policymakers recognized the need to attract and retain highly skilled foreign talent to maintain the country's competitive edge.
- The demographic composition of the United States was changing, with an aging population and a declining birth rate among native-born Americans. As a result, there was an urgent need for a younger workforce to support the country's social and economic systems.
- A rise of advocacy groups in the 1980s had a significant impact on shaping public opinion and influencing policymakers to adopt more compassionate immigration laws.
- The United States had become known as a place of refuge for many people fleeing persecution and conflict since the passage of the Refugee Act in 1980.

To fulfill these needs and uphold our image as a haven of opportunity, refuge, and freedom, the act raised the annual ceiling for immigration, allowing for more legal immigrants to enter the United States. The annual cap on family-sponsored immigrants increased, as did the number of employment-based immigrants. The new law also placed a greater emphasis on family reunification by increasing the allocation of visas for family-sponsored immigration. This change allowed for more family members to join their relatives who were already U.S. citizens or legal permanent residents, and in turn, a greater degree of confidence for prospective immigrants with advanced skills that they could likewise relocate along with their families without significant worry or inconvenience.

Recognizing the critical contributions that immigrants make to the economic growth and vitality of the United States, the Immigration Act of 1990 introduced a series of employment-based preference categories designed to attract skilled individuals from around the world. This significant shift in U.S. immigration policy was driven by the understanding that skilled professionals, priority workers, and investors could bolster the nation's workforce, foster innovation, and stimulate economic development.

These employment-based preference categories, which included Professionals (EB-2), Priority Workers (EB-1), and Investors (EB-5), were more than just a policy change; they were a strategic decision to attract the best and the brightest from across the globe that would fill specific needs within our economy. By welcoming professionals, priority workers, and investors, the United States aimed to foster innovation, strengthen its workforce, and drive economic prosperity. It demonstrated a commitment to leveraging the skills and resources of the global community to ensure the country's continued growth and success.

The act further introduced Temporary Protected Status, allowing the U.S. government to provide temporary immigration benefits to nationals from designated countries experiencing armed conflict, natural disasters, or other extraordinary conditions. It also established the Diversity Visa (DV) Program, which allocates a certain number of visas each year to individuals from countries with low rates of U.S. immigration, promoting diversity in the immigrant population.

Diversity Visa Program

The Diversity Visa (DV) program, often referred to as the visa lottery, remains one of the most prominent and impactful features of the Immigration Act of 1990. The real beauty of the DV program lies in its all-encompassing global reach. Contrary to some previous policies that specifically excluded immigration based on nation of origin, the DV program would instead use similar criteria to open doors, taking into consideration relevant factors from around the world that might restrict immigration, and fostering a better-rounded global community in America.

It extends an opportunity that transcends borders to individuals from countries with historically low rates of immigration to the United States, including African nations hampered by colonialism, economic woes, and internal strife, certain Asian countries such as Nepal and Uzbekistan, which are in varying degrees of development, and smaller European countries, some of which, such as Albania and Estonia, are still reestablishing national identities after decades of forced inclusion in former Soviet states. In doing so, the program recognizes that talent, ambition, and the potential to shape society are not limited to specific regions or nations, and ensures that war, politics, or other factors won't deprive entire populations of the opportunity to join in the American experience.

DV recipients contribute positively to the U.S. economy. They bring with them unique skills, experiences, and perspectives, which lead to innovation, entrepreneurship, and economic growth. Many become successful business owners, scientists, artists, and other professionals who make significant contributions to their communities and the nation. They further serve as impromptu ambassadors to their home nations, helping to spread knowledge and understanding of American systems and ideals internationally, while simultaneously bringing aspects of their own cultures to be known within our borders.

But the DV program is not without challenges. One of its most significant hurdles is the limited number of visas available each year. With only about 50,000 visas issued annually, the demand far exceeds the supply. This limitation results in a highly competitive process, leaving many eligible individuals without the opportunity to secure a Diversity Visa. Further complicating the issue, the DV program employs a random selection process, leading to concerns about the fairness and unpredictability of the program. Some argue that this approach may not necessarily select individuals with the most relevant skills, experiences, or qualifications.

The popularity of the DV program has also given rise to fraud and scams. "The American Dream" is a lofty concept aspired to by countless individuals and families around the globe. An unfortunate side effect is the lengths they may go to or risks they often take to attain it. Unscrupulous individuals and organizations exploit the dreams of aspiring immigrants, charging them exorbitant fees or making false promises of securing a Diversity Visa. These fraudulent practices can, and often do, lead to financial loss and shattered dreams. For example, in 2016, the U.S. Federal Trade Commission (FTC) reported that a scam operation had targeted thousands of individuals, falsely claiming to guarantee Diversity Visa approval for fees as high as $5,000. Many victims, desperate for a chance at U.S. immigration, paid these exorbitant sums only to receive fake or invalid documentation. Another common scam involves phishing emails or fake websites that impersonate official U.S. government entities, instructing applicants to pay a "processing fee" for their application—a violation of the program's actual free application process.

The U.S. Department of State has issued warnings about these scams, emphasizing that the lottery does not require fees for entry and that winners are notified only through the State Department's official portal. Despite these efforts, scams continue to proliferate, particularly in countries with high numbers of applicants, such as Ghana, Nigeria, and Bangladesh. Victims not only suffer financial losses but may also be put at risk for identity theft or other forms of exploitation.

Critics of the DV program, in addition to worries of fraud, have voiced concerns about its potential national security implications. They suggest that the randomness of the selection process could inadvertently open the door to individuals with malicious intent, compromising national security. Implemented years prior to the terrorist attacks of September 11, 2001, and subsequent threats from foreign agents such as bombings or anthrax, it is clear that our standards for national security have been drastically altered since this act came to be. It's important to note, however, that the DV program is not a lax gateway to the United States. The program's stringent background checks and security measures, and a rigorous vetting process, have proven to be effective barriers against potential threats entering through this passageway.

Illegal Immigration Reform and Immigrant Responsibility Act of 1996 (IIRIRA)

The Immigration and Nationality Act of 1965, enacted during the Civil Rights Movement, marked a significant shift in U.S. immigration policies. This transformation centered on human rights, family reunification, and attracting highly skilled individuals to bolster the nation's economy. Over the next three decades, most immigration legislation would reflect these principles.

But the world was changing.

The return of tough immigration laws, exemplified by the Illegal Immigration Reform and Immigrant Responsibility Act of 1996 (IIRIRA),[17] which was signed into law by President Bill Clinton, becomes clearer when we examine what was happening in the world at that time.

The late 20th century saw significant demographic shifts in the United States. The country was becoming increasingly diverse due to a surge in immigration, with many newcomers hailing from Latin American and Asian countries. This demographic transformation stirred debates about cultural assimilation, national identity, national security, and economic competition.

17. Pub. L. No. 104-208, Div. C, 110 Stat. 3009-546 (1996).

Economic downturns and job insecurities in the 1990s played an undeniable role in the resurgence of restrictive immigration policies. Some argued that the influx of immigrants, particularly those with lower skill levels, could strain social services, depress wages, and exacerbate unemployment issues. Welfare reform, aimed at reducing dependence on government assistance, raised questions about the eligibility of immigrants for welfare benefits and quickly became intertwined with the broader immigration debate.

The 1990s witnessed substantial global migration flows, including refugees from war-torn regions, such as Bosnia and Rwanda, and those seeking better economic opportunities. These international migration patterns drew attention to the need for coherent immigration policies. The era was further marked by growing concerns about national security, especially in the wake of the 1993 World Trade Center bombing and the Oklahoma City bombing. These events prompted a reevaluation of immigration policies and their potential role in safeguarding national security.

There were also huge shifts in public opinion during the 90s, with some segments of the population expressing concerns about the pace and impact of immigration. This had a dramatic impact on legislation. Political leaders, in response to these concerns, began to adopt tougher stances on immigration as a means of aligning with their constituencies, regardless of party affiliation.

The IIRIRA introduced a series of tough immigration measures, including stricter enforcement, expanded deportation rules, and limitations on access to social services, such as welfare and Medicaid. These measures addressed concerns related to the economy, national security, and the welfare system, reflecting the shift in the political and social climate of the United States at the time.

The act expanded the detention of immigrants, including legal permanent residents, for a broader range of offenses, and it limited the ability of detained immigrants to seek release through habeas corpus petitions. For certain categories of unauthorized immigrants who were apprehended near the U.S. border, IIRIRA introduced expedited removal procedures, allowing for swifter deportation without the full immigration court process.

The law imposed limitations on asylum claims, particularly for individuals who had arrived in the United States without proper documentation, such as a valid visa, passport, or other required paperwork, making it more challenging for asylum seekers to establish credible fear of persecution. Although this includes individuals who may have crossed the border without inspection at a port of entry or those who arrived with false or fraudulent documents, it fails to recognize that the reason for missing documentation is often related to the urgency with which the asylum seeker had to flee persecution or violence in their home country. In these situations, obtaining valid travel documents is likely impossible, and no provision was provided to address the discrepancy.

One of the most controversial changes of IIRIRA was the expansion of the definitions of aggravated felonies, which significantly broadened the range of offenses that could lead to mandatory detention and deportation. For instance, a one-time failure to appear for a criminal proceeding could now result in an individual being classified as having committed an aggravated felony. This classification subjected them to mandatory detention and removal, with no opportunity to contest their deportation or seek reentry into the United States.

The law also introduced changes to legal immigration processes, affecting the eligibility for adjustment of status and visas for family-sponsored and employment-based immigrants. These changes were designed to tighten immigration enforcement, but had far-reaching implications for many lawful immigrants.

One such major change was the introduction of unlawful presence bars, which penalized individuals who overstayed their visas or worked without authorization. Those who accumulated more than 180 days of unlawful presence in the United States became subject to a three-year bar on reentry, while those with more than one year of unlawful presence faced a ten-year bar. This meant that individuals seeking adjustment of status often had to leave the country to complete their process, but risked being barred from returning, effectively trapping many in a precarious legal limbo. Additionally, the permanent bar, which applies to individuals who reenter the United States without authorization after having been previously removed or after accruing more than one year of unlawful presence, has resulted in the separation of an estimated two million individuals from their families. Many of those affected by the permanent bar entered the United States as children.

The IIRIRA also imposed more stringent income requirements for sponsors of family-sponsored immigrants, requiring them to demonstrate that their income or assets were at least 125 percent of the federal poverty level. This aimed to ensure that immigrants would not become a public charge, but also made it more difficult for lower-income families to reunite.

The law would further redefine certain criteria for employment-based visas, tightening eligibility and increasing documentation requirements for both employers and prospective employees. Furthermore, the IIRIRA eliminated relief mechanisms, such as suspension of deportation for individuals who could prove long-term residence and good moral character, replacing it with the more restrictive cancellation of removal, which required a higher burden of proof.

The Illegal Immigration Reform and Immigrant Responsibility Act significantly altered U.S. immigration law and enforcement. It has been widely criticized for aspects of its implementation and its impact on immigrant communities. Support and opposition came from various quarters for different reasons.

Law and order advocates viewed IIRIRA as a necessary step in enforcing immigration laws and deterring unauthorized immigration. They argued that stricter enforcement measures were essential to maintain the integrity of U.S. immigration laws. The act was seen as a means to enhance border security. It received support from those concerned about the flow of unauthorized immigrants and illegal drugs across the U.S.-Mexico border, as it authorized increased funding for border enforcement. Some supporters were also motivated by concerns that undocumented immigrants were accessing public benefits, and they saw IIRIRA as a way to restrict access to such benefits.

Immigrant advocacy organizations and civil rights groups, on the other hand, strongly opposed IIRIRA. They argued that the act was punitive, disproportionately targeting immigrant communities, and undermining due process rights.

Many of these critics were concerned about the impact of the law on immigrants and refugees, particularly provisions related to detention and deportation, such as the introduction of expedited removal procedures. They argued that it did not adequately consider humanitarian concerns, and it increased the potential for errors and unjust deportations. IIRIRA was further criticized for its potential to separate families, particularly provisions that made it easier to deport individuals for a wider range of offenses, even relatively minor ones. Critics argued that the act failed to ensure adequate legal representation for immigrants facing deportation, which would inevitably lead to unfair outcomes.

By this point, you may be noticing a pattern in the evolution of U.S. immigration law. If we examine the historical progression of these laws, we see that they tend to become tougher during economic downturns, and the "cracking down" on immigrant populations is largely in response to public opinion in times of crisis. Here are a few possible factors contributing to this phenomenon:

- During economic downturns, there is often a perception that immigrants, especially those with lower skill levels, are competing with native-born Americans for scarce job opportunities. There is often a call for economic protectionism of domestic industries and jobs. Some argue that stricter immigration controls are necessary to safeguard American industries and preserve jobs for U.S. citizens.
- Economic crises also strain social services, and some argue that immigrants, particularly those who may rely on public assistance, place an additional burden on the system.
- National security concerns take precedence during economic downturns. There can be worries that lax immigration enforcement might allow individuals with malicious intent to enter the country. This can lead to calls for stricter border security and immigration control measures.
- When people are facing economic hardship, they may be more susceptible to anti-immigrant rhetoric. This can contribute to a climate in which tougher immigration laws are seen as necessary to protect the economic well-being of the native population.
- These laws may be seen as a way to protect the economic interests and security of the nation, even if the relationship between immigration and economic problems is more nuanced than portrayed. The tough laws instill a sense of control, even if the "control" may be misdirected.
- Economic crises can create opportunities for politicians to advance their agendas by blaming immigration for economic challenges. They may propose and pass stricter immigration laws as a way to demonstrate their commitment to addressing the crisis, or simply to distract from other issues for which they don't have answers. Any of the above scenarios could be intentionally or unintentionally

exacerbated or caused in their entirety by this type of scapegoating and misdirection by government, political, or other agents.

Here are some specific examples of periods when economic challenges or crises coincided with changes in immigration policy. While economic conditions were not the sole factors driving these changes, they were certainly influential in shaping the debates and policy decisions related to immigration.

- Great Depression (1930s): The Great Depression, which began in the late 1920s and continued into the 1930s, was a period of severe economic hardship in the United States. During this time, immigration laws became more restrictive, reinforcing earlier quotas and limiting immigration. The most notable policy shifts, however, came with the mass deportation and repatriation campaigns of the 1930s, during which it is estimated that between 400,000 and two million people of Mexican heritage were forcibly removed or pressured to leave the United States, even though many were legally residing in the country.
- Recession of the Early 1990s: The early 1990s recession, which resulted from a combination of factors, including the savings and loan crisis and a downturn in the real estate market, saw increased attention to immigration issues. The Immigration Act of 1990, which raised the annual cap on legal immigration, was followed by the Illegal Immigration Reform and Immigrant Responsibility Act of 1996, which introduced stricter enforcement measures.
- Great Recession (Late 2000s): The financial crisis of 2008 and the subsequent Great Recession prompted concerns about unemployment and job competition. While comprehensive immigration reform was proposed in 2009, it did not pass, despite efforts to address key issues in the immigration system. Among the proposed measures were pathways to citizenship for undocumented immigrants, enhanced border security, reforms to visa programs, and stricter enforcement mechanisms. The failure to pass these reforms left states dealing with immigration issues on their own, leading to the enactment of strict state-level laws, such as Arizona's SB 10701. This controversial law included provisions requiring law enforcement officers to determine immigration status during

> lawful stops if there was "reasonable suspicion" that an individual was undocumented. Fortunately, many provisions of SB 10701 were challenged in court and ultimately struck down in the landmark Supreme Court case *Arizona v. United States* (2012).[18]

IIRIRA was a particularly controversial piece of legislation, and opinions on it were divided along political, ideological, and humanitarian lines. It remains a topic of discussion and debate in the broader context of U.S. immigration policy and reform.

9/11 and the Homeland Security Act of 2002

The events of September 11, 2001, had a profound and direct impact on the creation of the Homeland Security Act of 2002[19] and the establishment of the Department of Homeland Security (DHS). The terrorist attacks revealed significant shortcomings in the U.S. government's preparedness to prevent, respond to, and mitigate domestic security threats, particularly those related to terrorism. As a result, there was a compelling need to reorganize and coordinate efforts to enhance national security, particularly in terms of knowing who was gaining entry to America, as well as how. The Homeland Security Act of 2002 was passed by Congress and signed into law by President George W. Bush on November 25, 2002.

The most notable outcome of this act was the creation of the DHS, a cabinet-level department designed to centralize and coordinate various federal agencies responsible for homeland security. The 9/11 attacks demonstrated the lack of coordination among various federal agencies responsible for different aspects of national security, such as intelligence, border control, and emergency response. The fragmentation of responsibilities undoubtedly contributed to lapses in communication and coordination, which may have allowed preventable security breaches to occur.

In response, a total of 22 federal agencies and organizations, including the Immigration and Naturalization Service (INS), the U.S. Coast Guard, and the Federal Emergency Management Agency (FEMA), were brought together under one umbrella, to improve communication, coordination,

18. 567 U.S. 387 (2012).
19. Pub. L. No. 107-296, 116 Stat. 2135 (2002).

and the ability to respond to a wide range of security threats, including terrorism, natural disasters, and the emerging concern of cybersecurity issues.

The act emphasized the importance of intelligence and information sharing between federal, state, and local agencies, as well as with private-sector entities, to facilitate the early detection and prevention of potential threats. It further established U.S. Customs and Border Protection (CBP) and U.S. Immigration and Customs Enforcement (ICE) within DHS, with an emphasis on enhancing border security and immigration enforcement. It also created the Transportation Security Administration (TSA), responsible for security in all modes of transportation, including aviation, rail, and maritime, which has had a profound impact on every U.S. traveler, regardless of immigration status. Increasingly, immigration concerns were having a larger-than-ever presence in the daily lives of the average American.

The 9/11 attacks created a sense of urgency, resulting in bipartisan support for the Homeland Security Act. It was evident that a more cohesive and coordinated approach was essential to prevent future attacks. Members of both political parties recognized the need for a restructured government agency to address homeland security in a more efficient manner.

The combination of fear, political pressure, and haste, however, is not the best recipe for effective governance. Not surprisingly, DHS has been a subject of controversy and debate since its creation in 2002. Critics have raised concerns about the expansive scope of DHS's authority. They argue that it has the potential to infringe on civil liberties and individual privacy due to its broad surveillance and law enforcement powers, and that it has in fact done so at various junctures.

Immigration policies and practices have been among the most significant controversies for DHS. This includes the handling of undocumented immigrants, the separation of families at the border, and the treatment of asylum seekers. Some of the leading controversies surrounding DHS and its practices are listed here:

- Controversies have arisen over the use of force by DHS agencies, particularly CBP. Incidents involving the use of force, including lethal force, have raised concerns about accountability and oversight.
- The conditions in immigration detention centers, where individuals are held while their immigration status is being determined,

have been a subject of controversy. Reports and images of overcrowding, substandard conditions, and allegations of mistreatment have drawn public outrage.

- DHS has been criticized for its role in domestic surveillance, including the warrantless monitoring of citizens and non-citizens, with specific ethnic groups as targets at times. Concerns about potential violations of civil liberties and privacy rights have been raised.
- The use of emergency declarations to fund border security measures and the reallocation of funds from other government agencies to DHS have sparked legal and political controversy.
- The effectiveness and civil liberties implications of DHS's efforts in countering domestic terrorism have been debated. Critics argue that some policies have the potential to infringe on free speech and individual rights.
- The appointment of leadership positions within DHS has been politically contentious. The qualifications and ideologies of individuals in top roles have led to disputes.
- DHS, through FEMA, plays a critical role in responding to natural disasters. The department's handling of disaster responses, including Hurricane Katrina, has faced criticism and scrutiny.

There is no question that DHS operates in a complex and challenging environment, and its role in homeland security and immigration enforcement remains a topic of ongoing debate and discussion. Its policies and practices are scrutinized from both security and civil liberties perspectives, leading to a broad range of opinions and controversies.

Secure Fence Act of 2006

Continuing the trend of enhanced border control and surveillance, alongside tougher penalties for immigration violations, the Secure Fence Act of 2006[20] was signed into law by President George W. Bush on October 26, 2006. The vast expanse of the U.S.-Mexico border stretches more than 1,900 miles, and the defining feature of the Secure Fence Act was to authorize the construction of extensive physical barriers along that border.

20. Pub. L. No. 109-367, 120 Stat. 2638 (2006).

It mandated the construction of at least 700 miles of fencing along the southwest U.S. border, targeting areas with the highest rates of smuggling and unauthorized border crossings. This initiative utilized a range of physical barriers, from steel fencing to vehicle barricades, all underscored by the strategic use of lighting and cutting-edge surveillance technologies. It was an ambitious plan, aimed at preventing unauthorized entry into the United States, but proved to be equally divisive.

The contentious debate that ensued involved a range of concerns. Critics voiced apprehension about the potential environmental impact of these new barriers, as they cut across ecosystems and disrupted wildlife migration patterns. The notion of a "fortified" border raised humanitarian questions, as it potentially placed asylum seekers and those seeking a better life in precarious situations. Even riskier alternatives to traditional crossings could ensue, fraught with danger.

Cost effectiveness was another issue. Skeptics questioned whether the financial investment truly aligned with its intended outcomes. Were the substantial resources allocated for the construction of these barriers genuinely enhancing border security, or could alternative strategies prove more efficient? The physical effectiveness of various barriers also came into question, as some were observed to be easily bypassed despite the large expenditures for their deployment.

Since the passing of the Secure Fence Act in 2006, border fencing has remained a controversial and politically divisive issue. An even bigger wall became a central promise of Donald Trump's 2016 presidential campaign. While a partial barrier already existed, the Trump administration spoke of significant enhancements, building upon the framework established by the Secure Fence Act. His claim was aspirational: a stronger physical barrier to deter unauthorized immigration, combat drug trafficking, and bolster national security, and with a promise that Mexico—and not America—would foot the bill.

Trump's ambitions led to a series of executive orders prioritizing the construction of the new wall, directing the allocation of funding and resources to realize the vision. But the proposal faced an uphill battle, navigating challenges in securing funding from Congress and encountering a slew of legal hurdles. Courts deliberated on the use of specific funds, impacting the progress of construction.

A Trump strategist, Steve Bannon, even created a crowdsourced effort to solicit funds from private citizens to build Trump's wall, which raised more than $25 million. With no legal avenue for private funds to build such a wall, however, no action came from this effort—other than Bannon pleading guilty in 2025 to defrauding the donors.

In the end, the realization of a new and improved border wall remained elusive, but not without transformation. New barriers emerged, particularly in areas where existing ones were insufficient to address pressing border security concerns. This enhanced border consisted of a composite structure—part physical wall, part fencing, part vehicle barricade.

Today, the U.S.-Mexico border is characterized by an eclectic mix of materials. There are towering sections of steel mesh that reach a height of 15 feet, providing border agents with a vantage point to monitor the other side. Other sections are composed of solid landing mats, remnants from the Vietnam War. They were chosen for their cost-effectiveness, but pose a distinctive challenge as they obscure visibility and complicate surveillance efforts.

Vibrant murals and paintings adorn certain sections of the barrier, often conveying messages of hope, unity, and shared humanity in pure defiance of the very structures meant to contain and suppress them. San Diego's "Friendship Park" is situated in an area along the fence where families and loved ones separated by the border are permitted to speak and even touch through the fencing at certain times during the month. The mesh and steel barrier becomes a place of reunion, albeit a temporary one.

At the western extremity of the border, the Pacific Ocean assumes the role of a natural barrier, yet fencing extends into the water, effectively dividing San Diego and Tijuana. Although attempts to swim around this section occasionally occur, they are typically met with custody by border patrol agents or require rescue, given the extensive surveillance. This particular area is considered one of the most secure sections of the fence, yet enforcement remains an evolving challenge, as drug smugglers have gone so far as to construct makeshift "narco-submarines" capable of carrying thousands of pounds of cargo, in efforts to elude detection and reach American soil.

The efficacy of the border wall remains a subject of continual debate. Advocates emphasize its role as a deterrent and cite increased apprehensions in areas with barriers. Critics assert that investments in technology and additional personnel could represent a more cost effective and environmentally sound approach, highlighting that illegal crossings often occur through tunnels, boats, and routes unobstructed by barriers.

The border wall serves as an integral component of the broader conversation on immigration and border policy in the United States. It encapsulates the ongoing challenges presented by unauthorized migration, the humanitarian concerns for those seeking a better life, and the debate surrounding the efficient allocation of resources. It signifies a tangible reminder of the ongoing discourse on immigration reform—a delicate balance between security and compassion in an increasingly complex and interconnected world.

Deferred Action for Childhood Arrivals (DACA)

Established through executive action by President Barack Obama on June 15, 2012, the Deferred Action for Childhood Arrivals[21] (DACA) is a significant and often debated immigration policy. DACA is not a law, but rather a program implemented by the U.S. Department of Homeland Security (DHS).

Designed to provide temporary relief from deportation and work permits to undocumented individuals who were brought to the United States as children, DACA eligibility is based on certain criteria. Applicants must have arrived in the United States before the age of 16, have continuously resided in the United States since June 15, 2007, and meet educational or military service requirements. They must also have no significant criminal record.

Approved DACA recipients are protected from deportation for a renewable period of two years. During this time, they are also eligible to apply for work authorization, allowing them to work legally in the United States. DACA status can be renewed every two years, provided recipients continue to meet the eligibility requirements and have not engaged in criminal activities.

Recipients can obtain Social Security numbers, which allows them to work, pay taxes, and access certain benefits. DACA also provides opportunities for recipients to pursue higher education, as they can attend colleges and universities and apply for financial aid in some states.

21. Memorandum from Janet Napolitano, Sec'y of Homeland Security, to David Aguilar, Acting Comm'r, U.S. Customs and Border Protection, et al. (June 15, 2012) [DACA Policy Memo].

Deferred Action for Parents of Americans and Lawful Permanent Residents (DAPA)

In November 2014, President Obama announced an expansion of deferred action programs, including the introduction of the Deferred Action for Parents of Americans and Lawful Permanent Residents (DAPA).[22] DAPA aimed to provide temporary relief from deportation and work authorization for certain undocumented *parents* of U.S. citizens or lawful permanent residents. To qualify, applicants had to meet specific criteria, pass background checks, and demonstrate that they were not enforcement priorities for removal.

DAPA was intended to address family unity by protecting parents of U.S. citizens and lawful permanent residents from deportation and allowing them to contribute to society through legal work. Like DACA, DAPA was not a path to citizenship, but rather a temporary measure to provide stability for families.

But the future of DACA and DAPA are uncertain.

DAPA faced significant legal challenges from the start. In 2015, a coalition of states filed a lawsuit,[23] arguing that the program was an overreach of executive authority. The case reached the U.S. Supreme Court[24] in 2016, resulting in a 4–4 deadlock that left in place a lower court ruling blocking DAPA's implementation. Consequently, DAPA was never enacted.

In 2021, the state of Texas sued the U.S. government,[25] contending that the original 2012 DACA program, established by the Obama administration, was unlawful. In 2022, Judge Hanen, a federal judge in Texas, initially ruled in favor[26] of this argument, but the 5th U.S. Circuit Court of Appeals sent the case back to Judge Hanen, asking him to reconsider his decision in light of a new rule issued by the Biden administration. In 2023, Judge

22. Memorandum from Jeh Charles Johnson, Sec'y of Homeland Security, to León Rodríguez, Director, USCIS, et al. (Nov. 20, 2014) [DAPA Policy Memo].

23. Texas v. United States, 86 F. Supp. 3d 591 (S.D. Tex. 2015), *aff'd*, 809 F.3d 134 (5th Cir. 2015).

24. United States v. Texas, 579 U.S. ___ (2016) (per curiam), *aff'g by an equally divided court*, Texas v. United States, 809 F.3d 134 (5th Cir. 2015).

25. Texas v. United States, No. 1:18-cv-00068 (S.D. Tex. 2021).

26. Texas v. United States, 549 F. Supp. 3d 572 (S.D. Tex. 2021); Texas v. United States, No. 1:18-cv-00068, 2023 WL 5955356 (S.D. Tex. Sept. 13, 2023).

Hanen again ruled against the DACA program, concluding that the 2021 DACA regulation proposed by the Biden administration closely resembled the 2012 DACA program and, in his view, was therefore unlawful.

Since its inception in 2012, DACA has provided temporary relief and opportunities for hundreds of thousands of young undocumented individuals who have grown up in the United States. While Judge Hanen ruled against the program, he also made a provision allowing existing DACA recipients to continue renewing their DACA status. First-time applications, however, could no longer be processed.

It's important to note that DACA does not provide a pathway to permanent residency or citizenship, and it does not offer the same level of benefits as comprehensive immigration reform. It is a temporary, renewable status that can be terminated by the government at any time, which applies only to a set group of individuals in very specific circumstances.

DACA has been a subject of political and legal controversy since 2012. Some argue that it provides a humane solution for undocumented individuals who were brought to the United States as children, having no say in their current circumstances, and knowing no other home. Others view it as executive overreach or even an incentive for illegal immigration. The only thing that's clear is that DACA's long-term future remains very much uncertain.

The Transition from an Industrial to a Service-Oriented Labor Market

Over the course of American history, the nation's labor markets have undergone significant transformations, and these changes have left prominent marks on immigration policy. The United States' economy evolved from primarily agrarian in its early days to industrial and eventually service-based.

The shift from industrial to service-oriented economies had significant implications for immigration policy. During the industrial era, immigrants were drawn to work in factories, mines, and on construction projects, including the roads, bridges, and rails that would accelerate that economic expansion. They played a crucial role in building the nation's infrastructure, particularly during the rapid urbanization of the late 19th and early 20th centuries. But the nation has largely moved away from industrial work.

According to the U.S. Bureau of Labor Statistics (BLS), the service sector accounts for about 80 percent of U.S. employment today,[27] encompassing a wide range of industries, including healthcare, education, finance, and technology. While manufacturing, industrial work, farming, and other traditional roles still exist and support critical regional economies, the service sector is undoubtedly the driving force behind the modern U.S. economy as a whole.

This decline in industrial work has had several major impacts on immigration patterns and trends, including new occupational preferences among immigrants and an increased demand for skilled workers. Our country's change in occupational demand led to a shift in the composition of immigrant flows to the United States and dramatically influenced immigration policies. Visa programs like the H-1B visa for highly skilled workers were established in response to the changing nature of the labor market.

With the emergence of our new knowledge-based economy, which places a premium on skills, education, and innovation, there was a growing demand for highly skilled professionals to fill positions in technology, science, engineering, and other specialized fields. In response to the changing labor market and the need for foreign talent, the United States established the H-1B visa program in 1990, which allows U.S. employers to temporarily employ foreign workers in specialty occupations. The H-1B has become a vital pathway for highly skilled immigrants. It allows U.S. employers to sponsor foreign workers, often in STEM (Science, Technology, Engineering, and Mathematics) fields. H-1B visa holders are typically well-educated and bring valuable skills and experience in specialized fields to the American workforce.

India has consistently been one of the leading sources of H-1B visa applicants. Indian professionals, particularly in the fields of information technology, engineering, and medicine, have made substantial contributions to the U.S. economy. Chinese immigrants, especially in STEM fields, have also been significant contributors to the highly skilled workforce in the United States. Many Chinese nationals come to the United States for advanced degrees and professional opportunities. South Korean nationals

27. U.S. Bureau of Labor Statistics, *Employment by Major Industry Sector* (updated Aug. 2025), https://www.bls.gov/emp/tables/employment-by-major-industry-sector.htm.

also frequently apply for H-1B visas, with a notable presence in engineering, biotechnology, and academia.

While highly skilled immigrants have undoubtedly played a major role in driving innovation, entrepreneurship, and economic growth in the United States, these shifting dynamics have had dire consequences for unskilled immigrant workers and the issue of undocumented immigration. As the American economy transitioned toward a knowledge-based and technology-driven model, opportunities for low-skilled immigrant workers to secure stable employment diminished, and they faced increasing challenges in finding jobs that would provide a sustainable income. But the decline in low-skilled job opportunities did not deter immigrants from seeking safety and economic prospects in the United States. As a result, many immigrants, unable to secure legal immigration status, found themselves in the ranks of the undocumented, and now without even the dubious job prospects of generations past.

While these individuals may in fact have documents of identity from their home nation or otherwise, the term "Undocumented" typically means they lack American documents and the legal status that those documents represent. Due to their legal vulnerability, these workers are more susceptible to exploitation, abuse, and mistreatment by employers. They often work in low-wage jobs, earning less than their documented counterparts for similar work, and undocumented immigrants may be subjected to hazardous working conditions without proper safety measures or employment benefits. Living under the constant threat of deportation, and without the ability to seek relief from law enforcement or government agencies, undocumented immigrants experience significant legal uncertainties, which can create a climate of fear and anxiety. Access to quality healthcare, housing, education, and other services can be difficult or impossible to attain, further diminishing the quality of life of many immigrants who lack legal status.

While the preference for highly skilled immigrants is often highlighted for its economic benefits, low-skilled immigrants also make essential contributions to the U.S. economy. They perform critical roles in industries that rely on manual labor, such as agriculture, which is integral to food production, and construction, which contributes to infrastructure development. According to the Migration Policy Institute (MPI),[28] there were

28. Migration Policy Institute, *Unauthorized Immigrant Population by State and Country of Origin, 2019–2021* (updated July 2023), https://www.migrationpolicy.org/data/unauthorized-immigrant-population/state/US.

approximately 11.2 million undocumented immigrants living in the United States in 2021, the most recent year for data collection. These figures do not account for the record number of border crossings in 2022 and 2023, however, so that number is likely to be much higher. The contributions of undocumented workers to various industries, while often overlooked, are substantial.

A comprehensive approach to immigration reform could address the situation of undocumented immigrants, providing them with a pathway to legal status while also aligning immigration policies with the evolving needs of the U.S. labor market. But policymakers continue to grapple with finding a balance between economic demand for low-skilled labor and the protection of American jobs, and ensuring fair treatment and working conditions for all immigrants.

Mohammad Gulab's Story

In the remote mountains of Afghanistan in June 2005, Mohammad Gulab made a decision that would forever alter the course of his life. A humble man from the small village of Sabray, Gulab encountered a wounded Navy SEAL, Marcus Luttrell—the sole survivor of a devastating ambush during a mission gone wrong. Guided by his belief in Pashtunwali, a traditional code of honor that mandates offering protection to anyone in need, Gulab risked everything to shelter Luttrell from the pursuing Taliban.

Pashtunwali, the code of the Pashtun people—an ethnic group native to Afghanistan and Pakistan—is both law and legend. Rooted in the conviction that humanity transcends all else, this ancient creed compels its followers to extend sanctuary to those in need, even at great personal risk. It is a code that defies time and circumstance, embodying the spirit of selflessness and resilience. While the Pashtuns are predominantly Muslim, Pashtunwali serves as a deeply ingrained cultural and moral foundation, operating alongside and often beyond formal religious practice.

For Mohammad Gulab, this ancient code was not just a set of ideals, but a way of life. When he found Marcus Luttrell, bleeding and hunted, he did not hesitate. Offering refuge was not a choice but an obligation, one he upheld with quiet determination despite the obvious threats to his village, his family, and himself.

Unfortunately, but not surprisingly, Mohammad Gulab's decision to save the Navy SEAL made him a target of relentless Taliban attacks, forcing him and his family into a decade-long fight for survival. While Luttrell's story gained worldwide attention and brought him immense benefits, Gulab was largely left to bear the crushing weight of his courage in isolation.

Luttrell's memoir, Lone Survivor, *and its subsequent film adaptation, catapulted him to fame and financial success. The narrative, centered on his harrowing ordeal and Gulab's selfless act of saving him, resonated deeply with American audiences. Luttrell's story of resilience earned him admiration, lucrative speaking engagements, book royalties, and a platform that transformed him into a celebrated hero. But the very publicity that glorified Luttrell also amplified the risks to Gulab and his family. As Luttrell's fame grew, so did the Taliban's resolve to exact revenge on the Afghan villager who defied them.*

While Luttrell was safe in the United States, Gulab was anything but in Afghanistan, where his heroism made him and his family prime targets. They faced constant attacks, including bombings, sniper fire, and ambushes, leaving them in constant fear for their lives. Gulab lost his home, his livelihood, and his peace of mind. The dangers extended to his children, one of whom was injured by shrapnel during a Taliban attack. According to Gulab, despite these threats, Luttrell, whose life had been saved at the ultimate risk to Gulab and his family, did not take any meaningful steps to help them escape to America.

In fact, Gulab says his attempts to reach out to Luttrell for help only strained their relationship. Disagreements over the portrayal of events in Lone Survivor *and financial disputes further alienated the two men. While Luttrell built a secure and prosperous life, Gulab felt abandoned, forced to survive and protect his family without adequate support. It was not Luttrell who ultimately helped Gulab escape to the United States in 2015, but rather a network of compassionate strangers, U.S. government and military officials, and dedicated legal advocates. Recognizing the profound risks Gulab had taken to save an American soldier, these kind individuals, officials, and his immigration team worked tirelessly to ensure he and his family found the safety and stability they deserved.*

When Gulab arrived in Texas with his wife and some of their children, the family was not fully intact. Several of the children remained in Afghanistan by choice, clinging to their home and familiar surroundings. However, the rapidly deteriorating security situation in Afghanistan following the Taliban's resurgence has left those who stayed behind in constant fear for their lives. What once seemed like a manageable separation has now become desperation to reunite the family and ensure their safety.

For Gulab's family who remained in Afghanistan when Gulab fled, the reality of daily life is often grim. With targeted violence, economic collapse, and the suppression of basic freedoms, Gulab's children, who once believed they could carve out a future in their homeland, have come to the heartbreaking realization that remaining is no longer an option. Now, all of Gulab's children wish to join their family in the United States, but the path to bring them here has been anything but straightforward. The process has been challenging, to say the least.

Although Gulab's son Irshad initially came to the United States with his father in 2015, his journey to build a safe and secure life here had just begun. After settling in the United States, Irshad fell in love and married his wife, Sunbal, in Afghanistan. Their marriage brought hope for the future, but it also tethered him to a homeland that was becoming increasingly dangerous. In 2021, as Kabul fell to the Taliban in a moment of chaos and despair, Irshad returned to Afghanistan to rescue his pregnant wife and bring her to safety.

Arriving in a country on the brink of collapse, Irshad found himself racing against time. He did everything in his power to secure passage for his wife, but the unfolding chaos made that impossible. Red tape, overwhelmed embassies, and the sheer danger on the ground left Irshad unable to bring her to safety before the Taliban regained control. With the clock ticking, he faced an agonizing choice: stay and risk his life, or escape to safety while he still could, and come up with a plan to get his wife and unborn child to safety.

In the chaotic final days of the U.S. withdrawal, Irshad managed to secure a seat on one of the last evacuation flights out of Afghanistan. As he boarded the plane, the weight of his decision was unbearable—he was leaving the woman he loved and their unborn child behind in a country spiraling into violence and oppression. The guilt and heartbreak were compounded by the uncertainty of when, or if, he would see them again, but this may have been their only foothold to an eventual life together in America.

Shortly after Kabul fell, Irshad's wife gave birth to their son, Mudasser. With the Taliban tightening their grip on Afghanistan, their situation became increasingly dire. They lived in constant danger, with limited access to resources and no clear path to safety. Fortunately, this part of the story has a very happy ending.

Thanks to the courage and ingenuity of good Samaritans, who are unnamed to protect their safety, Irshad's wife and infant son eventually escaped to a third country. Although they remained there in limbo for several years, Irshad was finally able to reunite with his wife and meet his now three-year-old son for the first time in January of 2025. This emotional reunion marked a new chapter for Irshad's family.

It has now been nearly 20 years since Mohammad Gulab saved Marcus Luttrell's life in 2005, an act of extraordinary courage that forever altered his own fate. While Gulab's daughter-in-law and grandchild have finally joined the family in the United States, some members of Gulab's family remain outside of the United States, facing dire circumstances. This is not only tragic but deeply unjust. That an American can achieve fame and financial rewards by publicizing this story, while the Afghan savior who made it possible faces relentless suffering and displacement, is a disturbing reflection of moral failure and systemic indifference. It is hard to imagine a cause that the U.S. government should be more sympathetic toward, not simply to reward Gulab's selfless actions, but to make a statement to the international community that the United States will steadfastly recognize and support those who are imperiled for taking such heroic actions.

The true story of heroism here lies not in Marcus Luttrell's survival, but in the bravery and selflessness of Mohammad Gulab and his family, as well as the good Samaritans who have risked their own safety to support them. Their compassion, sacrifice, and determination to ensure justice for Gulab and his family remind us what true courage looks like in the face of adversity.

Despite the tireless efforts of Gulab, his legal team, and a network of supporters in the United States and abroad, the journey toward reunification is far from complete. Each delay for Gulab's family outside of the United States means more time spent in dangerous conditions, more nights filled with fear, and more days where hope is tested. The stakes couldn't be higher. Reuniting this family is not just about bringing loved ones together—it is a matter of survival and the chance to finally live in peace after years of unimaginable sacrifice.

At Wildes & Weinberg, we have always believed in Mohammad Gulab and his family. We are deeply inspired by their decision to put a stranger's life before their own well-being and by their extraordinary resilience over the past 20 years. They have faced unimaginable hardships with grace and dignity. This is why we have fought for their rights from the very beginning, consistently providing pro bono and reduced-rate representation. In addition to reuniting Irshad with his wife and child, our team helped him secure U.S. citizenship, ensuring he has the protections necessary to rebuild his life. It has been a privilege to stand by Gulab and his family on this journey, and we remain committed to supporting them as they embrace this new chapter in their lives.

A Note from Mohammad Gulab

I want to say from my heart how grateful I am to Michael Wildes and his team at Wildes & Weinberg for everything they have done for me and my family. When I helped Mr. Luttrell in 2005, I acted because of my faith and my belief in doing what is right. I never thought that choice would bring such hardship to my life and to the lives of my family.

Since then, we have faced many struggles that I could never have imagined. Through all of it, Michael Wildes and his team have stood with us. They did not just help with the legal work—they also gave me hope when it was so hard to find. Their efforts to reunite my family and help us begin a new life in the United States have been a great light during some of the darkest times. They made it possible for my son Irshad to be with his wife and meet his son for the first time, something I could only dream of before.

To Michael, his team, and the many good people who have helped us along the way, including those who put themselves at risk to support us, I cannot thank you enough. Your kindness and courage remind me that there are still people in this world who care deeply about others. It is because of you that my family has a chance to live in peace, without fear, and to hope for a better future.

I pray that one day all of my children will be safe here with me in the United States. Until that day, I am truly thankful for everyone who continues to fight for us and stand by our side. Thank you for believing in me, for helping my family, and for showing what true goodness looks like. May God bless you all.

CHAPTER 2

Echoes of the Past: Key Cases

Immigration law in the United States is not a static entity; it is a dynamic and evolving field that has been influenced by social, political, and economic circumstances, as well as by a series of landmark legal battles. In this section, we will explore not only the specific circumstances and individuals involved in these influential cases, but also the resulting principles and precedents that continue to shape and reshape the policies of today.

United States v. Wong Kim Ark (1898): Establishing Birthright Citizenship

Long before debates over birthright citizenship became a contemporary political flashpoint, the landmark Supreme Court case *United States v. Wong Kim Ark*[1] established the constitutional foundation for the principle that anyone born on U.S. soil is a citizen, regardless of their parents' immigration status. This 1898 decision profoundly shaped the interpretation of the 14th Amendment and remains a cornerstone of American immigration law—for now.

At the heart of *Wong Kim Ark* was a simple yet groundbreaking question: Is a child born in the United States to non-citizen parents automatically a U.S. citizen under the Constitution?

The case began when Wong Kim Ark, born in San Francisco in 1873 to Chinese immigrants, returned from a trip to China and was denied reentry to the United States on the grounds that he was not a citizen. This denial

1. 169 U.S. 649 (1898).

came during a time of rampant anti-Chinese sentiment, fueled by the Chinese Exclusion Act of 1882, which sought to restrict Chinese immigration and strip Chinese immigrants of many rights. The federal government argued that Wong Kim Ark, though born in the United States, was not a citizen because his parents were subjects of the Chinese Empire and not U.S. citizens or permanent residents.

The primary issue was the interpretation of the Citizenship Clause of the 14th Amendment, which states: "All persons born or naturalized in the United States, and subject to the jurisdiction thereof, are citizens of the United States and of the State wherein they reside." The question turned on the meaning of the phrase "subject to the jurisdiction thereof."

Arguments Against Citizenship for Children of Non-Citizens

- Allegiance to Foreign Powers: Opponents argued that children of foreign nationals inherited the allegiance of their parents and were thus not fully subject to U.S. jurisdiction, as their primary loyalty lay with another country.
- Policy Concerns: Some feared that granting citizenship to children of non-citizens, especially those perceived as undesirable immigrants, would undermine the nation's cultural and racial identity.
- Intent of the Amendment: Critics contended that the 14th Amendment was designed primarily to grant citizenship to formerly enslaved individuals, not to expand rights to the children of immigrants.

Arguments in Support of Birthright Citizenship

- Common Law Precedent: Supporters pointed to the long-standing English common law principle of jus soli (right of the soil), which recognized birth within a sovereign territory as the basis for citizenship.
- Textual Clarity: Advocates for Wong Kim Ark argued that the plain language of the 14th Amendment unambiguously granted citizenship to all born in the United States, except for children of diplomats or occupying forces, who were explicitly excluded.

- Equal Rights: Proponents emphasized that denying citizenship based on parental status created a second class of people, inconsistent with the egalitarian principles enshrined in the Constitution.

In a 6–2 decision, the Supreme Court sided with Wong Kim Ark. The majority opinion held that the 14th Amendment enshrined the principle of jus soli into U.S. law and guaranteed citizenship to nearly all individuals born on U.S. soil, regardless of their parents' nationality or immigration status. The Court clarified that being "subject to the jurisdiction" of the United States applied broadly, excluding only narrow exceptions, like foreign diplomats and enemy occupiers.

The decision in *Wong Kim Ark* laid the groundwork for birthright citizenship as it is understood today, affirming that the 14th Amendment protects the right of all those born in the United States to be recognized as citizens. At a time of intense anti-immigrant sentiment, the case upheld the Constitution's commitment to equality and fairness, principles that remain deeply contested in ongoing debates about immigration and citizenship.

Lennon v. I.N.S. (1975)[2]

In 1975, a case emerged that not only captured the public's attention, but also permanently impacted immigration law as a whole. *Lennon v. I.N.S.* was not just about the world-famous Beatles musician John Lennon; it was a turning point that illuminated the intersection of celebrity status, political activism, immigration policies, and the government's use of something known as Prosecutorial Discretion. The *Lennon* case ultimately paved the way for future immigration laws, including the Deferred Action for Childhood Arrivals (DACA) program.

The story began in the early 1970s, when John Lennon, the iconic former member of The Beatles, and his wife, Yoko Ono, found themselves on the federal government's radar. Their vocal and influential anti-Vietnam war activism drew the attention of President Richard Nixon and his administration, which in turn sought to deport Lennon from the United States, where he had been living for years. The government's motivation to remove

2. 527 F.2d 187 (2d Cir. 1975).

Lennon was clear: His political activities and prominence in the anti-war movement posed a significant threat to their agenda.

During the late 1960s and early 1970s, the United States was deeply embroiled in the Vietnam War, a conflict that had sparked widespread protests and dissent. John Lennon and Yoko Ono became prominent anti-war activists and used their celebrity status to advocate for peace, organizing events, protests, and campaigns that attracted national and international attention.

John Lennon was a cultural icon and a voice of his generation. His music, along with his outspoken political views, had an undeniable impact on American youth. The Nixon administration was rightfully concerned that Lennon's influence could sway public opinion, particularly among young voters. In 1971, the 26th Amendment to the U.S. Constitution had lowered the voting age in America to 18 years old, codifying the mantra of "old enough to fight—old enough to vote." As the 1972 presidential election approached, the government feared that the musician's activism could potentially undermine Nixon's reelection campaign.

To target Lennon, the government seized upon his prior drug-related offenses as a pretext for deportation. While Lennon had in fact faced drug-related charges in the past, the timing of the government's action raised suspicions. As it happens, my own father, Leon Wildes, led John Lennon's legal defense. He argued that the charges, which dated back several years, were abruptly and suspiciously resurrected by immigration authorities.

The timing of these actions, coinciding with Lennon's vocal anti-war activism during the Nixon era, was seen as highly problematic. My father contended that the government's tactics were a clear attempt to silence Lennon's political dissent, highlighting the fact that the years-old drug-related charges had at no prior point presented a problem with Lennon's immigration status, and had Lennon not been a high-profile figure and an anti-war activist, the drug-related charges likely would not have been used as a pretext for deportation. The Lennon case raised a critical question: whether the government's immigration enforcement was politically motivated.

My father strategically and famously invoked the concept of Prosecutorial Discretion, which essentially grants the government the power to decide how immigration laws are enforced, as a central pillar of Lennon's defense. He demonstrated how the government's efforts to deport Lennon were politically motivated and emphasized that immigration enforcement should not be used as a tool to suppress political activism or target individuals based on their beliefs. He built a case that went far beyond the drug-related charges, focusing on the broader implications of political motivation in immigration enforcement. This strategy aimed to set a precedent that has effectively prevented countless politically motivated deportations in the decades since.

What followed was a fierce legal battle that culminated in a landmark decision by the U.S. Court of Appeals for the Second Circuit in 1975.[3] The court overturned the government's deportation efforts against Lennon, but its ruling focused narrowly on interpreting a provision of the Immigration and Nationality Act (section 212(a)(23)), specifically distinguishing between hashish and marijuana for the purposes of excludability. While the court acknowledged Lennon's argument that the deportation was politically motivated, it did not make a determination on that issue, as the claim was not fully presented for review. However, the court's decision left the door open for further judicial scrutiny of selective enforcement claims, emphasizing that immigration laws should not be used to target individuals based on their political activities or beliefs.

There is no denying that John Lennon's activism posed a challenge to President Nixon's campaign and presidency, given its potential to influence public opinion and mobilize young voters. While Lennon's claims of political targeting were not fully addressed by the court, the case highlighted the importance of safeguarding against politically motivated enforcement of immigration laws and has since been cited in countless discussions about Prosecutorial Discretion in immigration policy.

The recognition of the government's potential to abuse its immigration enforcement powers for political gain set a significant precedent. It highlighted the need for safeguards to prevent immigration enforcement from being influenced by political motives, ensuring that deportation decisions are based on established legal principles and individual circumstances. But saying that we need safeguards against political motives and actually implementing those safeguards are two very different things.

Fortunately, my father's efforts brought forth more than simple talking points, and the high-profile nature of the case ensured the outcome was heard far and wide. By calling attention to the government's abuse of power

3. Lennon v. Immigration and Naturalization Service, 527 F.2d 187 (2d Cir. 1975).

and taking action to halt it in its tracks, my father helped usher in a new era of immigration law. Some of the resulting changes include:

- Prosecutorial Discretion Guidelines: Guidelines were established to govern the exercise of Prosecutorial Discretion in immigration matters. These guidelines help immigration officials make consistent, non-politically-motivated decisions regarding enforcement actions. They require immigration authorities to consider factors such as the severity of the individual's offense, their ties to the community, and their family situation before initiating deportation proceedings. Examples of PD guidelines include the 1981 INS Operating Instructions, the 1996 Illegal Immigration Reform and Immigrant Responsibility Act (IIRIRA), the Morton Memos[4] (2011), the 2014 DHS Enforcement Priorities,[5] and the 2021 DHS Guidance.[6]
- Deferred Action Programs: The recognition that children should not be held responsible for their parents' immigration decisions, a principle underscored by the *Lennon* case, led to the creation of programs like Deferred Action for Childhood Arrivals (DACA). DACA provides protection from deportation and work permits to undocumented individuals who were brought to the United States as children. It ensures that immigration actions are not politically motivated and that individuals can continue their lives and contribute positively to society.
- Immigration Court System: The *Lennon* case reinforced the need for an immigration court system that operates with transparency and fairness, even amid potential political pressures. It drew attention to the risks of using immigration enforcement as a tool for political retaliation, highlighting the importance of impartial adjudication. While immigration courts are supposed to apply

4. John Morton, Director, ICE, Exercising Prosecutorial Discretion Consistent with the Civil Immigration Enforcement Priorities of the Agency for the Apprehension, Detention, and Removal of Aliens (June 17, 2011); and Prosecutorial Discretion: Certain Victims, Witnesses, and Plaintiffs (June 17, 2011).

5. Jeh Charles Johnson, Secretary, DHS, Policies for the Apprehension, Detention and Removal of Undocumented Immigrants (Nov. 20, 2014).

6. Alejandro Mayorkas, Secretary, DHS, Guidelines for the Enforcement of Civil Immigration Law (Sept. 30, 2021); implemented Nov. 29, 2021 [Mayorkas Memo].

laws consistently based on legal principles and individual circumstances, it's important to note that immigration judges are part of the executive branch, which also oversees removal procedures, as opposed to the judicial branch, which (along with the legislature) was designed to serve as a potential check on the powers of the executive branch. This dual role raises ongoing concerns about maintaining judicial independence within the system.

- Oversight and Accountability: The *Lennon* case emphasized the need for oversight and accountability in immigration enforcement. Independent oversight bodies and organizations play an integral role in monitoring immigration actions to ensure that they are not politically motivated. These entities provide a check on government actions and advocate for the rights of individuals facing deportation.
- Public Awareness and Advocacy: Public awareness and advocacy have grown in importance with regard to preventing politically motivated immigration actions. Civil society organizations, human rights groups, and advocacy networks play a significant role in raising awareness about cases that may involve political motives and pressuring for transparent and just immigration decisions.
- Legal Challenges: The legal community, inspired by the success of my father and his legal team, continues to play a pivotal role in challenging immigration actions that appear politically motivated. Legal challenges and court cases are essential tools for ensuring that individuals are not targeted for their political beliefs or activism.
- Transparency and Documentation: Transparency in immigration enforcement is necessary for preventing politically motivated actions, a lesson learned during Lennon's high-profile battle. His case revealed how the lack of clear documentation and public accountability in immigration decisions could enable misuse of the system for political purposes. It quickly became evident that decisions were influenced by external pressures, prompting widespread criticism and calls for reforms. The *Lennon* case also reinforced the need for policies and individual decisions to be thoroughly documented, allowing for scrutiny and accountability.
- Community to Congressional Oversight: Entities ranging from local activists to elected officials can take on oversight roles in immigration matters. Community organizations often work to ensure that

> individuals are not targeted for political or unjust reasons, while members of Congress can advocate for fair and impartial immigration policies. A transparent process allows for anyone to join the cause to help ensure the immigration system cannot be manipulated for personal or political gain.

The *Lennon* case highlighted the importance of considering underlying motives of immigration enforcement actions, and this principle played a significant role in shaping the foundation of DACA. In fact, the influence of this case can be traced directly to DACA's creation, which was established more than three decades later in 2012. In addition to protecting children from being held responsible for the immigration decisions of their parents, DACA prevents individuals from being targeted or deported due to political affiliations, activism, or other non-criminal factors.

The legacy of *Lennon v. I.N.S.* reminds us that the government's actions in immigration matters must be just, consistent, and free from political manipulation. It serves as a testament to the power of the law to ensure that immigration enforcement is fair and impartial, protecting the rights of all individuals who come to the United States seeking a better life. The government's use of Prosecutorial Discretion should be guided by established legal principles, due process, and fairness. Not politics.

The *Lennon* case, with my father at the helm, is also a powerful example of the importance of legal advocacy in immigration matters. It illustrates how a skilled legal team, armed with knowledge of immigration law and a commitment to justice, can challenge politically motivated actions by the government and ultimately protect the rights of individuals. A defendant with less means for legal challenge than Lennon, or with a less skilled and tenacious legal team, may not have been fortunate enough to attain the same result and avoid deportation. Fortunately, these legal precedents now stand to benefit all who might face undue political pressures in their own immigration matters. The case's legacy endures in the form of legal principles that safeguard against the abuse of immigration enforcement for political purposes.

How to Be a Changemaker

I cannot overstate the importance of standing up to the government when immigration policies are inhumane, particularly those motivated by political agendas, and refusing to accept "no" when a client's civil or human rights are at stake. If you are an immigration law student or practicing attorney, your actions have the potential to profoundly affect not only the lives of your clients, but also the evolution of immigration law and policy. Legal advocacy is a powerful force for justice, and you can contribute to this cause by engaging in the following actions.

Upholding the Rule of Law

The rule of law is the cornerstone of justice and equality in immigration matters. No one, regardless of their background—or fame—should face deportation based on political motivations. An immigration lawyer's dedication to upholding the rule of law ensures fairness and accountability in the application of immigration policies.

Protecting Civil and Human Rights

Immigration law often involves defending cases where an individual's civil and human rights are at risk. Aggressively advocating for these rights, no matter the odds, is essential. This work demonstrates the power of legal advocacy in safeguarding individuals' rights to due process and protecting them from politically motivated actions.

Challenging Injustice

Challenging injustice, even and especially when it is driven by the government, is not only a duty, but also an achievable goal. Immigration lawyers play a critical role in opposing unjust or inhumane policies and actions. The legal system can be used as a tool to address and rectify these injustices.

The Role of Knowledge and Expertise

In the *Lennon* case, my father and his legal team relied on their deep understanding of immigration law to challenge the government's actions effectively. Their knowledge and experience were pivotal to their success. For law students and practitioners, continuous education and the development of expertise in the field are essential for impactful advocacy. Immigration law is a specialized field with countless nuances, where even minor mistakes can be costly and permanently impact immigration status.

Persistence and Determination

The *Lennon* case was not won easily; it required years of steadfast determination. As such, it exemplifies the need for immigration lawyers to be steadfast in their commitment to their clients' rights. The journey is frequently long and challenging, but persistence can lead to justice.

Leaving a Legacy

Groundbreaking cases extend their impact far beyond the courtroom. The *Lennon* case is a powerful example of the impact that legal advocacy can have in shaping immigration law and policy. Immigration lawyers have the potential to leave a lasting legacy that advances justice and fairness in the immigration system.

Building a Just Society

Ultimately, immigration lawyers serve as legal advocates working to create a just and equitable society. By contributing to the development of a system that respects the rights and dignity of all individuals, regardless of their background or beliefs, we fulfill a higher purpose—ensuring justice for all.

Plyler v. Doe (1982):[7] Paving the Way for Equal Protection

In the early 1980s, *Plyler v. Doe* was a Supreme Court case that would dramatically shape immigration law and, more importantly, how we treat undocumented children in the United States. At its core, the case revolved around one question: Should the immigration status of a child dictate their access to public education?

Plyler v. Doe originated in Texas, where state laws at the time allowed local school districts to deny enrollment to undocumented children, deeming them ineligible for the free education that their U.S.-citizen counterparts enjoyed. The key issue was whether this disparity in educational access violated the 14th Amendment's Equal Protection Clause.

7. 457 U.S. 202 (1982).

The Equal Protection Clause was intended to shield against discrimination by affirming that no state shall "deny to any person within its jurisdiction the equal protection of the laws." In essence, it means that all individuals, regardless of their background, are entitled to equal protection under the law.

In the context of *Plyler v. Doe*, the clause was the touchstone upon which the case hinged. The Supreme Court was tasked with determining whether the denial of educational opportunities to undocumented children solely based on their immigration status amounted to a violation of this protection.

The case captured the nation's attention and garnered immense legal and public interest. Public opinion was very much divided. On one side, Texas authorities argued that denying undocumented children access to public education was a permissible exercise of their authority. On the other side, the children and their supporters contended that such exclusion perpetuated discrimination and inequality. At the heart of this debate were the following arguments.

Arguments in Support of Denying Access

- Rule of Law: Supporters of denying access often cited the rule of law. Many believed that the enforcement of immigration laws and regulations necessitated denying certain benefits, including public education, to those who did not have lawful immigration status.
- Limited Resources: Some argued that public education resources were limited, and it was essential to allocate them to lawful residents and citizens. They contended that providing education to undocumented children could strain already overburdened school systems.
- Taxes: Concerns were raised about the financial burden placed on taxpayers to fund the education of undocumented children. Opponents argued that providing such education would result in increased costs for taxpayers, who were already shouldering high expenses.

Arguments in Support of Providing Access

- Preventing a Permanent Underclass: Supporters of access to education contended that by providing education to undocumented children, the United States could help prevent the creation of a permanent underclass of individuals with limited opportunities. They believed that education was an avenue for these children to break the cycle of poverty and contribute positively to society.

- Long-Term Benefits: Proponents argued that educating undocumented children could lead to long-term benefits for society. An educated workforce was seen as an investment that could enhance the nation's economic productivity and social cohesion.
- International Human Rights: Some supporters framed the issue as a matter of international human rights. They believed that denying education to children based on their immigration status contravened fundamental principles of human rights and dignity.

In a historic decision, the Supreme Court ruled in favor of the plaintiffs. The Court held that the Texas laws denying undocumented children access to public education were unconstitutional and violated the Equal Protection Clause of the 14th Amendment. The ruling declared that all children, regardless of their immigration status, had a right to equal educational opportunities.

The case not only reaffirmed the principle that the Constitution's Equal Protection Clause applied to all individuals within U.S. borders, but also extended this protection to undocumented children. The decision emphasized that immigration status should not be a barrier to essential services like education, and that society has an interest in educating all children, regardless of their legal status. *Plyler v. Doe* is another example of how immigration laws can shape not only our immigration system, but American society as a whole.

Jean v. Nelson (1985):[8] A Pivotal Case for Detained Immigrants

In recent years, the topic of detained immigrants and their treatment in detention centers has made headlines. But the mistreatment of immigrants in detention centers is nothing new. In 1985, the case of *Jean v. Nelson*

8. 472 U.S. 846 (1985).

revolved around the treatment of detained Haitian immigrants, particularly those seeking asylum in the United States. It raised critical questions about due process protections for detained non-citizens and the government's obligations in handling asylum claims.

The petitioner, "Jean," was the named representative of "a class of undocumented and unadmitted aliens from Haiti." "Jean," along with other detained Haitian nationals, challenged the government's actions in seeking asylum and the mistreatment of detained immigrants.

"Nelson" refers to David A. Nelson, who was the Commissioner of the Immigration and Naturalization Service (INS) at the time. The INS, now known as U.S. Citizenship and Immigration Services (USCIS), was responsible for immigration enforcement and processing asylum claims. The government's actions in detaining and processing asylum claimants, specifically involving Haitian nationals, were central to the legal dispute.

The proceedings ultimately resulted in the Supreme Court's decision, which firmly established that due process protections apply to non-citizens in detention facing deportation. It further clarified that detained immigrants possess rights that must be safeguarded, reinforcing the principle that fairness and justice should not be confined by citizenship boundaries.

During the legal proceedings, several advocacy groups and legal organizations became involved in supporting the interests of detained Haitian nationals, including "Jean." These groups played a critical role in challenging the government's policies and actions, advocating for the rights of detained immigrants. Briefs of amici curiae were filed by the American Civil Liberties Union, the American Immigration Lawyers Association, Amnesty International U.S.A., the Asian American Legal Defense and Education Fund et al., Metropolitan Dade County et al., the NAACP Legal Defense and Educational Fund, Inc., the National Association for the Advancement of Colored People et al., the National Coalition for Haitian Refugees et al., the Procedural Aspects of International Law Institute et al., and the Lawyers Committee for International Human Rights et al.

In addition to these larger organizations, individual legal advocates and attorneys were instrumental in representing detained immigrants. They provided counsel, pursued legal challenges, and worked to ensure that due process rights were upheld.

These individuals, groups, and organizations played a vital role in advocating for the rights and fair treatment of detained Haitian immigrants, establishing important legal principles in the process and illustrating the power of advocacy groups in shaping immigration law.

The Supreme Court's ruling in *Jean v. Nelson* marked a significant shift in immigration law and policy. It reaffirmed that the government's actions in detaining and deporting non-citizens must adhere to the fundamental principles of due process. However, concerns about the mistreatment of detained immigrants, the conditions in detention centers, and the length of detention have continued to be subjects of debate and legal challenges. While *Jean v. Nelson* established the principle of due process, ensuring that these rights are consistently upheld and that detention practices meet humane standards remains a subject of ongoing advocacy and litigation.

In recent years, there have been countless reports of inadequate medical care, substandard living conditions, and issues related to the treatment of detained immigrants in various detention facilities. Advocacy groups, legal organizations, and individuals continue to advocate for the rights and humane treatment of detained immigrants, but problems persist.

Medical Neglect at ICE Detention Facilities

A 2019 report by the Department of Homeland Security's Office of Inspector General[9] documented severe deficiencies in medical care at multiple ICE detention centers. It highlighted instances of delayed or denied medical treatment, lack of necessary medications, and poor responses to medical emergencies.

Substandard Living Conditions

A 2020 study by the ACLU[10] detailed overcrowded conditions in detention centers, with reports of detainees being forced to sleep on floors and denied access to basic hygiene supplies such as soap and toilet paper, particularly during the COVID-19 pandemic.

9. U.S. Department of Homeland Security, Office of Inspector General, Concerns About ICE Detainee Treatment and Care at Four Detention Facilities, OIG-19-47 (June 3, 2019).

10. American Civil Liberties Union, Immigration Detention in the United States: Overview of Conditions & Legal Obligations (2020), https://immigrantjustice.org/wp-content/uploads/2025/05/Justice-Free-Zones_Immigrant_Detention_Report_ACLU-HRW-NIJC_April-2020.pdf.

Death of Immigrants in Custody

In 2017, a report by Human Rights Watch[11] found that inadequate medical care contributed to multiple deaths in ICE custody. The report cited cases where detainees' illnesses were ignored or mismanaged, leading to preventable fatalities.

Family Separation and Detention of Children

A 2018 report by Amnesty International[12] criticized the treatment of children detained at U.S.–Mexico border facilities. The report documented instances of children being held in cold, overcrowded cells without proper bedding, nutrition, or emotional support.

Sexual Abuse in Detention

A 2021 investigation by *The Intercept*[13] revealed widespread allegations of sexual abuse and harassment in ICE detention facilities, with many cases involving guards or facility staff. Advocates highlighted systemic failures in investigating and addressing these abuses.

Detention of Pregnant Women

A 2018 report by the Women's Refugee Commission[14] found that pregnant detainees faced inadequate prenatal care, including being denied access to necessary medical attention and facing harsh conditions that endangered their health and the health of their unborn children.

---

11. Human Rights Watch, *Systemic Indifference: Dangerous and Substandard Medical Care in U.S. Immigration Detention* (May 8, 2017), https://www.hrw.org/report/2017/05/08/systemic-indifference/dangerous-substandard-medical-care-us-immigration-detention.

12. Amnesty International, *USA: Catastrophic Immigration Policies Resulted in More Family Separations than Previously Disclosed* (Oct. 11, 2018), https://www.amnestyusa.org/reports/usa-catastrophic-immigration-policies-resulted-in-more-family-separations-than-previously-disclosed/.

13. Zeba Warsi, *"Immensely Invisible:" Women Fighting ICE's Inaction on Sexual Abuses*, Futuro Media (July 21, 2023), https://futuroinvestigates.org/investigative-stories/immensely-invisible/immensely-invisible-women-fighting-ices-inaction-on-sexual-abuses/.

14. Women's Refugee Commission, *Joint Complaint on ICE Detention and Treatment of Pregnant Women* (Sept. 26, 2017), https://www.womensrefugeecommission.org/research-resources/joint-complaint-ice-detention-treatment-of-pregnant-women/.

Furthermore, many detained immigrants face significant challenges in accessing legal representation. According to a 2016 study by the American Immigration Council,[15] only 37 percent of all immigrants in removal proceedings were able to secure legal representation, and for detained immigrants, that number dropped to just 14 percent. This disparity is deeply concerning, as the presence of legal counsel can dramatically improve the outcome of a case.

The absence of legal counsel severely impacts a detainee's ability to protect their rights. The same study found that immigrants with legal representation were five times more likely to succeed in their cases than those without representation. This stark disparity illustrates the critical role of legal counsel in ensuring a fair process and preventing unjust deportations.

In some instances, detained individuals have been deported while their asylum claims were still pending, a situation that may deny them the opportunity to seek protection from persecution in their home countries. Without legal guidance, many fail to understand their rights or the intricacies of asylum law, leaving them at an overwhelming disadvantage in proceedings that can determine their future and safety.

These significant problems highlight the ongoing need for advocacy efforts by organizations and individuals who seek to ensure that detained immigrants are treated with dignity and respect, and in alignment with principles of due process and human rights. They also reinforce the need for continued scrutiny and reform of detention practices to mitigate instances of inhumane treatment and substandard living conditions.

While the *Jean v. Nelson* case itself did not directly address issues related to unsanitary and unsafe conditions in contemporary detention centers, it set a legal precedent that mandated fair treatment for detained individuals, irrespective of their immigration status.

In the pursuit of national security and immigration enforcement, it's important not to lose sight of our fundamental values. The United States is a nation built on principles of justice, fairness, and due process, and these principles should extend to all who find themselves within its borders, regardless of their citizenship status. *Jean v. Nelson* remains instrumental in

15. American Immigration Council, Immigration Detention in the United States by Agency (2016), https://www.americanimmigrationcouncil.org/wp-content/uploads/2025/01/immigration_detention_in_the_united_states_by_agency.pdf.

shaping immigration law and the treatment of detained immigrants, but the issue of immigrant detention remains highly controversial.

INS v. St. Cyr (2001)[16]

While *Jean v. Nelson* focused on the due process rights of detained immigrants, particularly those seeking asylum in the United States, *INS v. St. Cyr* addressed the rights of immigrants with lawful permanent resident (LPR) status to seek relief from deportation through judicial review. While *Jean v. Nelson* and *INS v. St. Cyr* are both rooted in the principles of due process and the fair treatment of immigrants facing possible removal, they address different legal questions and aspects of immigration law.

Enrico St. Cyr was the petitioner in the *INS v. St. Cyr* case. He was a lawful permanent resident of the United States who had been convicted of possession with the intent to distribute cocaine and faced deportation as a result of the conviction. St. Cyr sought to challenge his removal through judicial review.

The INS, the precursor to U.S. Citizenship and Immigration Services (USCIS), was the respondent in the case. The INS was responsible for enforcing immigration laws and had initiated removal proceedings against St. Cyr based on his criminal conviction.

The case revolved around Enrico St. Cyr's right to seek relief from deportation through judicial review and the government's position on whether he was eligible for such review. The Supreme Court's decision in favor of St. Cyr had significant implications for immigrants with LPR status. Enrico St. Cyr was able to prevail in his case, despite a serious criminal conviction, because he challenged the government's efforts to deport him on the grounds of a change in immigration law. His defense relied on the following key arguments:

- Statutory Change: After St. Cyr's criminal conviction, immigration laws underwent several changes. In particular, Congress enacted the Antiterrorism and Effective Death Penalty Act (AEDPA)[17] and

16. 533 U.S. 289 (2001).

17. Antiterrorism and Effective Death Penalty Act of 1996, Pub. L. No. 104-132, 110 Stat. 1214 (Apr. 24, 1996).

the Illegal Immigration Reform and Immigrant Responsibility Act (IIRIRA). These laws limited the ability of certain immigrants with criminal convictions to seek relief from deportation. However, St. Cyr's conviction occurred before the enactment of AEDPA and IIRIRA.

- Due Process and Retroactivity: St. Cyr's legal team argued that applying AEDPA and IIRIRA retroactively to his case would violate his due process rights. They contended that he had a legitimate expectation that the immigration laws in place at the time of his conviction would apply to his situation.
- Judicial Review: St. Cyr sought the right to have his case heard in immigration court, which was consistent with the immigration laws in place at the time of his conviction.

The Supreme Court ruled in favor of St. Cyr, concluding that he should be allowed to pursue relief from deportation through judicial review because the application of the new laws retroactively would violate his due process rights. This decision upheld the rights of immigrants with LPR status to seek relief from deportation and set a precedent that remains influential in contemporary immigration law.

Key Implications for Immigration Law Today

The Supreme Court's decision in *INS v. St. Cyr* reinforced the basic principles that protect the rights of individuals involved in deportation proceedings. Here are some of the key implications of this case for immigration law today:

- Right to Seek Relief from Deportation: One of the critical outcomes of *INS v. St. Cyr* was the affirmation of the right of LPRs to seek relief from deportation through judicial review. This ruling emphasized the importance of providing a fair and accessible process for immigrants with LPR status to challenge their deportation. As a result, LPRs can pursue legal remedies and have their cases heard before an immigration judge, contributing to a more just and transparent immigration system.
- Protection of Due Process Rights: The case underscored the significance of due process rights in immigration proceedings. It

emphasized that immigrants, even when facing deportation, are entitled to a fair and impartial process that allows them to present their cases and seek relief from removal. This principle remains a cornerstone of immigration law today, ensuring that individuals are afforded the opportunity to assert their rights.

- Judicial Review as a Safeguard: *INS v. St. Cyr* recognized judicial review as a critical safeguard in immigration proceedings, allowing for independent oversight of decisions made by immigration authorities. This mechanism helps prevent potential abuses of power and ensures individuals are not wrongfully deported. However, subsequent cases, such as *Patel v. Garland*,[18] have significantly limited the scope of judicial review in certain contexts, particularly when discretionary decisions by immigration officials are at issue. This development has created a more nuanced situation, in which the protections established in *INS v. St. Cyr* may not always fully apply, highlighting the ongoing tension between judicial oversight and administrative discretion in immigration law.
- Impact on Legal Challenges and Advocacy: *INS v. St. Cyr* has served as a foundational case in shaping legal challenges and advocacy efforts. It established a precedent that has been instrumental in arguments to protect the rights of immigrants, particularly those with LPR status, facing deportation. For example, it has been cited in cases challenging retroactive application of immigration laws and in efforts to preserve access to judicial review. The case continues to serve as a critical tool for immigration attorneys advocating for fair treatment.
- Ongoing Influence in Immigration Policy: *INS v. St. Cyr* has had a lasting influence on immigration policy and enforcement practices. It continues to shape the way immigration authorities interact with individuals in deportation proceedings, reinforcing the principles of fairness and justice.

---

18. 596 U.S. 328 (2022). In this case, the Supreme Court held that federal courts lack jurisdiction to review certain factual findings made by immigration officials in discretionary relief proceedings, significantly narrowing the scope of judicial review in immigration matters.

INS v. St. Cyr has been invoked in myriad legal contexts to emphasize the importance of due process and judicial review for immigrants who are facing deportation or removal proceedings. The case continues to influence legal arguments and decisions aimed at protecting the rights of non-citizen individuals within the United States.

CHAPTER 3

Immigration Today

Constantly evolving challenges and factors influence the ongoing debates and decisions that affect millions of individuals seeking a better life in the United States. The modern immigration debate is defined by several key issues, including but not limited to the challenge of keeping legislation and regulations up to date with current circumstances, national security concerns including the heightened threat of terrorism, and the influence of political campaigning and other divisive and inflammatory rhetoric.

No single event has had a more profound and far-reaching impact on the field of immigration law and policy during my career than the tragic events of September 11, 2001. The day after the attacks, I was at Ground Zero in my role as a volunteer EMT with an ambulance crew. Standing amid the devastation, staring in horror at the smoldering ruins of what had once been a thriving hub of commerce, culture, and human connection, it became clear to me and every other American that our world had been irrevocably changed.

These tragic events not only shook the very foundations of our nation, but also ushered in a new era of immigration policies and regulations that continue to affect immigration law today. In the aftermath of the attacks, the United States witnessed a seismic shift in its approach to national security, precipitating significant changes in immigration and visa policies. These changes were driven by an urgent need to enhance security measures, prevent potential threats, and maintain the safety and well-being of those living within the country's borders. All very legitimate objectives.

What came next, however, was highly problematic. While strong and swift action was surely called for to ensure the safety of the American people, fear and emotion got the better of many Americans, leading to racially fueled societal outrage, as well as overreach in our government's reaction.

The issue with our response to the attacks of 9/11 did not stem from our concurrent desire to protect both our loved ones and our freedom, but rather from the voices that started to conflate terrorism with immigration. I wholeheartedly acknowledge that offering refuge should never come at the cost of compromising our national security. However, it is equally imperative that we resist discrimination against millions of innocent individuals solely based on their religion or country of origin, or the crimes of a few bad actors. This principle is underscored by the fact that, as witnessed with Timothy McVeigh, Ted Kaczynski, and Dylann Roof, terrorism can just as easily be homegrown. The expression of fear and hostility within our nation toward Muslims and individuals perceived to be of Middle Eastern descent has not only contributed to a mounting global death toll over far too many years, but also undermines our own security. Our treatment of immigrants and those beyond our borders is intrinsically tied to the safety and well-being of this great nation. When we embrace people with respect, empathy, and compassion, we tend to elicit a similar response, which would serve to reduce the risk of violence, including acts of terrorism.

Conversely, when we respond with fear, disrespect, and bigotry, we increase the likelihood of conflict and violence. This applies to all people, not solely immigrants. Whether we examine the childhood and life experiences of an Islamic extremist, a gang member in Los Angeles, an abusive spouse, or a school shooter, we will likely find a history of mistreatment, abuse, neglect, poverty, or some manifestation of profound suffering. As such, our immigration policies and the compassion with which we treat those who seek refuge or a better life in the United States are not only humanitarian imperatives, but also essential components of a comprehensive national security strategy.

As an immigration lawyer, I believe it is critical to explore how these post–9/11 reforms have impacted the lives of countless immigrants and the practice of immigration law itself. As a witness to these events and consequences throughout my own lifetime and professional career, I feel an obligation to apply my own experiences and reflections to this study. Historical research is an admirable practice, but will never fully capture what we in the present can observe and document. We may become the record that future scholars will rely on, so especially in our areas of expertise, we should strive to understand and pass on that knowledge to the best of our abilities.

In the pursuit of heightened national security, countless measures have been implemented that continue to adversely affect innocent immigrants. The USA PATRIOT Act,[1] for instance, expanded the government's surveillance powers, including its ability to monitor phone and internet communications. While the intended targets were potential threats, the broad scope of these surveillance programs often resulted in the unjust scrutiny of innocent immigrants. In some cases, individuals were subjected to unwarranted surveillance, leading to unjustified suspicions and difficulties in their immigration processes.

Similarly, the No-Fly List, established to prevent potential terrorists from boarding planes, has mistakenly ensnared innocent individuals, including American citizens and lawful permanent residents. Many of these individuals were subject to severe travel restrictions and hardships in reuniting with their families or pursuing education and career opportunities abroad.

The post–9/11 era also witnessed a significant increase in immigration detentions. While some detainees were individuals who posed security risks, many innocent people were held in detention facilities for extended periods, without due process or the opportunity to challenge their detention. Innocent immigrants, including those seeking asylum from persecution in their home countries, found themselves detained for extended periods under harsh conditions.

While national security remains a top priority, it is essential to strike a balance that protects both the nation's security and the rights and well-being of those who seek a better life here. These policies must be implemented judiciously to avoid compromising the principles of justice, compassion, and respect that our nation holds dear.

Terrorism and National Security Concerns

Since the events of 9/11, national security concerns have prompted the implementation of rigorous security measures within the immigration system. These measures, including enhanced background checks, security

1. Uniting and Strengthening America by Providing Appropriate Tools Required to Intercept and Obstruct Terrorism (USA PATRIOT) Act of 2001, Pub. L. No. 107-56, 115 Stat. 272 (Oct. 26, 2001).

screenings, increased vetting processes, and detentions, aim to mitigate potential security risks and threats that could compromise the safety of the nation.

Although these mechanisms are components of a broader counterterrorism strategy to prevent those with malicious intentions from entering the country, their efficacy is often called into question. For starters, an overemphasis on rigorous vetting processes diverts resources from addressing other pressing immigration issues, such as the need for comprehensive reform and addressing systemic challenges, both of which are required for a more efficient system.

From invasive background checks for visa applicants to the use of biometric technologies, including facial recognition, at ports of entry, what is a waste of time and resources, what is a violation of human rights, and what is actually effective?

The implementation of stricter security measures, particularly at ports of entry, has raised valid concerns about potential violations of human rights. Profiling based on race, religion, or nationality, whether intentional or not, is common, leading to claims of discrimination and the erosion of civil liberties. Examples of these violations include:

- Enhanced Screening of Individuals from Specific Countries: Security protocols that target individuals from specific countries, often labeled as high-risk due to geopolitical considerations or past incidents, often contribute to racial profiling. Even if these measures are rooted in security concerns, they disproportionately affect individuals solely based on their nationality, regardless of their individual circumstances.
- Selective Secondary Inspections: Individuals are frequently subjected to secondary inspections based on their perceived ethnic or racial background, even in the absence of concrete evidence or suspicious behavior. Such practices result in unwarranted delays and increased scrutiny for individuals who may be targeted solely due to their appearance or cultural background.
- Use of Ethnic and Religious Appearance as Indicators: Security personnel, consciously or unconsciously, may use ethnic or religious appearance as indicators for potential security threats. This subjective approach leads to individuals being singled out based on stereotypes rather than specific evidence of wrongdoing.

- Disparate Impact on Minority Communities: Security measures that disproportionately impact minority communities, either due to their geographical origin or cultural background, are a form of systemic racial profiling. This contributes to a sense of alienation within these communities and undermines trust in the fairness of immigration and security processes.
- Inadequate Training and Bias: Instances of racial profiling can be exacerbated by inadequate training of security personnel and the presence of implicit biases. Unconscious prejudices may influence decision making, leading to disparities in how individuals are treated during security screenings.

Furthermore, strict security measures impede the flow of legitimate travel and trade. Lengthier processing times and increased scrutiny at ports of entry have economic repercussions and strain international relations. Addressing these concerns requires ongoing efforts to promote awareness, provide comprehensive training, and ensure that security protocols are both effective and fair, safeguarding the principles of justice and equal treatment for all individuals entering the country.

In addition to the intrusive security measures discussed earlier, unnecessary detentions have become far too common. Detaining immigrants without proper cause or due process violates human rights and contributes to an environment of fear and animosity, further eroding the trust between immigrant communities and authorities.

Instances of unnecessary detention often stem from overreliance on generalized criteria, such as nationality or immigration status, rather than evidence of individual wrongdoing. This approach results in the unwarranted and unjust incarceration of individuals who pose no security threat. These practices not only fail to address security concerns effectively, but also tarnish the reputation of the country on the international stage.

While these examples all revolve around human rights violations, it's important to recognize that when these violations occur on a large scale, they serve as an incubator for distrust, fear, and hatred among those who are targeted. Beyond human rights, it is in the best interest of national security that we improve relations with immigrants, both documented and undocumented, as well as foreign nationals living abroad.

The ripple effects of widespread human rights violations extend far beyond the immediate impact on the individuals directly affected. They sow the seeds of animosity, creating an environment where mutual distrust and fear flourish. This, in turn, poses a substantial threat to national security. By fostering an atmosphere of fear and division, these violations inadvertently contribute to an environment where hostility and resentment prevail.

Recognizing the interconnection between human rights and national security, we can see that safeguarding the rights and dignity of immigrants is not just a moral imperative, but a strategic necessity. Improving relations with immigrants, irrespective of their documentation status, and nurturing positive connections with foreign nationals abroad is an investment in building bridges, fostering understanding, and ultimately fortifying the nation against external threats. The need to address human rights violations goes beyond ethical considerations; it is a matter of national interest.

Bureaucratic Inefficiencies and Backlogs

Increased scrutiny has also resulted in bureaucratic inefficiencies and substantial backlogs in visa processing. Resulting delays and administrative hurdles often have significant consequences for individuals, families, and businesses, as well as a negative impact on U.S. tourism and international relations. These delays even limit the ability of our businesses to compete on a global scale. Specific challenges associated with bureaucratic inefficiencies and backlogs include:

- Extended Processing Times for Visa Applications: The increased scrutiny of visa applications translates into extended processing times. Individuals and families awaiting visa approvals often face prolonged periods of uncertainty, affecting important life decisions such as education plans, career opportunities, and family reunification.
- Administrative Delays in Security Clearances: Security clearances, which have become more intricate and detailed in the post–9/11 era, frequently contribute to bureaucratic bottlenecks. The thorough vetting processes result in delays as security agencies work through extensive background checks, impacting the timely issuance of visas.
- Inadequate Resources and Staffing: Limited resources and staffing within immigration and consular offices exacerbate inefficiencies. Insufficient personnel struggle to manage the increased workload associated with rigorous security measures, leading to delays in processing and decision-making.

- Backlogs in Visa Interviews and Appointments: The demand for visa interviews and appointments often surpasses the available slots, creating backlogs. This backlog is attributed to a combination of increased security protocols, high application volumes, and resource constraints, resulting in delays for individuals and families in scheduling and attending visa interviews.
- Complicated Administrative Procedures: The implementation of complex administrative procedures, particularly in response to security concerns, contributes to bureaucratic inefficiencies. Cumbersome documentation requirements and intricate application processes create confusion and result in errors that further prolong the visa processing timeline.
- Economic Impact on Businesses: Lengthy visa processing times pose challenges for businesses seeking to recruit international talent. Delays in obtaining work visas for skilled professionals hinder companies' abilities to meet project deadlines and capitalize on market opportunities, affecting the competitiveness of U.S. businesses on the global stage.
- Impact on Tourism and International Relations: Lengthy processing times and heightened scrutiny can discourage potential tourists from choosing the United States as their destination. This not only affects the tourism industry, but also strains international relations as travelers experience frustration and inconvenience, impacting our global image.

Addressing these bureaucratic inefficiencies and backlogs necessitates a careful balancing act between security imperatives and the facilitation of legitimate travel and immigration. Improved allocation of resources, streamlined administrative processes, and the implementation of technology to enhance efficiency are essential considerations to mitigate the negative consequences on individuals, families, businesses, and the broader economy.

Effectiveness of Counterterrorism Strategies

How effective are these counterterrorism strategies, really? Evaluating whether security measures truly enhance national security or inadvertently target innocent individuals remains a controversial topic.

Here are a few specific examples highlighting concerns about the effectiveness of certain counterterrorism measures:

- Mass Surveillance Programs: In addition to their potential infringement on privacy rights, mass data collection yields an overwhelming volume of information, making it difficult to identify credible threats. Resources allocated to comprehensive surveillance might be better used in targeted, intelligence-driven approaches that focus on specific individuals or groups with known links to extremist activities.
- Enhanced Screening Procedures: Stricter screening procedures at ports of entry, while intended to identify potential threats, can lead to extensive delays and bureaucratic inefficiencies. The time-consuming nature of enhanced screening procedures does not proportionally enhance security. Resources spent on these processes would be more effectively used to invest in advanced technologies that can efficiently identify legitimate security threats without causing unnecessary delays for travelers.
- Warrantless Searches and Detentions: Expanded powers allowing warrantless searches and detentions by immigration authorities raise concerns about due process rights. But these measures are also counterproductive, creating distrust within communities and deterring individuals from cooperating with law enforcement. Resources invested in community engagement and intelligence gathering would yield more valuable information without compromising civil liberties.
- Extreme Vetting Policies: Policies proposing "extreme vetting" of visa applicants have been criticized for their subjective nature and potential for discrimination. Furthermore, instead of enhancing security, they often alienate communities and hinder the free flow of information. Allocating resources to targeted vetting processes based on credible intelligence would yield more meaningful results.
- Border Wall Construction: The construction of physical barriers, such as border walls, is framed as a strategy to prevent illegal entry and enhance security, but the effectiveness of physical barriers in preventing terrorism is extremely limited. Resources spent on constructing and maintaining these barriers could be redirected to invest in technology and personnel for more dynamic border security solutions.

As immigration policies evolve, it is essential to consider not only the security benefits, but also the potential social and ethical implications of counterterrorism measures. A comprehensive policy analysis must assess the trade-offs and aim to ensure that these efforts align with the values and principles of the United States. Getting it right would increase the effectiveness of counterterrorism strategies while also reflecting the nation's commitment to civil liberties, inclusivity, and the protection of vulnerable populations.

Outdated Legislation and Regulations

One of the most pressing challenges within our modern immigration system is the presence of outdated legislation and regulations. Antiquated laws struggle to address contemporary issues and circumstances, leaving lawmakers and immigration advocates scratching their heads about the relevance and effectiveness of existing regulations.

The need for upgrades to our immigration policy over time should not come as a surprise, and should be planned for proactively at regular intervals, rather than with reactive stopgap solutions only after a real or imagined crisis comes to pass.

To adapt to the evolving needs of our nation and its immigrant population, we need comprehensive immigration reform and the elimination of redundant or contradictory policies. Here are just a few specific examples illustrating how outdated laws and regulations can impede the immigration system:

- Family-Based Immigration Quotas: The current family-based immigration system operates under quotas established by the Immigration and Nationality Act of 1965. These quotas allocate a limited number of visas for family-sponsored immigrants based on familial relationships. The family-based immigration system is plagued by lengthy waiting times and backlogs, as the quotas do not adequately reflect modern family structures and relationships. This outdated approach fails to address modern familial ties, leading to delays in visa processing and family reunification.
- Employment-Based Immigration Categories: Employment-based immigration categories have not kept pace with the changing economic landscape and workforce needs. Outdated employment categories often do not align with current demands for skilled workers

in specific industries. This mismatch hampers the recruitment of talent critical to the U.S. economy, hindering competitiveness and innovation in sectors where skilled labor is essential.

- Asylum and Refugee Laws: The asylum and refugee laws, designed to address humanitarian concerns, have struggled to adapt to modern geopolitical realities and global displacement crises. Most are based on the 1951 Refugee Convention,[2] which defines a refugee as someone fleeing persecution based on race, religion, nationality, membership in a particular social group, or political opinion. This definition excludes individuals fleeing more recently recognized forms of violence and oppression, such as climate-induced displacement, organized crime, and gender-based violence. Current asylum frameworks also fail to account for the increasingly transnational nature of modern crises. For example, refugees from protracted conflicts, such as in Syria, Afghanistan, or Sudan, face challenges in navigating inconsistent asylum processes across different jurisdictions. Furthermore, while displacement is a global issue, asylum laws are largely governed at the national level, leading to fragmented and inconsistent responses. Wealthier nations shift responsibilities to poorer countries through regional agreements, leaving frontline states disproportionately burdened.
- Mandatory Detention Provisions: The mandatory detention provisions under the Illegal Immigration Reform and Immigrant Responsibility Act (IIRIRA) of 1996 set forth strict guidelines for the detention of certain immigrants. These inflexible provisions contribute to the prolonged detention of individuals, including asylum seekers and vulnerable populations. Detention policies rooted in outdated legislation fail to consider alternatives to detention and the principles of due process.
- Lack of Clear Pathways for Undocumented Immigrants: The absence of a clear and comprehensive pathway for undocumented immigrants to attain legal status remains a persistent problem. Antiquated laws create situations where undocumented individuals face significant hurdles to regularization. This not only perpetuates a

2. Convention Relating to the Status of Refugees, July 28, 1951, 189 U.N.T.S. 137; as modified by the Protocol Relating to the Status of Refugees, Jan. 31, 1967, 606 U.N.T.S. 267.

shadow population, but also fails to acknowledge the contributions of long-term residents who have integrated into their communities.

- Country-Specific Quotas: The diversity visa program, which allocates visas based on a lottery system, has country-specific quotas that do not reflect current migration patterns or address global geopolitical shifts. Outdated country-specific quotas lead to disparities, limiting opportunities for individuals from certain regions while oversubscribing visas for others. The program fails to account for changing migration dynamics and the diverse backgrounds of potential immigrants.

Antiquated legislation and regulations must be addressed through comprehensive immigration reform in order to reconcile the evolving needs of the nation, with the imperative of respecting the rights of immigrants.

Political Campaigning and Rhetoric

Political campaigning and divisive rhetoric exert significant influence on public perception of immigration. Campaigns have employed immigration as a rallying point, capitalizing on the emotions, concerns, and aspirations of voters. The rhetoric surrounding immigration often mirrors broader political ideologies, from calls for stricter border controls to demands for a more compassionate and inclusive immigration system.

These polarized narratives often result in lasting effects on policy decisions, public discourse, and the experiences of immigrants. Examples of divisive political rhetoric surrounding modern immigration policies include the following.

"America First" Slogan

Rhetoric: The "America First" slogan, popularized during political campaigns, has been associated with a nationalist stance that emphasizes prioritizing the interests of native-born citizens over immigrants.

Impact: This rhetoric influences policy discussions on issues such as visa allocation, asylum policies, and trade agreements. It resonates with voters who prioritize domestic concerns and harbors skepticism about the perceived impact of immigration on jobs and social services.

"Build the Wall" Movement

Rhetoric: The rallying cry to "build the wall" gained prominence during the 2016 presidential campaign. It centered on constructing an enhanced physical barrier along the U.S.–Mexico border to address perceived security concerns.

Impact: This slogan became emblematic of calls for stricter border controls, influencing subsequent policy discussions on immigration enforcement, border security funding, and the Deferred Action for Childhood Arrivals (DACA) program.

"Secure Our Borders" Narrative

Rhetoric: Many political campaigns, across various levels of government, have emphasized the need to "secure our borders" as a core component of their platforms.

Impact: By foregrounding border security, campaigns seek to address public concerns about national security and economic impacts. This rhetoric influences policy debates on immigration enforcement strategies and resource allocation for border protection.

Calls for "Pathways to Citizenship"

Rhetoric: On the opposite side of the coin, some political campaigns advocate for inclusive immigration policies, emphasizing the importance of providing pathways to citizenship for undocumented immigrants.

Impact: This rhetoric appeals to voters valuing humanitarian principles and a more lenient approach to immigration. It shapes discussions on comprehensive immigration reform, the fate of undocumented individuals, and the broader concept of American identity.

Immigration rhetoric employed during political campaigns significantly contributes to the formulation of policy decisions. Campaign promises and priorities influence legislative agendas, executive actions, and resource allocations related to immigration. This affects the introduction, modification, and repeal of immigration laws and regulations.

Political rhetoric also shapes public discourse, framing discussions on issues such as national security, economic impact, and cultural identity. This, in turn, influences public perception and attitudes toward immigrants and immigration policies. It also has implications for international relations. Rhetoric that emphasizes isolationist or nationalist positions impacts diplomatic relations and cooperation on global migration challenges. As with any political content, it is important to consider the motivating factors behind this. While some surely come from genuine policy perspectives, scapegoating of immigrants in order to appeal to a more conservative and nationalistic audience has been a common political strategy throughout history in America and beyond. On the other hand, more accommodating viewpoints may seek to pander to certain minority communities in order to gain votes from those ranks. Any number of other scenarios that address specific election circumstances could similarly come into play.

It is a sad truth that immigration continues to be one of the most common "political footballs" utilized to manipulate public opinion in American politics. It is an effective tool in this manner because it is such an emotional issue, with a profound impact on scales as grand as national economies and global security, yet as intimate as individual families. This ability to capture the attention of the public will ensure this trend continues, casting yet another layer of intricacy onto the already complex issue of immigration policy.

Border Security and Enforcement

Another hallmark of immigration today is the constant debate over border security, which encompasses border walls, surveillance, human rights, and humanitarian considerations. Advocates of stricter border security emphasize the need to protect national borders and ensure compliance with immigration laws, while opponents raise concerns about the impact of border enforcement on civil liberties, family reunification, and the welfare of those seeking asylum or refuge.

Border Wall Construction

The construction of physical barriers, commonly referred to as border walls, has been a focal point of the broader discussion around border security. Advocates argue that walls are essential for deterring illegal border crossings and enhancing security, while opponents emphasize the environmental impact, the potential for wildlife disruption, and the symbolic message of exclusion.

The construction of the U.S.–Mexico border wall has been a major source of contention, with debates over funding, environmental assessments, and the effectiveness of physical barriers in deterring unauthorized entries.

Surveillance Technologies

The use of advanced surveillance technologies, including drones, sensors, and facial recognition, raises concerns about privacy, civil liberties, and the potential for unwarranted intrusions into the lives of border communities. Surveillance drones have been deployed along the U.S.–Mexico border, sparking debates over the balance between effective monitoring and respecting the privacy rights of individuals living in border regions.

Family Separation Policies

The "zero-tolerance" policy in the United States, which resulted in the separation of families at the border, triggered widespread condemnation and legal challenges, prompting a reassessment of the approach. Advocates argue that such measures deter illegal border crossings, while opponents highlight the severe emotional and psychological impact on children and parents. The resulting policy shifts included:

1. June 2018: Executive Order to End Family Separations[3]:
    - In response to public outrage, President Trump signed an executive order on June 20, 2018, directing officials to keep families together whenever possible during immigration proceedings.
2. June 2018: Court Order to Reunite Families[4]:
    - A federal judge in California issued an order requiring the reunification of separated families within 30 days. However, implementation was slow, and hundreds of children remained separated for months or years.

3. Exec. Order No. 13841, *Affording Congress an Opportunity to Address Family Separation*, 83 Fed. Reg. 29435 (June 20, 2018).

4. Ms. L. v. U.S. Immigration and Customs Enforcement, 310 F. Supp. 3d 1133 (S.D. Cal. 2018).

3. January 2021: Biden Administration's Task Force:
    - President Joe Biden issued an executive order[5] establishing a task force to locate and reunite separated families.
    - As of 2023, efforts continued to reunite remaining children with their families, but challenges persisted due to incomplete records and difficulties in locating parents.
4. Policy Shifts in Immigration Enforcement:
    - While the Biden administration formally ended family separations as a deterrent, debates over immigration enforcement and border security continue, with new policies focusing on alternatives to detention and humanitarian relief programs.

Use of Force and Border Patrol Practices

Instances of the use of force by border patrol agents and allegations of mistreatment of migrants have raised serious concerns about excessive force, human rights violations, and the treatment of individuals in U.S. custody. Incidents of border patrol agents using tear gas on migrants and allegations of inadequate conditions in detention facilities have also fueled debates about the ethical treatment of individuals at the border.

Asylum and Refugee Policies

Changes in asylum and refugee policies, including restrictive eligibility criteria and the prioritization of certain categories of asylum-seekers, raise questions about compliance with international humanitarian standards and the protection of vulnerable populations. The implementation of policies such as the Migrant Protection Protocols (MPP) in the United States, which require asylum seekers to wait in Mexico during immigration proceedings, have been criticized for its impact on vulnerable individuals.

Border Militarization

The militarization of border enforcement, involving the deployment of military personnel, raises concerns about the blurring of military and civilian roles, potential escalations of tensions, and the impact on local communities.

5. Exec. Order No. 14011, *Establishment of Interagency Task Force on the Reunification of Families*, 86 Fed. Reg. 8273 (Feb. 5, 2021).

Furthermore, the use of National Guard and military personnel in border enforcement operations calls into question the appropriateness of such deployments and their long-term implications.

Environmental Impact

Many border security measures, such as wall construction, have significant environmental consequences, including habitat disruption, barriers to wildlife migration, and alterations to ecosystems. The impact of border wall construction on the diverse ecosystems along the U.S.–Mexico border has led to numerous legal challenges and protests, emphasizing the importance of balancing security concerns with environmental conservation.

Detention Policies and Conditions

Conditions in detention facilities, including overcrowding, lack of access to medical care, and reports of mistreatment, prompt concerns about human rights violations, dignity, and the well-being of individuals in custody. High-profile cases of substandard conditions in detention facilities, including inadequate healthcare and sanitation, have shed light on the inhumane treatment of migrants and the need for reform.

Impact on Border Communities

Border security measures also have profound impacts on the daily lives of communities along the border, affecting economic activities, cultural exchange, and social cohesion. Increased border enforcement, including the presence of barriers and checkpoints, has raised concerns among border communities about the perception of living in a heavily militarized zone.

Pathways to Legalization

The term "regularization" refers to a country's policy response to the presence of undocumented immigrants residing in that country. In the United States, the process of regularization provides multiple benefits, including an increase in tax and Social Security revenues, a reduction in the "underground economy," and a decrease in the exploitation of immigrants.

According to the Center for Immigration Studies,[6] there were an estimated 11.35 million undocumented immigrants in the United States in January 2022, which is a 1.13 million increase from January 2021. This 11 percent spike can be attributed to:

1. Economic Recovery and Labor Demand: Following the economic downturn caused by the pandemic, the United States experienced a significant economic recovery in 2021. This resurgence led to increased demand for labor, particularly in sectors such as construction, agriculture, and service industries, which have historically relied on immigrant labor. The improved job market acted as a strong pull factor for individuals seeking better employment opportunities.
2. Perceptions of U.S. Immigration Policies: Changes in U.S. immigration policies and enforcement practices under the Biden administration may have influenced perceptions regarding the ease of entering and residing in the country. Some migrants might have interpreted these policy shifts as a more lenient stance toward immigration, encouraging attempts to cross the border.
3. Diverse Migrant Origins: There was an increase in migrants from countries experiencing political instability, economic hardships, and natural disasters. Notably, individuals from Venezuela, Colombia, Nicaragua, Haiti, and various African nations sought entry into the United States, contributing to the rise in undocumented immigrants.

Recent legislative proposals have sought to provide a path to legal status for certain undocumented immigrants. However, these proposals face significant challenges in gaining bipartisan support and navigating the legislative process. President Joe Biden's Build Back Better Plan (BBB)[7] was promoted as a transformational social spending package addressing a wide range of issues, including climate change, healthcare, and universal pre-K. While the BBB included a $100 billion investment to improve the asylum

6. *Estimating the Illegal Immigrant Population Using the Current Population Survey*, Center for Immigration Studies (Mar. 29, 2022), https://cis.org/Report/Estimating-Illegal-Immigrant-Population-Using-Current-Population-Survey#:~:text=We%20estimate%20that%20in%20January%202022%20there%20were%2011.35%20million,the%20number%20in%20January%202019.

7. The White House, *Fact Sheet: The Build Back Better Framework* (Oct. 28, 2021).

system and make immigration laws more humane, it did not specifically propose a path to citizenship for undocumented immigrants.

The USA Citizenship Act of 2021,[8] a separate legislative proposal introduced early in President Biden's administration, aimed to create the largest mass-legalization program for undocumented immigrants in U.S. history. This ambitious proposal sought to provide legal status to an estimated 11 million undocumented immigrants, including work permits, authorization for international travel, and access to state benefits such as driver's licenses. Approximately seven million individuals could have qualified under its provisions, offering significant advancements for immigrants from Central America, Mexico, and other regions.

Republicans stood in opposition to the issuance of work permits or any legalization measures due to the surge of new arrivals at the U.S.–Mexico border in 2021 and 2022. They were concerned that providing millions with work permits might incentivize further migration and argued that undocumented immigrants pose competition to Americans for low-wage employment opportunities. Conversely, some immigrant advocates also rejected the idea of work permits, instead advocating for full citizenship for long-standing residents.

Democrats argued that immigration is an economic imperative, especially with nationwide labor shortages during and since the pandemic, but the Senate had previously rejected a path to citizenship on two different occasions, saying that such a policy doesn't belong in a tax-and-spend bill.

While both the BBB and the USA Citizenship Act of 2021 reflected broader efforts to reform immigration laws, neither succeeded in advancing through Congress. The challenges of securing bipartisan support and enduring the legislative process have left these proposals as unrealized aspirations in the ongoing debate over immigration reform. Ultimately, the enormous costs associated with these proposals likely played a larger part in their failure to progress than did the policies themselves.

No legislation granting citizenship has been approved by Congress since the Immigration Reform and Control Act of 1986. This act, signed into law by Republican President Ronald Reagan, paved the way for nearly three million immigrants to obtain U.S. citizenship. Democrats have been eager to establish immigration protections and codify them in law to prevent legal

8. U.S. Citizenship Act of 2021, H.R. 1177, 117th Cong. (2021–2022).

challenges like the ones that have hampered the success of the Deferred Action for Childhood Arrivals (DACA) program.

In 2021, a federal judge in Texas ruled that DACA was unlawful, saying that President Barack Obama exceeded his authority when the program was created back in 2012. The same judge again ruled that DACA was unlawful in 2023, following the Biden administration's move to preserve the program and codify the policy into federal law. Although current DACA recipients, known as Dreamers, can continue to renew their benefits (at least for the time being), no new DACA applications are being accepted. The uncertain status of DACA has created a sense of insecurity and anxiety among recipients, severely impacting their educational and professional pursuits.

According to the Migration Policy Institute's 2022 Spotlight Report, about 46.2 million non-citizen immigrants live in the United States, of whom more than three-quarters (approximately 35 million) are legal residents.[9] These individuals contribute to the workforce through either lawful permanent residence or temporary visas designed for students and workers. Additionally, programs like DACA and Temporary Protected Status (TPS) provide temporary authorization to live and work in the United States to around one million unauthorized immigrants.

Public sentiment, electoral considerations, and partisan dynamics play a massive role in shaping the trajectory of legislative efforts around pathways to legalization and naturalization. Polls indicate a growing recognition among the U.S. public of the need for comprehensive immigration reform, with a significant percentage supporting pathways to legal status for undocumented immigrants. Still, as a country, we have failed to find the common ground necessary to pass meaningful legislation.

Economic Impact and Labor Market

It is common knowledge that immigration has significant economic implications, but the nature of those implications remains a divisive issue. Advocates emphasize the economic benefits of immigration, arguing that it drives innovation, entrepreneurship, and overall economic growth. Opponents

9. Jeanne Batalova, *Frequently Requested Statistics on Immigrants and Immigration to the United States*, Migration Policy Inst. (Mar. 13, 2024), https://www.migrationpolicy.org/sites/default/files/publications/FRS-PRINT-2024-FINAL.pdf.

express concerns about job displacement and wage suppression. Both have valid arguments. But what is the true net impact of immigration on the U.S. economy and labor market?

Job Competition

One of the primary concerns surrounding the topic of immigration is job competition. Advocates argue that immigrants contribute to economic vitality by filling gaps in the labor market, especially in industries facing shortages of skilled or unskilled workers. They contend that immigrants often take up jobs that native workers are unwilling or unable to perform, thus complementing the existing workforce.

Opponents, on the other hand, express concerns about job displacement. They argue that an influx of immigrant labor may lead to increased competition for jobs, potentially putting pressure on the wages and employment opportunities available to native workers. This perspective raises questions about the balance between meeting labor market demands and protecting the interests of the existing workforce. Let's examine the proven benefits and legitimate concerns surrounding the matter of job competition.

Proven Benefits:

- Filling Labor Market Gaps: Immigrants contribute to economic vitality by filling critical gaps in the labor market. For example, in the healthcare sector, where there is a constant demand for nurses and physicians, immigrants make up a significant portion of the workforce, addressing shortages and ensuring the delivery of essential services. In industries like agriculture, construction, and hospitality, immigrants also play a crucial role in filling labor gaps that might otherwise impede economic activities.
- Entrepreneurship and Job Creation: Immigrant entrepreneurs have played a substantial role in job creation. According to a study by the National Foundation for American Policy, immigrants founded more than half of the United States' billion-dollar startup companies, demonstrating their significant contributions to innovation, economic growth, and job creation.[10] More than half!

---

10. Stuart Anderson, *Immigrant Entrepreneurs and U.S. Billion-Dollar Companies*, Nat'l Foundation for Amer. Policy (July 2022), https://nfap.com/research/new-nfap-policy-brief-immigrant-entrepreneurs-and-u-s-billion-dollar-companies/.

- Economic Expansion: Immigrant labor, particularly in industries like technology and science, has been associated with increased productivity and economic expansion. For instance, Silicon Valley, a hub for technological innovation, has thrived with the contributions of a diverse immigrant workforce, leading to the creation of numerous high-tech jobs and driving the global tech industry.

Legitimate Concerns:

- Wage Pressure in Low-Skilled Jobs: Research by the National Academy of Sciences indicates that while high-skilled immigration tends to have positive effects on wages, the impact on low-skilled native workers is more nuanced, with potential downward pressure on wages in certain occupations.[11] This perspective adds complexity to the debate by intertwining economic considerations with issues of workers' rights and fair compensation.
- Job Competition in Specific Industries: In certain industries, such as construction and manufacturing, concerns arise about job competition and potential displacement of native workers. Studies by organizations like the Economic Policy Institute suggest that in specific occupations and geographic areas, increased immigration may contribute to job competition and hinder wage growth for some native workers.

Contributions to the Economy

Advocates highlight the positive economic contributions of immigrants. They argue that immigrants bring diverse skill sets, talents, and perspectives that drive innovation and entrepreneurship. Immigrant entrepreneurs, for example, have been credited with founding successful businesses that contribute significantly to the economy, creating jobs and fostering economic growth.

Opponents, however, question the extent to which immigrants contribute positively to the economy. Some argue that immigrants may strain public resources, such as education and healthcare, without proportionate

11. National Academies of Sciences, Engineering, and Medicine, *The Economic and Fiscal Consequences of Immigration* (2017), https://nap.nationalacademies.org/catalog/23550/the-economic-and-fiscal-consequences-of-immigration.

economic contributions. This debate extends beyond individual economic contributions to consider the overall impact on the national economy.

Proven Benefits:

- Entrepreneurship and Business Creation: Immigrants have a strong track record of entrepreneurship in the United States. According to the National Bureau of Economic Research, immigrants are more likely to start businesses than their native-born counterparts. Notable examples include companies like Google and Tesla, founded by immigrants or children of immigrants, demonstrating the substantial impact on innovation and job creation.
- Innovation in STEM Fields: Immigrants play a major role in driving innovation, particularly in science, technology, engineering, and mathematics (STEM) fields. Research by the National Foundation for American Policy indicates that immigrants contribute significantly to patent filings and breakthrough innovations. This innovation, in turn, has far-reaching effects on economic growth, creating new industries and employment opportunities.[12]
- Labor Force Growth: Immigrants contribute to the expansion of the labor force, which has positive effects on overall economic output. The Congressional Budget Office[13] reports that immigration has a positive impact on the economy by increasing the size of the labor force, contributing to economic growth, and partially offsetting the challenges posed by an aging population.

Legitimate Concerns:

- Access to Public Services: Opponents argue that immigrants, particularly those with lower socioeconomic status, may strain public resources such as education and healthcare. While studies, such as that by the National Academies of Sciences, Engineering, and Medicine mentioned earlier, indicate that the fiscal impact of immigrants is generally positive over the long term, concerns exist about

12. Stuart Anderson, *Immigrant Entrepreneurs and U.S. Billion-Dollar Companies*, Nat'l Foundation for Am. Policy (July 2022), https://nfap.com/wp-content/uploads/2022/07/2022-BILLION-DOLLAR-STARTUPS.NFAP-Policy-Brief.2022.pdf.

13. Congressional Budget Office, *The Impact of Immigration on the United States Labor Market and Economy* (2023), https://www.cbo.gov/publication/58620.

the immediate costs associated with providing public services to a growing immigrant population.

- Impact on Social Services: Critics also point to potential strain on social services, such as housing assistance and welfare programs, arguing that immigrants with lower incomes may rely on these services. However, studies like the National Academies of Sciences' report[14] suggest that the fiscal contributions of immigrants outweigh the costs, contributing positively to government finances over time.

The economic implications of immigration remain a hotly debated aspect of modern immigration law. The solution lies in finding a balance between harnessing the economic benefits of immigration, such as innovation and growth, while addressing concerns about job competition, wage suppression, and overall impacts on the labor market and national economy.

Humanitarian Considerations and Refugees

Global migration crises continue to place humanitarian considerations at the forefront of immigration debates. Challenges encompass the treatment of refugees, the legal obligations of nations to provide protection and assistance, and the ways in which the United States can balance its commitment to humanitarian values with its national security interests. Examining some of the most urgent refugee and humanitarian crises in recent history provides insight into both the successes and failures of U.S. responses.

Syrian Refugee Crisis

In 2011, a wave of protests against the Syrian government escalated into a full-scale civil war. The brutal conflict had a profound impact on its civilian population, with egregious violations of human rights and international law becoming tragically commonplace. As a result, millions of Syrians were forced to seek refuge in neighboring countries and beyond, creating one of the most significant refugee crises of our time.

14. *Supra* note 11.

The crisis has had a profound impact on modern immigration law and policy worldwide, prompting an increased focus on the role of resettlement programs and asylum policies in addressing the needs of those displaced. It also spurred debates on the responsibility of nations, including the United States, to provide humanitarian assistance and protection to those fleeing violence and persecution.

In response to the Syrian refugee crisis, the United States implemented measures to increase the number of Syrian refugees admitted through resettlement programs. However, these efforts were met with debates over security concerns and the balancing act between providing refuge and ensuring national security. The situation also reinforced the importance of international collaboration in addressing such crises.

During the height of the crisis, the United States responded by increasing its commitment to refugee resettlement. In fiscal year 2016, the Obama administration set a goal to admit 10,000 Syrian refugees to the United States. While this number was a notable increase from previous years, it constituted only a small fraction of the vast number of Syrian refugees at that time. The limited admission of Syrian refugees by the United States during the crisis can be ascribed to a confluence of factors, encompassing logistical challenges, security concerns, and political considerations.

Furthermore, the United States was not the sole actor in responding to the Syrian refugee crisis. International efforts, including those by neighboring countries and humanitarian organizations, played a substantial role in providing immediate assistance and shelter to millions of displaced Syrians. The United States took into account the collective response and sought to complement the efforts of other nations while addressing its own challenges.

Neighboring countries hosted a massive influx of displaced Syrians. Turkey, Lebanon, and Jordan, in particular, absorbed millions of refugees, straining their resources and infrastructure. In response, the United States provided substantial aid to these nations, further emphasizing the need for global cooperation and burden-sharing in addressing refugee crises. The collaboration underscored the interconnected and global nature of the crisis, emphasizing the importance of unified efforts in mitigating the impact of large-scale displacement. To date, the United States continues to be the largest humanitarian donor to the Syria response, providing nearly $15 billion in assistance throughout the region since the conflict began.[15]

The limited resettlement of Syrian refugees in the United States was also a result of remarks by some policymakers who expressed reservations about admitting large numbers of refugees, amplified by the fact that Syria is an Arab and primarily Muslim nation. Concerns about potential terrorist infiltration fueled opposition to more extensive resettlement efforts, and public sentiment played a role, with fears heightened by the global rise in terrorism and the uncertainty surrounding the backgrounds of individuals seeking refuge.

Despite limited resettlement in this country, U.S. support of Syrian refugees in other countries was robust. In addition to significant financial aid for humanitarian assistance, education, healthcare, and infrastructure in host countries, the United States also extended Temporary Protected Status (TPS) to eligible Syrians residing in the United States. TPS provided critical relief, allowing Syrians to live and work legally in the United States without fear of deportation while conditions in Syria remained unsafe.

This dual approach—offering direct support to refugees abroad and legal protections for those within U.S. borders—set a precedent for future policies, emphasizing the importance of addressing refugee crises both domestically and internationally to meet the challenges faced by those forced to flee their homes.

Rohingya Crisis

The Rohingya crisis represents one of the most severe and underreported humanitarian tragedies of the 21st century. The Rohingya are a predominantly Muslim ethnic minority from Rakhine State in Myanmar, historically marginalized and denied recognition as citizens by the Myanmar government. For decades, the Rohingya have endured systemic oppression, including restrictions on movement, limited access to education and healthcare, and exclusion from the political and legal frameworks of the country. This long-standing discrimination escalated into a full-blown humanitarian catastrophe in 2017.

15. *Syrian Refugee Response*, U.S. Dep't of State (Jan. 2017), https://2009-2017.state.gov/j/prm/policyissues/issues/refugeeresponse.

The immediate catalyst for the crisis was a violent military campaign by the Myanmar military, or Tatmadaw, in response to coordinated attacks by the Arakan Rohingya Salvation Army (ARSA), a Rohingya insurgent group, on police outposts. What followed was described by the United Nations as a "textbook example of ethnic cleansing."[16] The military's response included widespread reports of mass killings, sexual violence, and the destruction of entire villages. Human Rights Watch and other organizations documented the torching of hundreds of Rohingya settlements, forcing survivors to flee their homes under harrowing conditions.

In the span of just a few months, more than 700,000 Rohingya fled across the border into neighboring Bangladesh, joining the estimated 300,000 already displaced by previous waves of violence. This sudden and massive displacement overwhelmed international aid systems and highlighted the vulnerability of a stateless population systematically denied their rights for generations. The Cox's Bazar district in Bangladesh became the epicenter of the crisis, with the establishment of the world's largest refugee camp. Today, nearly one million Rohingya still reside in overcrowded and impoverished conditions, dependent entirely on international aid for survival.

The scale and gravity of the crisis prompted widespread international condemnation of Myanmar's actions, with many governments and human rights organizations labeling the events as genocide. The international community, including the United States, faced significant challenges in responding to the crisis within the confines of existing legal frameworks and immigration policies. The situation exposed critical gaps in international refugee protection systems, including the limitations of asylum mechanisms and the difficulty of addressing large-scale statelessness.

For the United States, the crisis not only highlighted the plight of the Rohingya, but also served as a sobering reminder of the global responsibility to protect vulnerable populations from atrocities. The international community, human rights organizations, and various governments have condemned the Myanmar military's actions as ethnic cleansing and genocide. A cooperative approach has far-reaching implications for the evolution of

16. United Nations Office of the High Commissioner for Human Rights, Report of the Independent International Fact-Finding Mission on Myanmar (Geneva: United Nations, 2018), https://www.ohchr.org/en/hr-bodies/hrc/myanmar-ffm/index. *See also* Human Rights Watch, *Burma: Military Burned Villages in Rakhine State* (September 17, 2017), https://www.hrw.org/news/2017/09/17/burma-military-burned-villages-rakhine-state.

international norms and agreements related to refugee protection, including how the United States engages in global efforts to address such crises.

The following is an overview of the U.S. response to the Rohingya refugee crisis from 2017 through 2023:

- Humanitarian Aid: The U.S. government has been a significant contributor to humanitarian aid for Rohingya refugees. Financial assistance has been directed toward providing essential services such as food, shelter, healthcare, and education in collaboration with international humanitarian organizations. The United States has also extended support to countries hosting Rohingya refugees, recognizing the strain on their resources. This assistance includes financial aid and collaborative initiatives aimed at enhancing infrastructure and services in host nations, particularly Bangladesh. Critics, however, argue that more targeted and sustained efforts are needed to address ongoing challenges faced by Rohingya refugees, including improved services around healthcare and education, and the psychological well-being of the displaced population.
- Diplomatic Engagement: The United States has engaged diplomatically to advocate for the rights and protection of Rohingya refugees on the international stage. This includes participation in forums and discussions aimed at finding diplomatic solutions to the crisis, promoting human rights, and holding those responsible for persecution accountable. However, critics contend that the United States could exert more diplomatic pressure on Myanmar to address the root causes of the crisis, including denying the Rohingya population citizenship, basic rights, and access to essential services. This systemic discrimination has contributed to the vulnerability of the Rohingya population and the perpetuation of a cycle of oppression. A more robust diplomatic approach is seen as essential for a long-term solution.
- Resettlement Programs: The United States has implemented resettlement programs for Rohingya refugees, offering them an opportunity for a new life in the United States. These programs, though constrained by various factors, represent a tangible effort to provide a safe haven for those in need. Since 2009, more than 16,000 Rohingya have been resettled in the United States, primarily from

> Malaysia. Despite these efforts, the number of Rohingya refugees resettled in the United States remains relatively low compared to the scale of the crisis. As of 2024, Bangladesh continues to host nearly one million Rohingya refugees who fled violence in Myanmar. Critics argue that the United States could do more to provide a haven for those fleeing persecution, considering its historical role in refugee resettlement in the years following the Holocaust. Similarities between the ongoing plight of the Rohingya people and that of Jews prior to the establishment of the State of Israel in 1948 are impossible to ignore.

Although the United States has offered substantial humanitarian assistance and advocacy in support of Rohingya refugees, the response to this crisis has drawn attention to the ongoing problems in the U.S. immigration system. Issues such as overly stringent vetting processes and restrictive immigration quotas have impeded the swift and comprehensive response needed to address the urgency of the crisis, creating barriers for Rohingya refugees seeking asylum.

In 2023, six years after the last wave of displacement, more than a million Rohingya refugees remain in exile, living in temporary shelters and relying entirely on humanitarian aid for food, water, and protection.

On a positive note, the Rohingya crisis has sparked immense global advocacy and human rights discourse, bringing to light the plight of the Rohingya and the necessity of protective measures. This increased awareness has influenced public opinion and, consequently, policymakers' considerations in shaping U.S. immigration policies responsive to humanitarian crises. The lessons learned from the Rohingya crisis have contributed to ongoing discussions and adaptations in U.S. immigration policies to better address the unique challenges presented by large-scale forced displacement and persecution. As a nation, however, we still have a long, long way to go.

Central American Migration

The surge in migration from Central America, particularly involving families and unaccompanied minors, has posed a unique set of challenges at the U.S. southern border. Many individuals from countries like Honduras, El Salvador, and Guatemala seek asylum, fleeing violence, poverty, and persecution.

This migration wave has triggered adjustments in U.S. immigration policies, particularly in asylum procedures. The goal is to find a balance between offering humanitarian relief and deterring irregular migration. While it is undeniable that monitoring and managing migration from our southern border is necessary, the political rhetoric surrounding this delicate situation urgently needs to change.

In October 2023, then former President Donald J. Trump—already a declared candidate to run again in the 2024 election, which he would ultimately win—once again shocked the public with his comments on undocumented immigrants, stating they were "poisoning the blood of our country." In a 37-minute video interview with *The National Pulse*, Trump expanded on his views regarding immigration at the southern border:

> Nobody has any idea where these people are coming from, and we know they come from prisons. We know they come from mental institutions and insane asylums. We know they're terrorists. Nobody has ever seen anything like we're witnessing right now. It is a very sad thing for our country. It's poisoning the blood of our country. It's so bad, and people are coming in with disease. People are coming in with every possible thing that you could have.[17]

Trump's comments are deeply troubling and condemnatory. Such xenophobic rhetoric, illustrated by the claim that undocumented immigrants are "poisoning the blood of our country," not only perpetuates harmful stereotypes, but also undermines the dignity of migrants seeking safety and a better life. This inflammatory language has real-world consequences, fostering an environment of fear and hostility that compromises the well-being of migrants and our nation as a whole.

Words matter, especially when spoken by politicians, celebrities, and anyone with a significant following in mainstream or social media. We must recognize the importance of a more compassionate and nuanced discourse surrounding immigration, one that respects the rights and humanity of all individuals, regardless of their immigration status. Failure to do so will only lead to more suffering and violence, further deepening divisions among our fellow countrymen and women.

---

17. Nathan Layne, *Trump Repeats 'Poisoning the Blood' Anti-Immigrant Remark*, Reuters (Dec. 16, 2023), https://www.reuters.com/world/us/trump-repeats-poisoning-blood-anti-immigrant-remark-2023-12-16/.

Russian Invasion of Ukraine

For nearly the entirety of the 20th century, Ukraine served as a pillar of the Soviet Union. In fact, it was positioned as the primary adversary to the United States during the Cold War. As the second-most populous and influential of the Soviet republics, Ukraine played a critical role, hosting a significant portion of the union's agricultural output, defense industries, and military assets, including the Black Sea Fleet and some of the nuclear arsenal. The decision of Ukraine to break away from the Soviet Union in 1991 dealt a final blow to the already faltering superpower.

Following its newfound independence, Ukraine sought to carve its own identity as a self-governing nation while simultaneously aiming to align more closely with Western organizations such as the European Union and NATO. Nonetheless, the nation struggled to manage its foreign relations while striving to bridge deep internal divisions.

In 2014, Russia's annexation of Crimea marked the first instance since World War II of a European state seizing the territory of another. The ongoing conflict in the Donbas region resulted in the highest death toll in Europe since the Balkan Wars of the 1990s, with more than 14,000 casualties. These hostilities represented a significant shift in the global security landscape, from a period of U.S. dominance to one shaped by conflict among powerful nations.

Many Russian politicians regard the separation from Ukraine as a major historical error, seeing it as a challenge to Russia's status as a global superpower. In February 2022, Russia initiated a large-scale invasion of Ukraine, with the objective of overthrowing the government aligned with Western powers led by Volodymyr Zelenskyy. Hundreds of thousands of Russians and Ukrainians have died in the nearly two years since the war began.

In response to the violence in Ukraine, President Biden introduced "Uniting for Ukraine," in April 2022, a simplified, fast-track approach to providing refuge for Ukrainian citizens fleeing Russia's invasion of their country. The initiative, which is still being utilized as of the writing of this book, builds on the humanitarian support provided by the United States to the many European countries that are also hosting Ukrainian citizens.

Uniting for Ukraine provides an opportunity for Ukrainians and their immediate family members to come to the United States and stay for a two-year period of "humanitarian parole." To be eligible for the program, the

Ukrainian citizen must have a U.S. supporter who agrees to support them financially during their stay. In November 2022, the Biden administration further announced that Ukrainians residing in the United States on parole are now automatically eligible to apply for work authorization.

Although the program is an innovative alternative to the more time-consuming process of resettlement, it is not without problems. Uniting for Ukraine places the care of refugees in the hands of private individuals, with no oversight beyond the initial vetting process. There are reports of unscrupulous sponsors requesting payment to serve as sponsors, a practice explicitly prohibited by the program. Some refugees have also found themselves stranded upon arrival in the United States due to last-minute sponsor withdrawals, a lack of follow-through on promises of financial or logistical support, or misunderstandings about sponsor responsibilities. For example, the *New York Times* reported cases where Ukrainian refugees arrived at airports only to find that their sponsors failed to meet them, leaving them temporarily homeless and dependent on local community groups or charities for immediate assistance.[18] Similarly, the *Washington Post* highlighted instances of refugees paying unvetted individuals through social media platforms in the desperate hope of finding a sponsor, only to be scammed.[19]

The two-year limit on humanitarian parole has also been called into question, as nobody knows how long the war will last. Furthermore, the decision to provide simplified access to parole for Ukrainians has drawn criticism since the United States does not offer similar programs to refugees from other nations, such as Afghans fleeing the Taliban, or Rohingya refugees who have been living in temporary camps for years.

Despite these serious issues, Uniting for Ukraine is a step in the right direction, highlighting the need for increased access to humanitarian parole in large-scale crises.

---

18. Kimiko de Freytas-Tamura, *These Ukrainians Arrived Under a Biden Program. They Ended Up Homeless*, N.Y. Times (Apr. 2, 2023), https://www.nytimes.com/2023/04/02/nyregion/ukraine-refugees-homeless.html.

19. Tatum Hunter, *Fake Lawyers Target Undocumented Immigrants through Social Media Scams*, Washington Post, May 10, 2025, at https://www.washingtonpost.com/technology/2025/05/10/immigration-scams/.

Ongoing Conflict Between Israel and Palestine

The establishment of the modern state of Israel is deeply rooted in historical, religious, and geopolitical factors. The idea of a Jewish homeland emerged in the late 19th and early 20th centuries in response to a surge in anti-Semitic persecution and the quest for self-determination among Jews worldwide. The Zionist movement advocated for the establishment of a Jewish state in the ancient land of Israel, known as Eretz Yisrael in Hebrew.

Following the atrocities of the Holocaust during World War II, the international community increasingly supported the establishment of a Jewish state, acknowledging the urgent need for a safe haven for Jewish survivors and the broader Jewish community. This culminated in the United Nations Partition Plan for Palestine in 1947, which proposed dividing the region into separate Jewish and Arab states, with Jerusalem designated as an international city. The plan was accepted by Jewish leaders but rejected by Arab leaders, leading to a war between the newly declared State of Israel and surrounding Arab nations.

On May 14, 1948, the State of Israel declared independence, marking a landmark moment in the history of the Israeli–Palestinian conflict. The establishment of Israel as a sovereign nation represented the realization of the Zionist dream and provided a homeland for the Jewish people after centuries of displacement and persecution.

However, the creation of Israel also resulted in the displacement of hundreds of thousands of Palestinian Arabs, leading to the Palestinian refugee crisis. This laid the groundwork for ongoing tensions and conflicts between Israelis and Palestinians, as both groups lay claim to the same territory and harbor deep historical and religious connections to the land.

In the 75 years since the creation of the State of Israel, there has been much violence on both sides, as well as several failed attempts at peace plans.

On October 7, 2023, Hamas, the militant Islamist organization and offshoot of the Muslim Brotherhood, launched an unprecedented attack on Israel, with hundreds of gunmen descending on communities near the Gaza Strip. More than 200 Israeli soldiers and civilians were taken as hostages and approximately 1,200 Israelis were killed in the attack.

In response to the attacks, Israel formally declared war on Hamas, mobilizing hundreds of thousands of troops, launching an aerial bombardment against militants in Gaza, and calling for civilians in northern Gaza to evacuate to the south. As of the writing of this book, a tenuous phased ceasefire agreement between Israel and Hamas has been reached, but tensions remain high as hostage and prisoner releases, disputed territory, and other delicate terms are negotiated.

Approximately one million Gazans are currently displaced as a result of the war, but people have been fleeing Palestine for decades. Despite the large number of displaced persons and refugees, only about 140 Palestinian refugees were resettled in the United States between 2019 and today. According to State Department data, less than 600 Palestinians have utilized the 1980 Refugee Admissions Program to move to the United States.

A report released by the Center for Immigration Studies[20] revealed that of the more than one million refugees resettled in the United States in the past two decades, only about 2,000 have been Palestinian. This is largely because the majority of refugees come to the United States via the United Nations High Commissioner for Refugees (UNHCR). Palestinian refugees, on the other hand, are usually processed through the United Nations Relief and Works Agency (UNRWA), an organization that does not provide resettlement as a service.

Despite the extremely low number of Palestinian refugees entering the United States, several 2024 presidential hopefuls used the conflict as a focal point of their primary campaigns. A few Republican lawmakers even introduced "The GAZA Act," with GAZA standing for "Guaranteeing Aggressors Zero Admission."

In addition to being xenophobic, such rhetoric fails to acknowledge that in most cases, civilians in Gaza are not only stuck there, but also are not seeking to leave. There is no need to ban the entry of people who are trapped, especially when many of those people would refuse to leave Gaza even if allowed. Palestinians are still haunted by the Nakba, or "catastrophe," of the first Arab-Israeli war in 1948, when hundreds of thousands of Palestinians had to flee. On top of not wanting to become refugees again, many would refuse to abandon Palestinian land—possibly permanently—even if given the choice.

The historical significance of Israel as a homeland for the Jewish people is deeply embedded in the collective consciousness of the global Jewish

20. Nayla Rush, *Opening the Door to Palestinian Refugees from Gaza?*, Center for Immigration Studies (May 7, 2024), https://cis.org/Rush/Opening-Door-Palestinian-Refugees-Gaza#:~:text=Included%20are%20several%20campuses%20that,Unallocated%20Reserve:%200.

community. As an immigration lawyer and an observant Jew, I stand in support of the State of Israel and unequivocally condemn any form of anti-Semitism. However, I am equally committed to advocating for the safety and dignity of the Palestinian people. The ongoing Israeli–Palestinian conflict has led to immense suffering for both Israelis and Palestinians, and it is crucial to recognize the humanity and rights of all individuals involved.

Just as I vehemently reject anti-Semitism, I reject all forms of racist and xenophobic rhetoric directed toward the Palestinian people. It is essential to acknowledge the legitimate aspirations of Palestinians for self-determination, safety, and prosperity. Embracing empathy and understanding the complexities of the Israeli–Palestinian conflict is critical in fostering meaningful dialogue and seeking peaceful resolutions.

I believe in promoting a future where both Israelis and Palestinians can co-exist in peace and security. This vision necessitates condemning all expressions of hatred, discrimination, and violence while working toward a just and lasting resolution for all those impacted by the ongoing conflict in the region.

***

Reviewing these modern refugee crises in order of occurrence allows us to witness an unfolding evolutionary process. Despite serious shortcomings and outright failings, the United States has continued to increase humanitarian assistance, as well as funding to countries that support large numbers of refugees, advocacy efforts, and, in some cases, refugee resettlement in the United States.

However, when it comes to resettlement, we can also see a distinct contrast in the reception of refugees from majority-Muslim countries, Mexico, and Central American countries compared to those from other regions. While it remains critical to protect national security through adequate vetting of immigrants and refugees, there is no doubting that our current system remains discriminatory, and severely broken. The security and well-being of our nation hinge not only on our ability to identify potential threats at our borders, but also on our ethical and compassionate response to those escaping violence and persecution. Finding a balance between these two aspects is paramount, as an imbalanced focus on vetting over humanitarian efforts poses equal risks to our fellow Americans.

In a hypothetical scenario, allocating 80 percent of our efforts to vetting and only 20 percent to humanitarian endeavors jeopardizes the safety of our nation, just as it would if the proportions were reversed. Failure to provide sufficient humanitarian relief on a global scale is inherently linked to the risk of conflicts with other nations. Recognizing this profound connection is crucial for gaining bipartisan support for comprehensive immigration reform that seeks equilibrium between protecting national security and upholding global human rights. Only through this understanding can we build a more compassionate and effective immigration system.

Other Controversial Topics Impacting Immigration Today

Sanctuary Cities

A city that limits its cooperation with federal immigration enforcement, aiming to create a safe haven for undocumented immigrants, is referred to as a "sanctuary city." While the specifics vary, these municipalities generally restrict the extent to which local law enforcement agencies can assist federal authorities in identifying and apprehending individuals based solely on their immigration status.

Sanctuary cities have been a hot topic in recent years, sparking debates and discussions across the political spectrum. The concept of sanctuary cities has often been a contentious issue, reflecting the vast disconnect between local governance and federal immigration policies. While every city and its elected leadership are legally bound to support the U.S. Constitution as well as state and local laws and law enforcement, there exists a great deal of discretion in their actions regarding immigrants and immigration authorities.

Local leadership in sanctuary cities tend to be vocal in educating immigrant communities on their rights, and in fostering confidence that they can continue to go to work and school and utilize public services without having their immigration status called into question by those agencies or local authorities. Some of the most notable sanctuary cities in the United States include San Francisco, Los Angeles, and New York City. These urban centers have adopted policies designed to foster trust between local law enforcement and immigrant communities. Such policies typically involve prohibiting police officers from inquiring about an individual's immigration status during routine interactions, and refusing to detain individuals solely at the request of federal immigration authorities without a warrant.

The controversy surrounding sanctuary cities centers on the perceived tension between local and federal authority, as well as concerns about public safety and national security. Critics argue that these policies can hinder effective collaboration between local and federal law enforcement agencies, potentially allowing undocumented individuals with criminal records to evade deportation. Proponents, on the other hand, assert that sanctuary city policies promote community safety by encouraging undocumented immigrants to report crimes and engage with local services without fear of deportation.

In the face of an ongoing national debate on immigration, sanctuary cities have shown compassion and pragmatism to immigrants living within their borders, demonstrating tangible benefits for both their residents and the broader community. These cities adopt policies designed to protect undocumented immigrants, fostering trust between law enforcement and immigrant communities. Multiple studies and real-world examples showcase the positive impact of sanctuary city policies.

Potential Benefits of Sanctuary Cities:

- Improved Public Safety: Contrary to the misconception that sanctuary cities compromise safety, research indicates that these communities experience lower crime rates. The rationale behind this is clear: When undocumented immigrants feel secure in reporting crimes or cooperating with law enforcement without fear of deportation, it creates a safer environment for everyone. For instance, the American Immigration Council reports that sanctuary policies are associated with lower crime rates and higher economic indicators.[21]
- Healthier economy: By providing a sense of security to undocumented residents, these cities empower a significant portion of the workforce to actively participate in the local economy. This, in turn, leads to increased economic productivity and growth. A report by the Immigrant Legal Resource Center highlighted the positive economic impact of sanctuary policies, including higher wages and increased tax contributions from undocumented workers.[22]

---

21. American Immigration Council, *Sanctuary Policies: An Overview* (Feb. 21, 2025), https://www.americanimmigrationcouncil.org/fact-sheet/sanctuary-policies-overview/#:~:text=A%202020%20study%20found%20that,in%20the%20non%2Ddetainer%20counties:.

22. Silva Mathema, *Providing Sanctuary: The Economic and Social Benefits of Policies that Offer Protection to Undocumented Immigrants* (San Francisco, CA: Immigrant Legal Resource Center, 2017), https://www.ilrc.org/sites/default/files/resources/sanctuary_report_final_2017-02-23.pdf.

- Services and Social Interaction: The threat of aggressive immigration actions can interrupt the flow of daily life for those with uncertain status in numerous ways. Similar to interactions with law enforcement, immigrants may fear to visit doctors or hospitals, and children may be held out of school. Health, education, housing, finances, and social and family interactions can all be greatly impacted.
- Inclusion and Diversity: By embracing and protecting immigrants, these cities foster a more vibrant and culturally rich community. The integration of diverse perspectives contributes to the dynamism of local culture, enriching the social fabric of the city. The success stories of thriving immigrant communities in sanctuary cities, such as San Francisco and Chicago, underscore the positive impact of inclusive policies.

The proven benefits of sanctuary cities extend beyond ideology, providing concrete evidence of improved public safety, economic vitality, and cultural enrichment. Yet there are some legitimate concerns.

Potential Drawbacks Associated with Sanctuary Cities:

- Potential for Federal Funding Cuts: Sanctuary cities risk losing federal funding, as there is often tension between local policies and federal immigration laws. The federal government has, at times, threatened to withhold funds from cities that do not fully cooperate with immigration enforcement efforts.
- Increased Risk of Criminal Activity: Critics of sanctuary cities express concerns that by limiting cooperation with federal immigration authorities, these cities may inadvertently harbor individuals involved in criminal activities, including those who are undocumented and have committed serious offenses.
- Legal Challenges and Uncertainty: The legal status of sanctuary city policies is often subject to challenges, creating uncertainty about the sustainability of these measures. Cities may face costly legal battles, and the lack of a standardized approach can result in varying interpretations of sanctuary policies.
- Potential for Exploitation: There are concerns that individuals with malicious intent may exploit sanctuary city policies to evade law enforcement. Critics argue that stricter immigration enforcement

is necessary to prevent individuals with criminal backgrounds from taking advantage of these policies.

- Impact on National Immigration Policies: Opponents of sanctuary cities argue that these local policies undermine the enforcement of national immigration laws. They believe that a uniform approach to immigration enforcement is essential for maintaining the integrity of the overall system.
- Challenges in Collaboration: The lack of collaboration between local law enforcement and federal immigration authorities may hinder efforts to address transnational criminal activities. Critics argue that seamless cooperation is crucial for ensuring national security.

Opposing arguments make some valid points, such as the potential for individuals with malicious intent to exploit sanctuary city policies. But studies indicate that crime has gone down, not up, in sanctuary cities.

Case in point, a 2017 study published in the *Journal on Migration and Human Security*[23] analyzed crime rates in more than 600 U.S. counties and found that counties with sanctuary policies experienced, on average, 35.5 fewer crimes per 10,000 people compared to non-sanctuary counties. Similarly, a 2019 study by the Center for American Progress[24] reviewed data from 11 sanctuary cities and found that these cities had both lower crime rates and stronger economies compared to cities without such policies.

San Francisco, a high-profile sanctuary city, has seen significant decreases in violent crime over the past two decades. According to the FBI's Uniform Crime Reporting Program, the city's violent crime rate dropped by more than 44 percent between 1993 and 2019,[25] even as it maintained its sanctuary city designation. Los Angeles, another prominent sanctuary city, has also experienced long-term declines in crime, with a 60 percent reduction in violent crime from the early 1990s to 2019.[26]

---

23. Tom K. Wong, *The Effects of Sanctuary Policies on Crime and the Economy*, 5 J. on Migration and Human Security 3 (2017), https://www.americanprogress.org/article/the-effects-of-sanctuary-policies-on-crime-and-the-economy/.

24. Michael D. Nicholson, *The Facts on Immigration Today: 2017 Edition*, Center for American Progress (Apr. 20, 2017), https://www.americanprogress.org/article/facts-immigration-today-2017-edition/.

25. Federal Bureau of Investigation, Crime in the United States 1993; and Crime in the United States 2019, Uniform Crime Reporting Program.

26. *Id.*

Critics often claim that sanctuary policies harbor undocumented immigrants who commit crimes, but available data paints a very different picture. A 2020 analysis by the Cato Institute[27] found that undocumented immigrants are 44 percent less likely to be incarcerated for violent crimes than native-born citizens. This aligns with the argument that sanctuary policies build trust between immigrant communities and local law enforcement, encouraging cooperation and the reporting of crimes without fear of deportation.

The debate over sanctuary cities highlights the broader challenges inherent in immigration law and policy. The ability to simultaneously uphold federal mandates and foster inclusive, secure communities remains a delicate task, requiring nuanced solutions that respect the rights and dignity of all individuals, regardless of their immigration status.

ICE

U.S. Immigration and Customs Enforcement (ICE) traces its roots back to the aftermath of the September 11 terrorist attacks. In response to the heightened concerns about national security, the Department of Homeland Security (DHS) was created in 2003, consolidating various agencies responsible for border protection, immigration enforcement, and other related functions. ICE was subsequently formed as a part of DHS, officially coming into existence on March 1, 2003.

ICE was established with the primary goal of ensuring the security of the United States through effective immigration enforcement; a noble mission, and a necessity at the time to address public apprehension as well as perform its stated role. Its objectives include investigating and enforcing the nation's immigration laws, combating transnational crime, and protecting the integrity of the immigration system.

But while ICE is intended to serve an important role in safeguarding national security and enforcing immigration laws, it has at times seemingly taken on a life of its own, spiraling out of control and often displaying a complete disregard for the rights and privacy of citizens and non-citizens alike. It has been highly scrutinized for its aggressive approach to immigration enforcement, particularly as it pertains to deportation policies. ICE's tactics

27. Michelangelo Landgrave, *Incarcerated Immigrants in 2017: Their Numbers, Demographics, and Countries of Origin* (Washington, DC: Cato Institute, Aug. 2020).

have led to the separation of families and the removal of individuals who pose little to no threat to public safety.

Critics argue that ICE operates with insufficient oversight and accountability, leading to instances of abuse of power and violations of civil liberties. The methods it uses to identify and apprehend undocumented immigrants have faced widespread criticism due to their far-reaching impact on local communities. One of the most significant concerns is that individuals are often hesitant to report crimes or seek essential services, fearing immigration enforcement repercussions.

ICE conducts targeted raids in residential neighborhoods. While such raids are intended to apprehend specific individuals, they undoubtedly instill fear and apprehension among the broader population in these communities. This environment of uncertainty dissuades individuals from engaging with authorities, even when they are victims or witnesses to criminal activities.

ICE also frequently conducts workplace raids as a means of identifying and detaining undocumented immigrants. While targeting individuals without legal status, such operations also create an atmosphere of fear within the entire workplace. Workers become reluctant to report abuses, hazardous conditions, or criminal activities for fear of being caught in the immigration enforcement net.

Utilizing tactics that stand in total contrast to those employed by sanctuary cities, ICE collaborates with local law enforcement agencies through programs like 287(g). Established under the Illegal Immigration Reform and Immigrant Responsibility Act of 1996, the 287(g) program was designed, in part, as a response to the rise of sanctuary cities and their policies of limiting cooperation with federal immigration authorities. The program allows ICE to deputize local officers to perform specific immigration enforcement functions, such as identifying and detaining individuals suspected of violating immigration laws during routine policing activities.

Proponents of 287(g) argue that it strengthens national security and aids in the removal of undocumented individuals who pose a public safety threat. However, the program has faced significant criticism for its broader implications. Critics highlight that it often results in racial profiling and the detention of non-violent offenders, including those apprehended for minor infractions such as traffic violations. This dynamic disproportionately impacts immigrant communities and undermines trust between these communities and local law enforcement.

The fear of deportation created by 287(g) hinders undocumented individuals from reporting crimes, cooperating with investigations, or serving as witnesses, thereby compromising public safety efforts. A 2013 study published in the *American Economic Journal*[28] found that jurisdictions participating in 287(g) experienced a decline in crime reporting among Latino communities, even as overall crime rates did not significantly decrease. Additionally, this fear erodes the relationships necessary for effective community policing, making it harder for law enforcement to address crimes that affect the broader population.

Significantly, 287(g) is an opt-in program that local law enforcement agencies may choose to utilize or not, underscoring the discretion that local leadership may employ in supporting aggressive immigration action or in fostering a sanctuary city or similar environment.

Furthermore, instances where ICE detains and deports undocumented individuals who are survivors of domestic violence are extremely concerning. This practice deters victims from seeking assistance, reporting abuse, or pursuing legal recourse, as the fear of deportation often outweighs their pursuit of justice.

There is no denying that the methods employed by ICE have created an environment of fear and apprehension within immigrant communities. This atmosphere not only hampers cooperation with law enforcement, but also discourages individuals from accessing essential services and reporting crimes, ultimately impacting the overall safety and well-being of entire communities.

Deafening Silence in Congress

No discussion about modern immigration law issues would be complete without mentioning the failure of Congress to address the need for comprehensive immigration reform that prioritizes keeping immigrant families together. Despite growing calls for action and pressing humanitarian concerns, legislative initiatives have repeatedly stalled, leaving millions of immigrant families in a state of uncertainty and vulnerability.

28. Catalina Amuedo-Dorantes and Esther Arenas-Arroyo, *Police Trust and Cooperation: Evidence from the U.S. Immigration Enforcement Program 287(g)*, 13 Am. Econ. J.: Economic Policy 3, 398–429 (Aug. 2021).

One notable example is the Deferred Action for Childhood Arrivals (DACA) program. Although DACA has provided temporary relief for more than 800,000 young, undocumented immigrants[29] who arrived in the United States as children, Congress has failed to pass a permanent solution, leaving DACA recipients in a perpetual state of limbo. The lack of legislative action not only jeopardizes the future of these individuals, but also disrupts the stability of their families, who live with the constant fear of separation. These are individuals who have contributed significantly to their communities and the broader society, who were minors with no ability to control their immigration circumstances, and who often have never known a home outside of America.

Congress has also fallen short in providing adequate protections for undocumented parents with U.S. citizen children. The absence of comprehensive immigration reform leaves these families vulnerable to the constant threat of deportation, tearing apart parents from their American-born children. The emotional toll and long-term consequences for the well-being of these children highlight the pressing need for legislative intervention.

The failure to address family reunification policies has further perpetuated a cycle of hardship for many immigrants. The backlog and inefficiencies in the current immigration system make it incredibly challenging for families to be reunited legally. The absence of effective legislation to streamline the immigration process exacerbates the pain and distress experienced by families separated by borders and bureaucratic hurdles.

Congress's failure to enact meaningful immigration legislation reflects a broader systemic issue. The lack of bipartisan consensus and political will to address the humanitarian aspects of immigration not only undermines the values of compassion and family unity, but also perpetuates a broken system that fails to serve the best interests of the nation and its residents. The practice of tying immigration reform to larger packages of legislation or budget items also continues to be a hindrance in addressing the very specific issues at hand.

***

Immigration attorneys, solely focusing on the current state of U.S. immigration law, run the risk of succumbing to hopelessness, questioning the

29. U.S. Citizenship and Immigration Services (USCIS), Number of Form I-821D, Consideration of Deferred Action for Childhood Arrivals, by Fiscal Year, Quarter, Intake, Biometrics and Case Status 2012–2022 (Department of Homeland Security, 2022).

purpose of it all. However, when we widen our lens to encompass the history of immigration law as a whole, we witness not only remarkable progress, but also the potential for an impactful and increasingly attainable path forward.

While we acknowledge the enduring presence of challenges such as political rhetoric, divisiveness, racism, xenophobia, and nationalist ideologies, we also recognize that these harmful forces have largely shifted from the forefront to the periphery. This shift creates an unprecedented opportunity for substantial, positive change—specifically through comprehensive immigration reform.

Humans crave immediate progress, whether it be in personal goals, like weight loss, or professional aspirations, like getting a promotion. We tend to grow disheartened when results do not materialize quickly, often leading to abandonment of the pursuit. Yet, the most significant advancements stem from perseverance, sustained dedication, and gradual, steadfast progress.

Modern immigration law may be fraught with challenges, but it is also ripe for the implementation of effective solutions. The following section of this book will explore these solutions, leading to a path forward that holds significant, and exciting, promise for all.

Martha's Story

In many ways, the U.S. immigration system has progressed from the exclusionary policies of the past to more inclusive and humanitarian principles. Nevertheless, immigration remains a contentious and widely debated issue, with polarizing arguments on both sides. Unfortunately, racism and bigotry continue to muddy the waters of this debate, hindering the ability of politicians, lawmakers, and the American people to find common ground for the way forward.

At Wildes & Weinberg, we believe in standing up for those who have given everything to protect the safety and well-being of others. That is why we are representing Martha Freire and her daughter, Amy, pro bono in their petition for a U-visa, and eventual U.S. citizenship. Many lives were saved as a result of the selfless actions of Martha's husband, who was killed in the 2019 terrorist attack in Jersey City. We firmly believe that his sacrifice should be honored in the most meaningful way possible—by ensuring that his family is granted the security and recognition they deserve.

Despite her husband's heroic actions and the devastating loss she has endured, Martha and her daughter remain in legal limbo, without the protections that should have been granted to them years ago. As part of our commitment to justice and our belief in the principles that this country stands for, we are working tirelessly to help Martha obtain a U-visa for herself and her daughter.

A U-visa is a special non-immigrant visa designed for victims of certain crimes who have suffered mental or physical abuse and are willing to assist law enforcement and government officials in the investigation or prosecution of criminal activity. The U-visa provides a pathway to legal status and, eventually, citizenship, offering protection and the opportunity to rebuild one's life in the United States. Given the extraordinary circumstances of Martha's case, we believe she more than qualifies for this relief.

By sharing Martha's story, we hope to shed light on the glaring issues in our immigration system and advocate for the change that is so desperately needed. Our goal is to secure the safety and security that Martha and her daughter deserve, and to ensure that her husband's legacy is honored in a way that befits his sacrifice.

Interview with Martha

Conducted by Amy Lane Singh

Martha, her husband, and their daughter, Amy, immigrated to the United States from Ecuador in 2016, driven by the hope of a brighter future. Back in Ecuador, they had a stable life; Martha worked as a social worker at one of the largest hospitals in the country, and her husband held a prominent position in finance. However, political turmoil and economic instability forced them to make the difficult decision to leave everything behind and start anew in America.

The transition to life in the United States was anything but easy. Upon arriving, they faced immediate challenges. With limited resources and no immediate job prospects, they moved in with friends in Union City, while Amy stayed with her cousin in another town. "It was hard for me because I had never left Amy's side," Martha recalled. They slept on couches, grappling with the harsh reality that their lives had drastically changed.

Martha's husband, once a respected professional, had to take on physically demanding jobs just to make ends meet. His first job in the United States involved fitting faucets onto hoses in a factory—a stark contrast to his previous career. "He worked there with gloves warming his hands. He had never done that type of work before, but he knew it was necessary," Martha said, describing the toll it took on him. Despite the blisters and exhaustion, he never complained, driven by the belief that they could make a life for themselves in this new country.

Martha also took on physically taxing work in a clothing factory, packing clothes for stores like Macy's and Nordstrom. It was a drastic change from her previous work in a hospital, but like her husband, she was determined to contribute to their family's survival. "It was a tough change, but well, we had to—you know, you come here to work hard and God decides what happens," Martha said with a quiet resolve.

Despite these hardships, they never lost sight of their goal: to build a life in America and secure a future for their daughter, Amy. They were determined to stay, work hard, and eventually become American citizens. Even when Martha's husband suffered severe injuries from a fall at work that left him unable to work for months, they didn't give up. They considered returning to Ecuador, but her husband, ever the optimist, told her, "No, Martha, wait, let's see what we can do." Tears fill Martha's eyes as she recalls these words of her husband, knowing how different things would be if they had gone back.

In December 2019, their dreams were shattered when terrorists attacked the Jewish-owned store in Jersey City where Martha's husband was working. The attack, a hate crime targeting the Jewish community, resulted in the deaths of several people, including Martha's husband, who was trying to help others escape. That day, as Martha recalled, "I felt something, I don't know how to explain it. I hugged him more tightly when I said goodbye." During the attack, instead of fleeing to save himself, her husband stayed behind to help others escape. "He could have left, but he didn't because he wanted to help," Martha recounted. At the time of the attack, dozens of elementary school students were present at an Orthodox Jewish school in an upstairs facility attached to the supermarket building. Investigators believe the synagogue and yeshiva may have been the ultimate target before the attackers veered off toward the store. His actions that day were nothing short of heroic, yet they cost him his life.

In the aftermath of the attack, Martha was devastated not only by the loss of her husband, but also by the unfulfilled promises that followed. She was told that her daughter, Amy, would receive free tuition for college, given that her father had died a hero. However, with the passing of time, these promises remain unfulfilled.

Martha expressed her deep disappointment and sense of abandonment: "There was a fund for Amy's education, but I don't know where that money is." Despite the numerous assurances of aid, no tangible support has been provided to her or Amy. While local officials memorialize those lost on the date of the attack each year, Martha feels forgotten, left to navigate the immense challenges of raising her daughter alone without the help she was promised.

The irony is cruel. Martha's husband, who died protecting Americans during a heinous act of hate, has not had his sacrifice fully honored by those he helped save. While recognized as a hero in words, the concrete support that was supposed to follow has been absent. Martha continues to struggle with the

U.S. immigration system, stating, "It has been four years since my husband was murdered . . . and I still do not have citizenship."

Martha's story exposes the deep flaws in the U.S. immigration system—a system that often fails to recognize the sacrifices made by immigrant families and the injustices they endure. It is a powerful testament to the need for reform, not only to honor the memory of those who have given everything for this country, but to ensure that their families are treated with the dignity and respect they deserve.

Despite the overwhelming loss and the hardships she has faced, Martha remains determined to secure a future for herself and her daughter in the country her husband died protecting. "Everything happens in God's time. God's time is just and perfect," she says, holding on to her faith and the belief that their sacrifices will not be in vain.

The U-Visa That Could Change Martha's Life

Created by Congress in 2000 as part of the Victims of Trafficking and Violence Protection Act, the U-visa recognizes the importance of supporting and protecting victims who are vital to the pursuit of justice, while also offering them a path to legal status in the United States. For Martha, the U-visa would be life changing.

Given the traumatic experience Martha and Amy have endured, and her willingness to cooperate with law enforcement in the aftermath, she is an obvious candidate for this relief. The U-visa would not only provide her with temporary legal status, but also allow her to apply for a green card after three years, putting her on the path to permanent residency and, eventually, citizenship.

This visa would offer Martha and her daughter the stability and security they desperately need. After years of living in uncertainty, the U-visa would protect them from deportation and allow them to remain in the United States legally. It would grant them work authorization, enabling Martha to support her family, now as a single parent, without the constant fear of losing her job due to her immigration status. Furthermore, the U-visa would provide Amy with the opportunity to continue her education in the United States, pursuing the dreams that her father worked so hard to make possible.

The U-visa also represents a form of justice for Martha's husband, whose heroic actions saved lives on that tragic day in Jersey City. By granting his family the protection and legal status they deserve, the U.S. government would be honoring his sacrifice in a meaningful way. It would send a powerful message that this country values the contributions and sacrifices of immigrant families.

For Martha and Amy, obtaining a U-visa is not just about securing legal status; it is about reclaiming the future that was stolen from them. It is about ensuring that they can live in the country Martha's husband died protecting, free from fear and with the opportunity to build the life they once dreamed of. The U-visa would give them the chance to move forward, to heal, and to find peace in the knowledge that her husband's sacrifice was not in vain.

At Wildes & Weinberg, we are committed to fighting for Martha's right to this protection. We believe that her story, and the stories of countless other immigrant families, highlights the need for compassion, justice, and reform in our immigration system. The U-visa could change Martha's life—and by sharing her story, we hope to inspire change that will benefit many others like her.

Glaring Problems with the U-Visa System

The U-visa was established with a noble intention. However, like many well-intentioned systems, the U-visa has not been immune to abuse and exploitation, leading to significant challenges that undermine its effectiveness and delay assistance to those who truly need it.

One of the most pressing issues with the U-visa system is the backlog of applications, which has reached crisis levels. As of recent years, tens of thousands of U-visa applications are pending, with applicants waiting years—sometimes a decade or more—for their cases to be processed. This backlog is a direct result of both the increasing number of applications and the statutory cap of 10,000 U-visas that can be issued each fiscal year, a limit that has not been adjusted since the program was established under the Victims of Trafficking and Violence Protection Act in 2000.

Immigration to the United States has grown substantially over the past two decades, and more individuals now come forward to report crimes, encouraged by programs like the U-visa. Unfortunately, the static cap of 10,000 visas per year is no longer sufficient to meet modern demand, leaving tens of thousands of victims in legal limbo each year. For perspective, as of 2023, there were more than 188,000 pending U-visa applications—a number that far exceeds the annual cap.

The inability to adjust the U-visa cap to reflect current immigration realities and the increasing number of crime victims creates a slew of problems. Applicants are often forced to wait in line for years, during which time they may lack legal status and work authorization, leaving them vulnerable to further exploitation and hardship. Even the granting of deferred action—a temporary measure to allow applicants to stay in the United States while awaiting their visa—is insufficient to provide long-term security.

Law enforcement agencies that rely on the cooperation of victims to prosecute serious crimes face challenges when victims are unable to access the protections and stability offered by the U-visa in a timely manner. Advocates have called for Congress to raise or eliminate the cap, emphasizing that doing so would enhance public safety and honor the United States' commitment to supporting victims of crime.

This is a stark contrast to racially and politically fueled dialogue that is frequently seen in the media, painting immigrants as a significant source of criminal activity. This legal recourse recognizing how often immigrants are victims as well as witnesses assisting in our criminal justice system is an absolute necessity, yet the sheer numbers and administrative backlog have hindered the effectiveness of the program.

Systemic inefficiencies in processing applications further exacerbate the problem. With demand expected to continue growing, the current system is woefully inadequate, leaving victims of serious crimes—including human trafficking, domestic violence, and sexual assault—waiting in uncertainty.

Another contributor to this backlog is the abuse of the U-visa system by individuals who exploit its provisions for personal gain rather than legitimate need. There have been documented cases where immigrants have falsely claimed to be victims of crime or abuse in order to obtain a U-visa, often with the guidance of unethical advisors.

An example of this issue is the case of Mohammad Reza Baniassadi, who operated the Law Offices of Reza Baniassadi in Chicago. Baniassadi faced federal charges, including one count of conspiracy to commit immigration fraud and five counts of submitting false applications for immigration benefits. The indictment alleged that Baniassadi, along with two of his employees, fabricated affidavits for their clients. These documents falsely claimed that the clients had been victims of spousal abuse, which would enable them to apply for a U-visa under false pretenses.

The fraudulent use of the U-visa system exploits the provision of immediate protection and work authorization that comes with a pending U-visa application. Once an application is filed, the applicant is often granted a form of deferred action, which can include temporary work authorization while their case is being processed. This creates an incentive for individuals to submit fraudulent claims as a means of obtaining legal status and work privileges in the United States, even if their cases are ultimately found to be without merit.

This exploitation of the system has several negative consequences. First, it undermines the integrity of the U-visa program. When the system is flooded with fraudulent claims, it becomes more difficult for immigration officials to identify and prioritize the cases of those who are in genuine need of protection. This not only delays justice for real victims, but also erodes public trust in the immigration system as a whole.

Second, the backlog caused by these fraudulent claims means that genuine victims are forced to wait years for their applications to be processed. During this time, they remain in a precarious legal status, unable to fully rebuild their lives or access the stability and security that the U-visa is supposed to provide. For individuals like Martha, whose husband died a hero protecting others, the delays caused by systemic abuse are particularly devastating, as they prolong the uncertainty and hardship that she and her daughter must endure.

Finally, the misuse of the U-visa system can lead to broader social and political consequences. As reports of fraud and abuse become more widespread, there is a risk that policymakers may push for stricter regulations or reductions in the number of U-visas issued each year. Such measures could further limit access to this vital form of relief, making it even harder for genuine victims to obtain the protection they need.

Addressing the glaring problems with the U-visa requires a systematic approach. Immigration authorities must be given the resources and tools necessary to effectively screen and process U-visa applications, ensuring that those who genuinely qualify for protection are prioritized. Additionally, there must be stricter penalties for those who submit fraudulent claims or advise others to do so, in order to deter abuse and maintain the integrity of the system.

There should also be ongoing efforts to educate both immigrants and legal practitioners about the proper use of the U-visa and the serious consequences of submitting false claims. By promoting a better understanding of the system and its intended purpose, we can help ensure that the U-visa remains a lifeline for those who truly need it, rather than a tool for exploitation. Only then can we truly provide the protection and support that individuals like Martha and her daughter deserve.

Developments Under the Second Trump Administration (2025)

While I was finalizing the manuscript for this book in late 2025, it became impossible to discuss "immigration today" without acknowledging the seismic shift brought about by the return of the Trump administration. In the span of just months, long-standing norms and legal pathways were reshaped through sweeping executive orders, unprecedented funding expansions, aggressive administrative actions, and rapid policy reversals. These changes are not minor adjustments at the margins; they represent a fundamental reorientation of the system, one whose consequences are being felt by families, employers, and entire communities in real time.

What follows is not an exhaustive catalog of every policy issued this year, but a focused account of the most consequential developments—changes that will define this moment in immigration history and shape the debates that lie ahead.

The "Invasion" Framework and the New Border Order

On January 20, 2025, President Trump signed an executive order titled "Protecting the American People Against Invasion," which revoked most Biden-era enforcement guidelines, directed federal agencies to "faithfully execute" the immigration laws against virtually all removable non-citizens, expanded the use of expedited removal, instructed ICE to revive and maximize 287(g) agreements with state and local police, and threatened to withhold certain federal funds from jurisdictions labeled as "sanctuary" cities or counties.[30]

On the same day, a companion order, "Securing Our Borders," authorized new or renewed construction of physical barriers at the U.S.–Mexico border, ordered detention "to the fullest extent permitted by law" instead of release, and paired immigration agents with thousands of active-duty troops and National Guard personnel at the southern border.[31] In practice, these measures were accompanied by the reinstatement of the Migrant Protection Protocols ("Remain in Mexico") and a sweeping bar on access to asylum for people described in presidential proclamations as participating in an "invasion" at the southern border.[32]

Within months, reported encounters between Border Patrol and migrants crossing between ports of entry dropped to historically low levels.

---

30. *Protecting the American People Against Invasion*, The White House (Jan. 20, 2025), https://www.whitehouse.gov/presidential-actions/2025/01/protecting-the-american-people-against-invasion/.

31. *Securing Our Borders*, The White House (Jan. 20, 2025), https://www.whitehouse.gov/presidential-actions/2025/01/securing-our-borders/.

32. *The "Migrant Protection Protocols": An Explanation of the Remain in Mexico Program*, Am. Immigr. Council (Feb. 1, 2024), https://www.americanimmigrationcouncil.org/fact-sheet/migrant-protection-protocols/.

In March 2025, U.S. Customs and Border Protection (CBP) reported just over 7,000 southwest border apprehensions—around a 95 percent decline from March 2024—followed by a further drop to roughly 6,000 encounters in June, figures that the White House touted as proof that the new restrictions and troop deployments are "delivering results on every front."[33]

Critics, however, emphasized that these record lows were achieved largely by closing off humanitarian channels—blocking or severely limiting access to asylum processing at the border and sharply curtailing parole-based pathways that had previously allowed some protection-seekers to enter lawfully.[34] Analysts agreed, noting that near-total restrictions on asylum and the deployment of military forces played a much larger role in driving those numbers down.[35]

Having spent more than three decades working within the immigration system, I understand the argument that a nation must have orderly borders. I also recognize that every administration has both the authority and the responsibility to enforce our immigration laws. For many Americans, the recent reduction in border crossings may appear to signal restored control, stability, and security. I appreciate why that result resonates, particularly among communities that have felt overwhelmed or unheard in recent years.

But it is equally important that we acknowledge what these numbers do not show. Enforcement can be effective without being indiscriminate, and border management can be strong without abandoning humanitarian values. When we rely almost exclusively on deterrence—military deployment, mass detention, expanded expedited removal, and the near-elimination of asylum access—we ignore the human beings whose lives hang in the balance.

---

33. Press Release, U.S. Customs & Border Prot., Most Secure Border in History: CBP Reports Major Enforcement Wins in June 2025 (July 15, 2025), https://www.cbp.gov/newsroom/national-media-release/most-secure-border-history-cbp-reports-major-enforcement-wins-june.

34. Tara Watson & Jonathon Zars, *100 Days of Immigration Under the Second Trump Administration*, Brookings Inst. (Apr. 29, 2025), https://www.brookings.edu/articles/100-days-of-immigration-under-the-second-trump-administration/.

35. Muzaffar Chishti & Kathleen Bush-Joseph, *In First 100 Days, Trump 2.0 Has Dramatically Reshaped the U.S. Immigration System, but Is Not Meeting Mass Deportation Aims*, Migration Pol'y Inst. (Apr. 24, 2025), https://www.migrationpolicy.org/article/trump-2-immigration-first-100-days.

My concern is not with the idea of securing the border; it is with the notion that security must come at the expense of compassion. A strategy that treats desperate people as invaders may produce short-term numerical results, but it does little to address the underlying forces that drive migration: political instability, corruption, famine, gender-based violence, and the absence of lawful pathways for those who genuinely need protection. In my experience, when we close the door entirely, we do not stop migration—we simply make it more dangerous, more chaotic, and more costly in both human and moral terms.

The "One Big Beautiful Bill" and the Rise of Mass Detention

The Trump administration also engineered a dramatic expansion of immigration detention. In mid-2025, Congress passed a budget package sometimes referred to as the "One Big Beautiful Bill Act," which set aside roughly $170 billion over several years for immigration enforcement, detention, and deportation. Of that amount, approximately $45 billion was dedicated to detention alone[36]—enough to roughly triple ICE's annual detention budget and nearly double bed capacity (from about 56,000 to well over 100,000) in detention facilities, most of them privately run. Those funds were explicitly tied to a presidential goal of deporting up to one million people per year.[37]

Amid this surge in detention funding, Congress enacted the Laken Riley Act, a sweeping mandate that dramatically expanded the categories of non-citizens subject to mandatory, no-bond detention. Designed and promoted as a public-safety measure, the law requires DHS to detain non-citizens accused—not convicted—of a wide range of criminal offenses. While the legislation's title invokes the murder of a Georgia college student by a man who was in the United States illegally, its operative provisions reach far beyond violent crime.

Under the act, individuals charged with offenses such as shoplifting, simple burglary, motor-vehicle theft, or driving under the influence must

36. *New Funding Increases Immigration Enforcement*, NAT'L IMMIGR. L. CTR. (Sep. 16, 2025), https://www.nilc.org/resources/new-funding-increases-immigration-enforcement/.

37. Muzaffar Chishti & Valerie Lacarte, *U.S. Immigrant Detention Grows to Record Heights Under Trump Administration*, MIGRATION POL'Y INST. (Oct. 29, 2025), https://www.migrationpolicy.org/article/trump-immigrant-detention.

be taken into ICE custody and held without the possibility of bond.[38] This represents a profound shift away from long-standing principles of individualized risk assessment. For decades, immigration judges evaluated whether a person posed a danger to the community or a flight risk before deciding on release. The Laken Riley Act overrides that system, transforming what were once discretionary decisions into automatic detention triggers.

The implications are far-reaching. Because the law applies at the charging stage, many non-citizens are detained before any adjudication of guilt, often based solely on arrests or allegations that may later be reduced or dismissed. In practice, this means that non-citizens who would ordinarily be released by state courts—because they pose minimal risk, have established community ties, or are first-time offenders—are instead transferred directly into immigration custody. For ICE, the law functions as an accelerant, filling beds at an unprecedented rate and dovetailing with the expanded detention capacity funded through the "One Big Beautiful Bill."

Aggressive Expansion of Interior Enforcement and the Largest "Mass Illegalization" in Modern U.S. History

In my opinion, one of the most consequential moves of 2025 has been the rapid dismantling of humanitarian parole programs created under the Biden administration. In March 2025, DHS announced plans to revoke parole and work authorization for roughly 500,000 to 530,000 Cubans, Haitians, Nicaraguans, and Venezuelans who had entered under the CHNV private-sponsorship processes, calling those permissions "unlawful" expansions of executive authority.[39] On May 30, 2025, the Supreme Court granted the administration's emergency request to proceed, lifting a lower-court injunction and allowing DHS to terminate parole status for these individuals; commentators have described this as the largest single "mass illegalization" event in modern U.S. history.[40]

---

38. Andorra Bruno et al., Cong. Rsch. Serv., R47901, Immigration Legislation and Issues in the 118th Congress (2024).

39. Diana Ramirez-Simon, *Trump Revokes Legal Status of 530,000 Cubans, Haitians, Nicaraguans and Venezuelans*, The Guardian (Mar. 21, 2025), https://www.theguardian.com/us-news/2025/mar/21/trump-revoke-legal-status-cuban-haitian-nicaraguan.

40. Press Release, U.S. Citizenship & Immigr. Servs., Litigation-Related Update: Supreme Court Stay of CHNV Preliminary Injunction (June 6, 2025), https://www.uscis.gov/newsroom/alerts/litigation-related-update-supreme-court-stay-of-chnv-preliminary-injunction.

By June 12, DHS began issuing formal termination notices and encouraging affected migrants either to depart the United States or to seek other forms of relief if eligible.[41] These measures effectively shut down most humanitarian pathways at the border and shifted the burden of protection back onto Mexico and other countries in the region.

At the same time, interior enforcement intensified. ICE has expanded its collaboration with state and local law enforcement under the revived 287(g) program, with the Day One "Invasion" order instructing ICE to authorize state and local officers to enforce immigration law during routine police duties, such as traffic stops.[42] Research showed that daily ICE arrests of Latino immigrants more than doubled in the first half of 2025 compared with the final year of the Biden administration, with internal targets reportedly set at roughly 3,000 arrests per day nationwide.[43]

Large-scale operations, such as an autumn 2025 sweep in Southeast Texas in which ICE reported more than 3,500 arrests in six weeks, including dozens of people labeled as murderers, gang members, or "child predators,"[44] drew intense media coverage and concern about collateral arrests of people with no criminal convictions. Such raids swept up thousands of people whose only alleged violation was civil immigration status, reinforcing concerns that the "worst of the worst" messaging obscured a much broader dragnet.

State-level enforcement also moved into new territory. In Texas, for example, the legislature previously enacted Senate Bill 4, which would have allowed state police and judges to arrest, prosecute, and order the removal of people suspected of entering the state unlawfully. That statute remained

41. Press Release, U.S. Dep't of Homeland Sec., DHS Issues Notices of Termination for CHNV Parole Program, Encourages Parolees to Self-Deport Immediately (June 12, 2025), https://www.dhs.gov/news/2025/06/12/dhs-issues-notices-termination-chnv-parole-program-encourages-parolees-self-deport.

42. Micaela McConnell, *287(g) Agreements With ICE Threaten Welcoming Communities*, American Immigration Council (Sep. 26, 2025), https://www.americanimmigrationcouncil.org/blog/287g-agreements-ice-threaten-communities/.

43. *UCLA Report Finds Latino Arrests by ICE Have Skyrocketed Under the Trump Administration's Second Term*, UCLA Luskin Sch. of Pub. Affairs (Oct. 28, 2025), https://luskin.ucla.edu/ucla-report-finds-latino-arrests-by-ice-have-skyrocketed-under-the-trump-administrations-second-term.

44. Press Release, U.S. Immigr. & Customs Enf't, ICE Arrests over 3,500 Criminal Illegal Aliens in Houston, Including the Worst of the Worst Pedophiles, Gang Members, and Murderers (Nov. 20, 2025), https://www.dhs.gov/news/2025/11/20/ice-arrests-over-3500-criminal-illegal-aliens-houston-including-worst-worst.

blocked after the Fifth Circuit held it unconstitutional in July 2025, reaffirming that immigration enforcement is principally a federal responsibility.[45] Yet the Trump Justice Department withdrew earlier federal challenges to SB 4 and similar laws in other states, signaling greater tolerance, if not outright encouragement, of state-driven enforcement initiatives.[46] At the same time, Texas entered into new 287(g)–style agreements under which roughly 3,500 state highway patrol officers were trained and authorized to perform federal immigration functions during traffic stops, raising fresh worries about racial profiling and pretextual policing.[47]

Another bombshell development was the granting of law enforcement authority to U.S. Citizenship and Immigration Services (USCIS), the agency historically responsible for administering immigration benefits such as naturalization, adjustment of status, family petitions, and humanitarian programs. Under a final rule that took effect on October 6, 2025, USCIS officers were given the power to initiate criminal investigations, make arrests for federal felonies or immigration violations, execute search and arrest warrants, and carry firearms.[48]

The practical effects of this change were soon being felt. Benefits interviews—long viewed as administrative, non-adversarial settings—came to carry heightened enforcement risks. Marriage-based adjustment applicants attending routine interviews, naturalization candidates appearing for civics exams, and asylees responding to requests for evidence now had to navigate an environment in which the very agency adjudicating their applications also possessed the power to detain them.

---

45. Uriel J. García, *Texas' Immigration Law Is Unconstitutional, Appeals Court Rules*, Tex. Trib. (July 4, 2025), https://www.texastribune.org/2025/07/04/texas-immigration-law-senate-bill-4-fifth-circuit-court-ruling/.

46. Uriel J. García, *Trump Administration Drops Challenge to Texas Law Targeting People Who Illegally Cross the Border*, Tex. Trib. (Mar. 19, 2025), https://www.texastribune.org/2025/03/19/texas-immigration-law-senate-bill-4-department-justice-lawsuit/.

47. *Texas DPS Troopers Gain Federal Authority to Enforce Immigration Laws Under New ICE Agreements*, Gonzalez Olivieri LLC, https://www.gonzalezolivierillc.com/immigration-updates/texas-dps-troopers-gain-federal-authority-to-enforce-immigration-laws-under-new-ice-agreements/ (last visited Mar. 30, 2026).

48. Frances Vinall, *Agency Handling Green Cards to Hire Armed Agents Who Can Arrest Immigrants*, Wash. Post (Sep. 5, 2025), https://www.washingtonpost.com/immigration/2025/09/05/uscis-law-enforcement-arrest-green-cards/.

While each of these developments had the potential to create devastating consequences, the dismantling of the CHNV humanitarian parole programs struck me with particular force—not only because of the scale, but also because of the message it sends. Parole has always been a discretionary tool, used by administrations of both parties to respond quickly to humanitarian emergencies, political upheaval, and regional instability. It was never meant to be a substitute for congressional action, but it has often served as a lifeline for people with nowhere else to turn. For more than half a million individuals from Cuba, Haiti, Nicaragua, and Venezuela—people who complied with every requirement, passed rigorous vetting, and entered lawfully—its sudden withdrawal created a level of instability and fear unlike anything I have seen in my career.

I understand the argument that parole cannot become an unbounded mechanism for large-scale migration. I also understand the concern that executive authority has, at times, expanded beyond what Congress envisioned. Those are legitimate debates. But even when the legal questions are complicated, the human consequences are clear. Families who built lives in the United States, who enrolled their children in school, who began working and contributing to their communities, are now being told not only that their status will end, but also that they should prepare to leave the United States—many returning to countries still marred by violence or economic devastation. Policy disagreements should not obscure the fact that real people are bearing the weight of these decisions.

The aggressive expansion of interior enforcement also raises serious concerns. Every administration has the right to enforce immigration law, and the public has a reasonable expectation that individuals who pose genuine risks to public safety will be prioritized. But reality on the ground tells a more complicated story. When thousands of individuals are swept into enforcement actions because of civil immigration violations—when parents, longtime residents, and people with deep community ties are arrested alongside those accused of serious crimes—we erode trust, not just in government, but in the very idea that the system is capable of distinguishing between danger and dignity.

State-driven initiatives like Texas's Senate Bill 4 add yet another layer of complexity. While states may understandably wish to respond to local pressures, immigration enforcement is, at its core, a federal responsibility—a principle reaffirmed by the courts for decades. Fragmenting that authority risks creating confusion, racial profiling, and inconsistent application of the law. It also places local officers in roles they were not trained to carry out, further straining community relationships.

High-Skilled Workers in the Crosshairs

Against this chaotic backdrop, the administration also turned its attention to legal immigration, particularly high-skilled temporary workers. On September 19, 2025, President Trump issued a proclamation imposing a $100,000 annual fee—per worker—on most new H-1B visa petitions and many requests for H-1B status filed from abroad, a dramatic increase from the prior filing fees of only a few hundred dollars.[49] Although the proclamation included narrow exceptions for petitions filed before a specified date and for certain existing visa holders, USCIS guidance confirmed that the new fee primarily applied to petitions entering the annual H-1B lottery.[50] In addition, heightened documentary requirements will make it significantly harder for employers to classify positions as "specialty occupations." The administration presented these changes as part of a broader effort to reduce reliance on foreign labor and to push employers to recruit and train U.S. workers instead.[51]

Business groups, universities, and major technology companies, however, warned that the fee would effectively shut small and mid-sized employers out of the program, hinder the United States' ability to attract global talent, and accelerate the offshoring of high-skilled jobs. These concerns intensified alongside a new White House–announced investor pathway—a $1 million "Gold Card" offering a route to permanent residence—deepening

49. Barbara Ortutay & Seung Min Kim, *Trump Signs Proclamation Adding $100K Annual Fee for H-1B Visa Applications*, ASSOCIATED PRESS (Sep. 19, 2025), https://apnews.com/article/h1b-visa-trump-immigration-8d39699d0b2de3d90936f8076357254e.

50. *H-1B FAQ*, U.S. CITIZENSHIP & IMMIGR. SERVS. (Sep. 21, 2025), https://www.uscis.gov/newsroom/alerts/h-1b-faq.

51. *Restriction on Entry of Certain Nonimmigrant Workers*, THE WHITE HOUSE (Sep. 19, 2025), https://www.whitehouse.gov/presidential-actions/2025/09/restriction-on-entry-of-certain-nonimmigrant-workers/.

the contrast between increasingly restricted humanitarian and worker visas and newly expanded options for the very wealthy.[52]

The decision to radically restructure the H-1B program entailed serious consequences. At a moment when global competition for scientific and technological leadership was never more intense, new barriers to the very talent that had driven the country's innovation for generations would be counterproductive. Instead of creating strategic pathways that help the United States compete in emerging fields—from artificial intelligence and biotechnology to quantum computing—the administration was pushing employers toward a system that was both prohibitively expensive and functionally inaccessible for all but the largest corporations.

In the next chapter, "Charting the Path Forward," we explore in detail why the United States must double down on attracting and retaining STEM talent from around the world. The data is unequivocal: Our K-12 STEM pipeline is struggling, our domestic workforce cannot meet the rapidly growing demand for high-skill labor, and competing nations have seized the moment by offering smoother, more welcoming immigration systems. Restrictive measures like the new H-1B fee move us in precisely the wrong direction. They undermine our ability to recruit the engineers, researchers, scientists, and technologists who are essential to maintaining leadership in critical and emerging technologies.

If we continue tightening the H-1B program while other countries open their doors, we risk losing the race for future innovation. The United States has always led the world by attracting the best minds, not turning them away. To safeguard our national security, strengthen our economy, and preserve our global standing, we must shift from an era of restriction to an era of intelligent, targeted investment in foreign talent. Anything less puts our long-term competitiveness at stake.

A Shrinking Pipeline—The Collapse of Student Visa Approvals

While the restructuring of the H-1B program has drawn the most public attention, an equally consequential shift is unfolding more quietly:

---

52. Will Weissert, *Trump's "Gold Card" Program Goes Live, Offering US Visas Starting at $1 Million per Person*, Associated Press (Dec. 10, 2025), https://apnews.com/article/trump-gold-card-website-live-us-visa-22edbd7e65d188bbf6c8ec1d5f78d11a.

a dramatic decline in student visas issued to foreign nationals seeking to study in the United States. Though less visible than employment-based visa changes, the steep drop in F-1 and J-1 approvals may ultimately pose an even greater threat to America's future innovation capacity.

Consular data reveals significant decreases in student visa issuance across multiple regions. In 2024 and 2025, approval rates for F-1 visas in key sending countries—including India, China, Nigeria, and Ghana—fell sharply due to heightened scrutiny, prolonged administrative processing, and increased denials for applicants previously considered low-risk.[53] Universities began reporting widespread disruptions as consulates delayed or refused visas even for students with full funding, established academic records, or prior lawful U.S. travel.[54]

These declines have an outsized impact on the United States because international students form the backbone of the American STEM pipeline. According to the National Science Foundation, foreign students account for more than half of all graduate-level enrollment in engineering, mathematics, computer science, and physical sciences, and represent the majority of Ph.D. candidates in emerging technologies such as artificial intelligence, quantum computing, and advanced materials.[55] When fewer students are admitted, fewer workers are available years later to join the U.S. scientific and technological workforce.

The timing of these visa reductions is especially troubling when viewed alongside the administration's broader restrictions on high-skilled immigration. As detailed in the previous section, the new $100,000 H-1B fee and tightened specialty-occupation rules make it far more difficult for employers to hire foreign graduates trained at U.S. universities. The combined effect is a one-two punch: fewer students entering U.S. programs today, and fewer opportunities for them to remain and contribute tomorrow.

Colleges and universities soon began raising alarms. A 2025 survey by the American Council on Education found that 96 percent of U.S.

53. *Monthly Nonimmigrant Visa Issuance Statistics*, U.S. DEP'T OF STATE, https://travel.state.gov/content/travel/en/legal/visa-law0/visa-statistics/nonimmigrant-visa-statistics/monthly-nonimmigrant-visa-issuances.html (last visited May 13, 2026).

54. Karin Fischer, *Even as Classes Begin, Some Foreign Students Are Still in Visa Limbo*, CHRON. OF HIGHER ED. (Sep. 5, 2025), https://www.chronicle.com/article/even-as-classes-begin-some-foreign-students-are-still-in-visa-limbo.

55. NAT'L SCI. FOUND., SCIENCE & ENGINEERING INDICATORS: HIGHER EDUCATION IN SCIENCE AND ENGINEERING (2019), https://ncses.nsf.gov/pubs/nsb20197.

institutions were concerned about the visa application process, citing delays and denials as the primary reason for declines in new international enrollments.[56]

NAFSA: Association of International Educators estimates that each cohort of international students contributes over $40 billion annually to the U.S. economy and supports more than 355,000 American jobs—revenues and roles now at risk.[57]

Other nations seized the moment. Canada, Australia, and several European countries streamlined student visa processing, expanded post-study work visas, and launched aggressive recruitment campaigns aimed specifically at students who would previously have chosen the United States. By narrowing access at our own borders, the United States ceded ground in a global competition that once overwhelmingly favored us.

As we explore more fully in Chapter 4, "Charting the Path Forward," the United States cannot maintain its leadership in critical and emerging technologies without a robust pipeline of foreign talent. Student visas are the first step in that pipeline. When these pathways constrict, the consequences are felt not only on campuses but also across laboratories, research institutions, startups, and national-security ecosystems for years to come. The decline in student visa approvals is not a peripheral issue. It is a direct threat to America's scientific future.

The Quiet Decline of Other Visa Categories

It is not just highly skilled workers or international students whose immigration pathways have constricted. Across nearly every temporary visa category, heightened scrutiny and dramatically slower processing began to reshape labor markets that depended on lawful immigrant workers. These reductions were less visible than headline-grabbing H-1B changes, but they quietly reverberated through industries that formed the backbone of the American economy.

56. *International Student Enrollment Slows as Concerns About the Visa Application Process Rise*, Am. Council on Ed. (Nov. 21, 2025), https://www.acenet.edu/News-Room/Pages/Open-Doors-2025.aspx.

57. Press Release, NAFSA: Ass'n of Int'l Educators, International Students Contributed $43 Billion to the U.S. Economy in 2024–2025; Fall 2025 Spending Down by $1.1 Billion (Nov. 17, 2025), https://www.nafsa.org/about/about-nafsa/international-students-contributed-43-billion-us-economy-2024-2025-fall-2025.

The H-2B program, which provides seasonal, non-agricultural labor to hotels, restaurants, landscaping firms, amusement parks, and coastal tourism centers, has been particularly strained. Annual supplemental visa allocations—long relied on to meet peak-season demand—now disappear within days. Employers have reported extraordinary levels of document requests, heightened fraud suspicions, and unpredictable adjudications.

The result?

- Businesses dependent on seasonal labor are unable to staff basic operations.
- Hotels reduce room availability; landscaping companies cancel contracts; amusement parks shorten seasons or eliminate attractions.
- Many small and mid-sized employers, particularly in rural or vacation-driven economies, face the real prospect of closures or permanent downsizing.

The H-2A program, which supplies foreign agricultural workers for crop cultivation, livestock care, and food processing, has also been reshaped by new compliance demands. Employers must now provide more extensive recruitment evidence, multi-year financial documentation, and expanded housing and transportation attestations. Processing times have lengthened, and audits have risen sharply.

The result?

- Farms face labor shortfalls during critical harvest windows.
- Crop losses increase; operational costs rise; and delays threaten supply chains that are already vulnerable to climate and market disruptions.
- The cumulative effect is felt at grocery stores nationwide, where reduced supply leads to higher food prices for American families.

Other industries hit extremely hard by the contraction include healthcare, manufacturing, and construction.

- Healthcare: Hospitals rely on a mix of H-1B physicians, J-1 waiver doctors, and TN professionals from Canada and Mexico. Delays and program limitations are hitting rural and specialty hospitals the hardest. As a result, we are seeing staff shortages, longer wait times, and declining access to critical care.

- Manufacturing: The manufacturing workforce includes a significant number of immigrant workers in production, machine operation, logistics, and food processing. Increased enforcement and reduced visa availability disrupt production lines, harming even U.S.-born workers whose jobs depend on stable output. The outcome is slower production, increased costs, and downstream job losses.
- Construction: One of the nation's most immigrant-dependent industries—especially among undocumented and temporary workers—construction now faces intensified audits and workforce disruptions. This has quickly resulted in project delays, labor shortages, increased costs, and heightened safety risks.

With the expansion of ICE operations and the new arrest authority granted to USCIS, the lines between benefit adjudication and enforcement have blurred in ways unseen in modern immigration history.

***

Taken together, the developments of 2025 do not replace the deeper structural problems outlined in Chapter 3—post-9/11 securitization, outdated quotas, and the enduring influence of political rhetoric—but they dramatically intensify them. The immigration system has become increasingly closed to humanitarian migration, more punitive in its interior enforcement, more reliant on large-scale detention, and less welcoming to many categories of legal workers, even as new pathways open for those with extraordinary financial means. At the same time, the enforcement-first approach of the current administration has emphasized the glaring absence of any broad legalization framework.

CHAPTER 4

Charting the Path Forward

Something must be done. Without thoughtful and considerable action, we risk an unprecedented period of regression that threatens to wreak havoc on immigrants, the U.S. workforce and economy, American innovation, and the security and well-being of our entire nation.

This section of the book explores different scenarios that could shape the future of U.S. immigration policies, with a focus on the potential outcomes. Through deep analysis, we present you with a balanced examination of the possibilities, encouraging constructive discussions and informed perspectives.

I do not deny, for one second, that we must be less reactionary and more proactive with regard to national security. However, we must also finally come to the realization that the morals of our nation are directly linked to national security. Embracing more humanitarian immigration policies is not only a moral imperative, but a strategic move that aligns with our core values and contributes significantly to the overall well-being of the American public.

Compassionate immigration policies acknowledge the humanity of those seeking refuge and a better life in this country. By prioritizing empathy and understanding, we create a system that treats immigrants with dignity and compassion. This approach not only upholds our commitment to human rights, but also sets a positive example on the global stage, enhancing our moral standing and soft power, which is our ability to influence and shape international relations through attraction and persuasion rather than coercion or force. "Hard power," on the other hand, relies on military strength and economic sanctions.

From a security perspective, inclusive immigration policies contribute to a safer and more secure nation. When people feel seen, acknowledged, and included, they are more likely to integrate positively into society. Inclusivity reduces feelings of alienation and disenfranchisement, factors that frequently contribute to radicalization or social unrest. By fostering a sense of belonging, we create a more united front against potential security threats.

Compassionate immigration policies also tap into the talents, skills, and diverse perspectives that immigrants bring to our nation. Immigrants have been integral to the cultural, social, and economic fabric of the United States throughout its history. Embracing this diversity not only enriches our communities, but also enhances our competitiveness on a global scale. A more diverse society births innovation, cultural exchange, and economic growth, making us more resilient and adaptable to the challenges of the modern world.

Regular, periodic analysis and modification of our immigration system are imperative for the well-being and prosperity of the American public. It reinforces the idea that our nation's strength lies in its ability to embrace and harness the collective potential of individuals, regardless of their origin. By leading with strength and heart, we not only honor our foundational principles, but also fortify the foundations of a secure, prosperous, and harmonious society for all.

But for immigration reform to be effective, we must consider a broad view of solutions that address multiple concerns, from enhanced border security to increased pathways to citizenship. Even more importantly, we must foster a constructive dialogue that appeals to people on all sides of this divisive issue. Without general consensus, we will remain in gridlock indefinitely. And that is an outcome we simply cannot afford.

Smart Border Security Measures

Integrating smart and technology-driven approaches to enhance border security is one potential solution in the larger discussion on comprehensive immigration reform. Smarter border security can include, but is not limited to, increased investment in surveillance technology, strategic infrastructure improvements, and collaboration with neighboring countries. By adopting a holistic view of border security, policymakers can strike a balance between safeguarding national interests and enabling efficient cross-border movement.

In addition to the benefits to national security and human rights, smart border security measures have substantial economic benefits. People are expensive, and people make mistakes. The use of technology reduces the need for a physical presence at borders, allowing that manpower to be reallocated to areas of greater need. Furthermore, effective technology is much less error prone than its human counterpart. A few examples of existing and potential technology solutions that could enhance border security include:

- Surveillance Technology: Investing in advanced surveillance technology, such as intelligent cameras, sensors, and radar systems, provides real-time monitoring of border areas. These technologies can autonomously detect and track suspicious activities, allowing border enforcement agencies to respond swiftly to potential threats. Machine learning algorithms can enhance the accuracy of threat detection, reducing false alarms and improving overall surveillance of even our most vulnerable borders.
- Unmanned Aerial Vehicles (UAVs) or Drones: Deploying drones for border patrol and surveillance has already proven to be a highly effective solution. Drones equipped with high-resolution cameras and infrared sensors can cover vast areas, including challenging terrain, providing border control agencies with valuable data. Additionally, autonomous drones can be programmed to follow predefined routes, monitor specific regions, and transmit real-time video feeds to central command centers.
- Biometric Identification Systems: Implementing biometric technology, such as facial recognition and fingerprint scanning, enhances identity verification processes at border crossings. This not only improves the accuracy of identifying individuals, but also facilitates faster and more secure border clearance. Biometric databases can be integrated with international databases to strengthen collaboration with neighboring countries in tracking and apprehending individuals with security concerns.
- Smart Fencing and Infrastructure: Enhancing physical barriers with smart technologies, such as sensors embedded in fences, can create a more responsive and adaptive border security system. Smart fencing can detect breaches, tunneling attempts, or tampering, triggering immediate alerts to border patrol agents. Integrating these

systems with artificial intelligence (AI) enables predictive analytics, allowing authorities to anticipate potential threats based on historical data.

- Geospatial Intelligence (GIS): Utilizing geospatial intelligence tools can enhance border mapping, monitoring, and situational awareness. GIS technology integrates data from various sources, including satellite imagery and ground sensors, to create comprehensive and real-time visualizations of border regions. This enables authorities to make informed decisions, allocate resources effectively, and respond rapidly to changing security dynamics.
- Blockchain for Secure Data Sharing: Implementing blockchain technology can enhance the secure sharing of data and information among relevant agencies. This decentralized and tamper-proof system ensures the integrity of data, allowing for trust and collaboration between countries sharing border regions. Blockchain can also streamline communication and coordination efforts, leading to more effective cross-border security initiatives.

Human-Centric Smart Border Policies

As effective as the implementation of technology is proving to be, smarter border policies involve a lot more than just advancements in technology. They also require an advancement in the way we think about human rights. Protecting the rights of refugees and asylum seekers is not only compassionate, it strengthens the security of our borders and our nation. Examples of human-centric smart border policies include the following.

Compassionate Detention Policies

To achieve smarter border controls, we must implement policies that prioritize access to proper healthcare, legal representation, and dignified living conditions. By integrating electronic monitoring, case management, and support from community organizations, we can find a balance between security concerns and respect for the rights and dignity of individuals within the immigration system.

Comprehensive healthcare initiatives within detention facilities are an important starting point. This includes providing timely medical assessments, ensuring access to mental health services, and addressing the unique healthcare needs of vulnerable populations, such as children and pregnant women. By implementing meaningful healthcare policies, we can demonstrate our commitment to treating detainees with dignity and respect for their well-being.

In addition to healthcare, offering detainees legal assistance is essential for protecting their right to due process. This can be accomplished by partnering with legal aid organizations, providing pro bono services, and offering legal orientation programs within detention facilities to inform detainees about their rights and available legal avenues.

Creating dignified living conditions is equally imperative. This can be achieved through thoughtful policies that establish standards for hygiene, nutrition, and appropriate accommodations. Guidelines prohibiting overcrowding and ensuring adequate personal space contribute to an environment that respects the humanity of every individual in detention.

Exploring alternatives to traditional detention, such as community-based programs, should also be prioritized. These programs place individuals under supervision while awaiting immigration proceedings, offering a more dignified and less restrictive approach to detention, and reducing the problem of overcrowding.

Environmental Considerations

I cannot stress enough that the deployment of border control infrastructure must be designed (or redesigned) with a keen awareness of environmental impact. Past designs failed to do this, but smarter controls incorporate eco-friendly solutions, minimizing disruption to ecosystems and wildlife. Sustainable practices in construction and maintenance contribute to an approach that respects the environment while addressing security concerns.

Utilizing solar-powered surveillance technology, for instance, can dramatically reduce the carbon footprint associated with traditional power sources. Green roofing on infrastructure facilities provides insulation and promotes biodiversity by creating habitats for local flora and fauna. And implementing sensor-based monitoring systems that can detect and differentiate between human and animal movement helps minimize unnecessary disturbances to wildlife.

Border fortifications can also have a substantial impact on local infrastructure and ecosystems. The massive structures often utilized can alter waterways and contribute to flooding or drought conditions, impacting human populations as well as animal and plant life. They can destroy native habitats and impede migration routes, threatening biodiversity loss that can have widespread impact. Organizations such as the Center for Biological Diversity have weighed in to propose design strategies that can minimize or mitigate the impact, but ultimately the authority resides with the U.S. government to implement responsible projects in the area.

By combining these technology and human-centric solutions, border security can evolve into a more sophisticated and adaptive system. Collaboration with neighboring countries and other organizations saves time, money, and resources, while the integration of technology is cost effective, enhances security, and contributes to a more agile and responsive border management system.

Often the problem isn't a lack of manpower and resources; it's the gaping wound of political division in the United States. We are too busy fighting with each other to come to the table and create a system that works for everyone, on all sides of the equation. Without bipartisan cooperation and a shared commitment to reform, we will continue to face the same challenges, unable to harness the full potential of innovative solutions that could transform our immigration system almost overnight.

Pathways to Legal Status

There is a common, and understandable, misconception that increasing pathways to legal status will lead to an influx of immigrants who will take jobs from hard-working Americans and overwhelm our vetting systems. On the contrary, by facilitating efficient legal pathways to permanent residency, we actually discourage unlawful entry and contribute to a more orderly immigration system overall.

Increasing pathways to legal status will almost certainly have significant positive impacts on the U.S. economy and national security. For starters, providing legal pathways encourages immigrant entrepreneurs to establish businesses, leading to job creation and economic stimulation.

Consider the following statistics: Nearly half of all Fortune 500 companies were founded by immigrants or their children,[1] immigrants are

---

1. *The "New American" Fortune 500: The Role of Immigrants in America's Largest Companies*, Partnership for a New American Economy (June 2011), https://www.americanimmigrationcouncil.org/wp-content/uploads/2013/07/new-american-fortune-500-june-2011.pdf.

80 percent more likely to start companies in the United States than their American-born counterparts,[2] and more than eight million Americans are employed by immigrant-owned businesses.[3]

As these numbers so powerfully illustrate, increasing immigrant-established new businesses will be a massive boon to the U.S. economy, resulting in more—not fewer—jobs for American workers.

Another key benefit of increasing pathways to legal status is increased productivity and innovation. When individuals have legal status, they are significantly more likely to contribute actively to the labor market, filling critical gaps in industries facing labor shortages. These are jobs that American-born workers can't or don't want to fill.

Furthermore, a well-regulated legal immigration system enhances national security by improving the ability to screen and vet individuals entering the country. When people have legal avenues to pursue residency, they are much more likely to undergo thorough background checks, reducing the risks associated with undocumented individuals who would otherwise circumvent the vetting process. Strengthening legal pathways allows authorities to focus resources on effective screening, ensuring that those who enter the country do so through transparent and secure channels.

Increasing legal pathways also promotes social integration and civic participation, fostering a sense of belonging and loyalty to the nation. This integration is vital for national security, as individuals who feel included in society are more likely to cooperate with law enforcement agencies, report suspicious activities, and contribute positively to the overall safety of the community.

To increase pathways to legal status in a manner that improves our economy and national security, we must dramatically reduce processing times, eliminate bureaucratic hurdles, and adjust visa quotas to better align with economic demands. Next, I discuss various methods of achieving these goals.

---

2. Robert W. Fairlie, Arnobio Morelix, E. J. Reedy, and Joshua Russell, *The Kauffman Index: Startup Activity National Trends - 2016*, Kauffman Foundation (Aug. 2016), https://www.kauffman.org/wp-content/uploads/2019/09/kauffman_index_startup_activity_national_trends_2016.pdf.

3. *New Data Shows Immigrant-Owned Businesses Employed 8 Million Americans; Immigrants Wield $1.1 Trillion in Spending Power*, Am. Immigration Council (Mar. 12, 2019), https://www.americanimmigrationcouncil.org/uncategorized/new-data-shows-immigrant-owned-businesses-employed-8-million-americans-immigrants-wield-1-1-trillion-in-spending-power/#:~:text=In%202017%20alone%2C%20households%20led,%2C%20and%20helping%20communities%20thrive.%E2%80%9D.

Exploring a Merit-Based Immigration System

To really overhaul our immigration system, an examination of the feasibility and implications of transitioning to a merit-based system must be seriously considered. This would involve reshaping visa allocation to prioritize skills, education, and qualifications. By shifting toward a merit-based approach, we would essentially be aligning our immigration policies with economic priorities and the evolving needs of the workforce. The benefits to a merit-based system include:

- Aligning with Economic Demands: By tailoring immigration policies to prioritize individuals with skills and qualifications in high demand, the United States can address specific gaps in the labor market, ensuring that incoming immigrants contribute meaningfully to the nation's economic growth.
- Streamlining Administrative Processes: The focus on objective criteria such as education, work experience, and language proficiency can simplify the evaluation of visa applications, making the system more transparent and efficient. This streamlining would contribute to quicker processing times and reduced bureaucratic complexity.
- Fostering Economic Growth: By attracting highly skilled and qualified individuals, the United States can enhance its competitive edge in global markets, stimulate innovation, and drive technological advancements. This influx of talent can contribute to the overall prosperity of the nation.
- Adapting to Labor Market Needs: Policymakers can adjust the criteria based on evolving economic demands, ensuring that the immigration system remains adaptive and responsive to changing industries and emerging sectors. This adaptability enhances the overall resilience of the workforce.
- Addressing Skill Gaps: The merit-based approach allows for a targeted and strategic selection of immigrants with expertise in areas where there is a shortage of qualified professionals. This can contribute to the development of a highly skilled and specialized workforce.

While a merit-based visa system emphasizes skills and qualifications, it's essential to acknowledge the potential social and cultural impacts of such policies on U.S. immigration patterns. As we learned in Chapter One, history has shown us the consequences of overlooking these factors. In the past, exclusionary immigration policies that prioritized certain skill sets or ethnic backgrounds without considering broader social and cultural implications led to societal division, discrimination, and missed opportunities for growth.

By failing to account for the importance of diversity and inclusivity, these policies perpetuated inequality and hindered the development of a truly multicultural society. Therefore, finding a balance between attracting talent and promoting diversity is not only ethically imperative, but also essential to a cohesive and thriving community. Policies that prioritize both skilled immigration and family reunification can help ensure that the United States continues to benefit from a well-rounded and culturally diverse society.

Addressing Undocumented Immigrants

An effective approach to immigration reform simply cannot ignore the presence of undocumented immigrants. Implementing pathways to legal status for certain undocumented individuals, particularly those with longstanding ties to their communities and a clean record, must be explored. Here are a few potential solutions.

Earned Legalization Programs

Establishing earned legalization programs allows undocumented immigrants to earn legal status through specific criteria, such as length of residency, continuous employment, community involvement, military service, and educational attainment. This approach considers the contributions and ties individuals have developed over time, providing a path to legal status for those with clean records and a commitment to being productive members of society.

Let's consider length of residency, for example.

Meet Maria. She has been living in the United States for the past eight years. She came to the country as a teenager with her family. Despite her undocumented status, she has built a life here, attending school, working, and participating in community events. Under the earned legalization program, Maria would be eligible to apply for legal status due to her substantial residency.

Continuous employment is another useful criterion.

Meet Victor. He's been working as a landscaper for the past seven years. He pays taxes using an Individual Taxpayer Identification Number (ITIN) and has never been involved in any criminal activity. Despite his undocumented status, Victor has consistently held a job and contributed to his community. Through an earned legalization program, Victor could demonstrate his eligibility for legal status based on his continuous employment history.

Community Service Programs

Community service also provides an innovative pathway to citizenship, recognizing the positive impact that individuals have on their communities. Programs could incentivize citizenship through documented community contributions, such as volunteer work, participation in local initiatives, and engagement in community-building activities.

Meet Ana. She regularly volunteers at her local food bank and helps organize community clean-up events. Despite her undocumented status, Ana is deeply involved in her community and is well-respected by her neighbors. An earned legalization program could recognize Ana's contributions and provide her with a pathway to legal status based on her active involvement in community initiatives.

Emphasizing community service as a pathway to citizenship can be complemented by civic education and integration initiatives. These programs could provide resources and support to help undocumented immigrants understand civic processes, cultural nuances, and the responsibilities associated with being a contributing member of American society. Furthermore, integration strategies can be tailored to the specific needs and dynamics of individual communities, fostering a sense of belonging and shared responsibility. This approach not only ensures a smoother transition, but also creates a sense of belonging and shared values.

Community Sponsorship Programs

Community sponsorship programs require local communities to take an active role in supporting undocumented individuals' journey to legal status. Community members, organizations, or religious institutions can sponsor and vouch for individuals with clean records, emphasizing their positive contributions to the community. This approach builds on the concept of community integration and support. Following are a few examples of how a community sponsorship program could function.

- Local Community Organizations: Non-profits, immigrant advocacy groups, and civic clubs could spearhead community sponsorship efforts. These organizations would work closely with undocumented individuals seeking legal status and with community members willing to sponsor them.
- Individual Sponsorship: Individuals within the community can sponsor undocumented individuals by vouching for their character, employment history, and community involvement. Sponsors could be neighbors, colleagues, teachers, or anyone familiar with the individual's circumstances and contributions.
- Religious Institutions: Churches, mosques, synagogues, and other religious institutions can play a significant role in community sponsorship programs by leveraging their networks and resources to support undocumented individuals.

An effective community sponsorship program would also implement mechanisms for monitoring sponsored individuals' progress and evaluating the program's effectiveness, ensuring accountability and identifying areas for improvement. For example, a community's sponsorship advisory board, comprised of representatives from sponsoring organizations and community members, could meet regularly to review sponsored individuals' progress and address any challenges they may encounter.

Community sponsorship programs empower local communities to take an active role in supporting undocumented individuals' journey to legal status, creating a sense of belonging, solidarity, and mutual support within the community. Fortunately, most communities have enough concerned citizens and organizations to operate a community sponsorship program effectively and make a real difference. We just need to start the conversation.

Entrepreneurial Visas

Creating visas specifically tailored for undocumented individuals with entrepreneurial aspirations can unlock economic potential and contribute to job creation. These visas could be designed to support individuals who want to start or invest in businesses, provided they meet certain criteria and have a clean record. This approach aligns with economic interests and encourages entrepreneurship.

How would it work?

Undocumented individuals interested in starting or investing in businesses would submit detailed proposals outlining their business ideas, market research, financial projections, and potential impact on the local economy. Those who have previously launched successful businesses or demonstrated entrepreneurial acumen in other ventures would likely be prioritized for visa approval.

Although investment potential should not be the primary consideration, individuals willing to make significant investments in businesses or startups that have the potential to create jobs and stimulate economic growth could be given priority consideration for visa approval.

Yoel, an undocumented immigrant with savings accumulated from years of working in construction, is interested in investing in a tech startup specializing in renewable energy solutions. His investment would not only provide critical funding for the startup's growth, but also create job opportunities in the emerging green energy sector. When applying for an entrepreneurial visa, Yoel presents documentation of his investment capital and the potential economic benefits of his investment.

Furthermore, visa candidates with unique and innovative business concepts that have the potential to transform industries or solve pressing societal challenges could be deemed eligible for visa approval.

Gloria, an undocumented immigrant with a background in software engineering, develops a groundbreaking mobile app designed to connect local farmers directly with consumers, eliminating the need for intermediaries and ensuring fair prices for both producers and consumers. Her innovative business idea has the potential to revolutionize the agricultural industry and empower small-scale farmers. Gloria applies for an entrepreneurial visa, showcasing her app prototype and outlining its potential impact on the agricultural sector.

Educational Pathways

Expanding educational pathways would allow undocumented individuals with clean records to pursue higher education without fear of legal consequences. By implementing policies that grant access to in-state tuition, scholarships, and financial aid for undocumented students, we can create opportunities for personal and professional growth.

This approach is also in perfect alignment with U.S. economic interests. Expanded educational pathways would attract and retain individuals who can contribute to the nation's growth and prosperity through innovation, productivity, and the creation of new jobs. Here's how it could work:

- Access to In-State Tuition and Financial Aid: One key aspect of expanded educational pathways is granting undocumented immigrants access to in-state tuition rates and financial aid for higher education. This ensures that they can afford to attend colleges and universities without facing exorbitant out-of-state tuition fees and financial barriers.
- Conditional Legal Status: Providing undocumented immigrants with conditional legal status while they pursue higher education would allow them to remain in the country lawfully and work legally. Of course, they would need to meet certain criteria, such as maintaining enrollment in an accredited educational institution and making satisfactory academic progress.
- Merit-Based Pathways to Permanent Residency: Educational achievements, such as completing a degree program or acquiring specific skills through vocational training, could serve as pathways to permanent residency. Undocumented immigrants who graduate from accredited institutions or obtain certifications in high-demand fields could be eligible to apply for adjustment of status to become lawful permanent residents (green card holders).
- Legal Assistance and Support Services: Expanding educational pathways to legal status would also involve providing undocumented immigrants with access to legal assistance and support services to navigate the complex immigration system. This includes assistance with applying for legal status, understanding eligibility requirements, and obtaining necessary documentation.
- Public Awareness and Advocacy: Raising public awareness about the benefits of expanding educational pathways to legal status for undocumented immigrants is critical. Advocacy efforts would help garner support for policy changes and initiatives aimed at providing undocumented individuals with opportunities to pursue higher education and contribute to society.

Improving Temporary Work Programs

Temporary work programs have long been an integral part of the U.S. economy, filling labor gaps and providing opportunities to skilled and unskilled foreign workers alike. Expanding these programs would have far-reaching benefits. Temporary work programs recognize the significant economic contributions foreign workers can make while maintaining ties to their home countries, while also creating a system that aligns with the evolving needs of the U.S. economy. But while existing programs provide some serious benefits, they are not without problems.

Take the H-2A visa program for agricultural workers, for example. This program allows employers in the agricultural sector to hire foreign workers on a temporary basis to fill seasonal or temporary agricultural jobs that domestic workers are unable or unwilling to perform. The H-2A program benefits both employers and foreign workers by addressing labor shortages in the agricultural industry, while providing foreign workers with employment opportunities and the ability to support their families. However, the program is widely criticized for its complex regulatory requirements, lengthy processing times, and potential for exploitation of foreign workers by unscrupulous employers.

Another example is the H-1B visa program for skilled workers in specialty occupations, which allows U.S. employers to hire foreign workers in occupations such as technology, engineering, and healthcare when there is a shortage of qualified domestic workers. The H-1B program has been praised for its role in filling critical skill gaps in the U.S. labor market and driving innovation and economic growth. However, it has also faced criticism for displacing American workers, depressing wages in certain industries, and enabling the outsourcing of jobs to foreign countries.

The H-2A and H-1B are two highly beneficial and necessary temporary work programs, but the need for revision and expansion of these programs and others like them is urgent. To realize comprehensive reform, we must begin by:

- Assessing Program Effectiveness: An improved temporary work system demands a thorough review of existing programs. By assessing their effectiveness, identifying shortcomings, and gauging their alignment with current economic demands, policymakers can lay the groundwork for meaningful improvements that benefit both foreign workers and the U.S. economy.

- Expanding Visa Categories: In response to changing economic needs, there is merit in exploring the expansion of visa categories within temporary work programs. This expansion could cater to diverse industries and skill sets, providing a more flexible and adaptable system that meets the demands of sectors ranging from agriculture and hospitality to technology and healthcare.
- Addressing Seasonal Labor Needs: For industries that experience seasonal fluctuations in demand for labor, innovative temporary work programs can be designed to accommodate these cycles. This approach ensures that foreign workers can contribute during peak periods while also maintaining ties to their home countries during off seasons, promoting stability and sustained economic participation.
- Implementing Rotational Work Schedules: To enhance the balance between economic contribution and familial ties, policymakers should consider rotational work schedules. This approach would allow foreign workers to engage in temporary employment for defined periods, followed by a return to their home countries. Such schedules create a cyclical pattern that aligns with the needs of U.S. industries while respecting the importance of maintaining cultural connections.
- Strengthening Labor Standards for Foreign Workers: An overhaul of temporary work programs should prioritize the strengthening of labor standards and protections for foreign workers. This includes fair wages, safe working conditions, and avenues for addressing grievances. By ensuring that workers are treated ethically and justly, policymakers can create a system that fosters trust and cooperation.
- Strengthening Labor Standards for American Workers: We must also strengthen labor standards and protections for American workers. Policymakers can achieve this by implementing robust labor market testing requirements, which require employers to demonstrate that there are no qualified domestic workers available to fill job vacancies before hiring temporary foreign workers. Furthermore, strict enforcement mechanisms should be in place to hold employers accountable for labor violations and ensure compliance with labor standards.

- Providing Access to Social Services: Enhancing the well-being of foreign workers involves providing access to social services during their temporary stay. This can include healthcare, educational opportunities for accompanying family members, and community support programs. Such initiatives contribute to the overall welfare of temporary workers and their families.
- Preventing an Undue Financial Burden on American Taxpayers: To minimize taxes associated with providing access to social services, one idea is to require employers participating in temporary work programs to contribute to a dedicated fund that covers the cost of social services for their foreign workers. This fund could be financed through modest fees or assessments on employers based on the number of temporary workers they employ. Additionally, partnerships with community-based organizations, healthcare providers, and educational institutions could leverage existing resources and infrastructure to provide cost-effective social services tailored to the needs of temporary immigrant workers and their families.

Of course, this level of assessment and revision requires the collaborative efforts of multiple stakeholders, including government agencies, policymakers, industry representatives, and advocacy groups. To complicate the situation further, policymakers already face numerous competing priorities. Despite this massive challenge, the reform of temporary work programs is essential, as legalizing and standardizing these practices holds benefits for all parties involved. This is why advocacy groups, immigration lawyers, and others with expertise in relevant areas must be invited to the table.

Advocacy groups pull a lot of weight in Washington. With a clear roadmap of effective immigration reform at their disposal, advocacy groups can and will play a major role in assessing and enacting the reform of temporary work programs. Some examples of established advocacy groups with influence in this particular area of need include:

- National Immigration Law Center (NILC): The NILC is a prominent advocacy organization focused on advancing and defending the rights of low-income immigrants in the United States. They have extensive expertise in immigration policy and could contribute valuable insights into the impact of temporary work programs on immigrant workers and their families. The NILC could advocate for reforms that prioritize the rights and well-being of temporary workers, including measures to prevent exploitation and abuse.

- National Guestworker Alliance (NGA): The NGA is a worker-led organization that advocates for the rights of guest workers and fights against labor trafficking and exploitation in temporary work programs. They have firsthand experience working with temporary workers and could provide valuable perspectives on the shortcomings of existing programs. The NGA could advocate for reforms that strengthen protections for guest workers, enhance enforcement mechanisms, and hold employers accountable for labor abuses.
- American Immigration Lawyers Association (AILA): AILA is a professional association of immigration lawyers and advocates who specialize in immigration law and policy. They have a deep understanding of the legal complexities surrounding temporary work programs and could offer expert analysis and recommendations for reform. AILA could advocate for reforms that streamline administrative processes, improve access to legal representation for temporary workers, and ensure compliance with labor and immigration laws.
- United Farm Workers (UFW): The UFW is a labor union representing farmworkers in the United States. They have been at the forefront of advocating for the rights of agricultural workers, many of whom are employed under temporary work programs such as the H-2A visa program. The UFW could advocate for reforms that provide farmworkers with greater job security, fair wages, and improved working conditions, as well as pathways to permanent residency for agricultural workers.
- National Council of Agricultural Employers (NCAE): The NCAE is a trade association representing agricultural employers and agribusinesses in the United States. They have a vested interest in ensuring the availability of a reliable workforce through temporary work programs. The NCAE could advocate for reforms that address labor shortages in the agricultural sector, streamline the recruitment process for guest workers, and provide employers with greater flexibility in hiring foreign workers.

These advocacy groups, along with others with expertise in immigration policy, labor rights, and workforce development, must collaborate to assess the effectiveness of temporary work programs and advocate for meaningful reforms that benefit both workers and employers.

When it comes to the need for policy changes in immigration law, I have to say, immigration lawyers are the most passionate, knowledgeable, and effective advocates out there. Unfortunately, most of us are taught to simply "do your job," which typically translates to "use precedent, without question, to address the needs of the client in front of you."

As lawyers, most of us massively underestimate our individual and collective power to make change. We are on the front lines of problems within the immigration system. We should all be playing a major role in assessing immigration programs and policies and enacting change. One of the most important lessons I teach my law students at the Benjamin N. Cardozo School of Law in New York is simple: You do not need to take "no" for an answer.

In Chapter Five of this book, "Empowering Advocates and Future Lawyers," I make it abundantly clear that the solution to just about every problem within the U.S. immigration system is in the hands of immigration lawyers. We are an army of thousands strong, and we have the power and responsibility to advocate for, influence, and implement meaningful change.

Strengthening Humanitarian Protections and Refugee Policies

One of the most important and challenging questions of the modern immigration debate is: How can the United States strengthen its commitment to providing refuge for those fleeing conflict and persecution, while ensuring that those who enter our borders are properly vetted? When envisioning a more effective and compassionate approach, we must also explore the potential implications for global migration patterns, balancing the moral imperative of offering sanctuary to those in dire need with the safety and well-being of our nation.

Implementing policies to provide refuge for those in need requires a careful approach that addresses humanitarian concerns while prioritizing national security. To achieve this delicate equilibrium, comprehensive background checks and thorough vetting processes must remain part of the admission procedures for refugees.

Through advanced screening technologies, intelligence sharing with international partners, and collaboration with relevant security agencies, we can bolster the effectiveness of security measures. Prioritizing cooperation between federal, state, and local authorities is essential. To strengthen and streamline humanitarian policies and increase national security, we must begin by:

- Strengthening Humanitarian Relief Programs: Humanitarian relief programs address the unique circumstances of certain undocumented individuals, such as those who have been victims of crime or exploitation. Providing more avenues for individuals to apply for legal status based on humanitarian grounds ensures a compassionate response to vulnerable situations.
- Increasing Refugee Quotas: An integral step in strengthening humanitarian protections is the significant increase of refugee admission quotas. By expanding the number of refugees admitted annually, the United States will play a leading role in addressing the global refugee crisis and providing a safe haven for individuals escaping persecution, violence, and untenable living conditions.
- Implementing Expedited Processing for Vulnerable Populations: To address urgent humanitarian needs, policymakers must explore expedited processing for vulnerable populations, including victims of violence, religious minorities, and LGBTQ+ individuals facing persecution. Streamlining procedures ensures that those in imminent danger receive timely protection, reflecting a commitment to human rights and compassion.
- Adopting a More Inclusive Definition of Persecution: This type of forward-looking approach acknowledges the evolving nature of threats worldwide, encompassing new forms of violence, environmental challenges, and systemic discrimination. Broadening eligibility criteria ensures that individuals facing a spectrum of hardships can find refuge in the United States.
- Extending Protections to Climate Refugees: Recognizing the growing impact of climate change, humanitarian protections should extend to those displaced by environmental factors. This includes individuals forced to flee due to rising sea levels, extreme weather events, or environmental degradation.
- Strengthening International Partnerships: An effective strategy for addressing global migration patterns involves strengthening international partnerships. By collaborating with other nations, the United States can create a coordinated response to refugee crises,

share the responsibility of providing refuge, and work toward sustainable solutions that address the root causes of displacement.

- Engaging in Diplomatic Solutions for Conflict Resolution: Addressing the root causes of refugee flows requires a commitment to diplomatic solutions for conflict resolution. The United States can help prevent the displacement of populations and create conditions conducive to the safe return of refugees to their home countries by actively engaging in international efforts to promote peace and stability.
- Implementing Robust Vetting Processes: Prioritizing national security requires the implementation of rigorous vetting processes to screen individuals seeking humanitarian protections or refugee status. Enhanced background checks, intelligence sharing, and risk assessments mitigate potential security risks while upholding humanitarian principles.
- Fostering Integration and Community Engagement: Strengthening national security involves fostering integration efforts and community engagement initiatives for resettled refugees and asylum seekers. Through the promotion of social cohesion and facilitating access to support services, the United States mitigates potential security concerns and promotes inclusive societies.

Strengthening humanitarian protections contributes to the creation of safe avenues for migration. It reduces the reliance on perilous journeys and irregular migration routes, and emphasizes the importance of structured and humane migration pathways that prioritize safety and dignity.

The United States has the opportunity to shape a model for global compassion by leading with empathy and responsibility. A commitment to effective humanitarian protections sets an example for other nations and reflects the United States' dedication to global justice. Our great nation must stand as a leader in a world where the right to seek refuge is recognized and protected for all individuals fleeing persecution and conflict.

Strengthening Bonds by Improving Family Reunification Policies

Many undocumented immigrants find themselves in multigenerational situations, where family ties span several generations. When we prioritize family unity, we create a more peaceful society. There are countless benefits to improving family reunification policies. Some of the most compelling include:

- Strengthening Social Fabric: By placing a greater emphasis on keeping families together, we create a sense of stability and community. This approach recognizes the integral role of family in shaping individuals' experiences, leading to a more interconnected and supportive society.
- Economic Contributions of Family-Based Immigrants: Family-based immigrants, often motivated by the desire to contribute to their communities and provide a better life for their loved ones, tend to actively engage in the workforce and entrepreneurial ventures. This influx of motivated individuals contributes to local economies and overall national prosperity.
- Promoting Cultural Diversity: As families reunite across borders, they bring with them diverse traditions, languages, and perspectives. This infusion of cultural richness enhances American society, creating an environment where different backgrounds are celebrated and contribute to our collective identity.
- Addressing Mental and Emotional Well-Being: Separation from family members contributes to stress and anxiety, impacting individuals' ability to integrate into their new communities. Improving family reunification policies supports the mental health of immigrants, facilitating a smoother transition and a sense of belonging. It also helps create safe, peaceful communities.
- Strengthening Community Support Networks: When families are united, they form a foundational support system that extends into the broader community. This network becomes a resource for newcomers, providing guidance, assistance, and a sense of belonging as they navigate the challenges of adapting to a new environment.

So the real question is, how can we strengthen immigration policies to prioritize family reunification while simultaneously protecting national security? Here are some possible answers:

- Streamlining Visa Processes: Simplifying and expediting the visa application and approval process for family members would reduce lengthy separation periods and facilitate timely reunification.

- Expanding Visa Categories: Broadening the scope of eligible family members and expanding visa categories to include extended relatives ensures that families are not arbitrarily separated based on narrow definitions of familial relationships.
- Increasing Quota Numbers: Adjusting immigration quota numbers to better reflect the demand for family-based visas prevents excessive wait times and ensures that families can reunite in a timely manner.
- Improving Access to Legal Assistance: Providing immigrants with greater access to affordable or pro bono legal assistance would help them navigate immigration laws and procedures, facilitating successful reunification efforts.
- Strengthening Protections for Vulnerable Populations: Implementing safeguards and special considerations for vulnerable populations, such as unaccompanied minors, elderly relatives, and individuals fleeing persecution, ensures that they are not unfairly excluded from the family reunification process.
- Enhancing Integration Services: Investing in integration services, including language classes, cultural orientation programs, and job training initiatives, supports immigrants in successfully integrating into their new communities.
- Promoting Family Unity as a Policy Priority: Advocating for family unity as a fundamental principle of immigration policy at the legislative and administrative levels would ensure that decision-making processes prioritize the preservation and strengthening of family bonds.
- Enhancing Background Checks and Screening Procedures: Implementing rigorous background checks and screening procedures for family-based immigrants ensures that individuals with potential security risks are identified and properly vetted before admission into the country.

Although the U.S. government holds much of the power when it comes to immigration policy, local communities—including immigrants themselves—are far from powerless. By harnessing the collective knowledge, skills, and resources within immigrant communities, immigrants can take an active role in facilitating their family's reunification. Doing so reduces the strain on government resources, which has the potential to lead to policy changes in favor of family reunification. A few examples of how immigrants can lend a hand in the reunification of their family and other families include:

- Community Sponsorship Programs: Community-based sponsorship programs allow established immigrant volunteers to assist newly arrived family members with the immigration process. These volunteers can provide guidance, support, and practical assistance, reducing the burden on government agencies and resources.
- Virtual Support Networks: Virtual support networks and online communities allow immigrants to connect with each other and share resources, advice, and experiences related to the immigration process. This digital support system can help streamline information sharing and provide emotional support during the often complex and stressful process of reunification.
- Language and Cultural Support Services: Language and cultural support services within immigrant communities help newly arrived family members acclimate to their new environment. Immigrants who are fluent in both English and their native language can serve as interpreters and cultural liaisons, facilitating communication and integration for their family members.
- Legal Assistance Clinics: Legal assistance clinics within immigrant communities, staffed by volunteer lawyers and paralegals, allow for the provision of pro bono or low-cost legal advice and assistance with immigration paperwork. These clinics can help ensure that families have access to reliable legal guidance throughout the reunification process.
- Financial Planning Workshops: Financial planning workshops or seminars within immigrant communities help families prepare for the financial aspects of immigration, such as application fees, travel expenses, and resettlement costs. Immigrants with experience navigating the U.S. financial system can share their knowledge to empower others in their community.
- Peer-to-Peer Mentoring Programs: Peer-to-peer mentoring programs allow established immigrants to mentor newly arrived family members on various aspects of life in the United States, including

education, employment, housing, and healthcare. These mentorship programs can provide personalized guidance and support tailored to the specific needs and challenges faced by immigrant families.

- Document Translation Services: Document translation services within immigrant communities can assist family members with translating important documents, such as birth certificates, marriage certificates, and educational transcripts, for immigration purposes. This can help ensure that paperwork is accurately completed and submitted, reducing the likelihood of delays or complications in the reunification process.

Scenarios for DACA and the Potential Legal Status of Dreamers

This section explores various scenarios related to the Deferred Action for Childhood Arrivals (DACA) program, considering the potential continuation, expansion, or modification of this critical initiative. As we examine these scenarios, we explore how reopening and expanding DACA offers benefits not only to recipients, often referred to as Dreamers, but also to the American public as a whole.

A scenario involving the reopening of a pathway to permanent residency and citizenship for DACA recipients offers the best solution. Providing a route for Dreamers to obtain legal permanent residency and eventually citizenship recognizes their long-standing contributions and commitment to the United States. Doing so also provides immense economic and cultural benefits.

Unfortunately, new DACA applications still remain in limbo. Although DACA renewals and Advance Parole applications continue to be accepted and processed, the current ruling signals the potential end of a program that has been a lifeline for hundreds of thousands of young immigrants and their families.

Judge Hanen's ruling is not final. If the current appeal is also denied, the case will likely proceed to the Supreme Court. But given the Supreme Court's current makeup and past immigration rulings, there's a very good possibility that the justices will rule against DACA. This would be a massive loss for these young immigrants, but also for our nation as a whole. If DACA is permanently discontinued, the 600,000 current recipients may lose their ability to work legally and could even face deportation. If DACA renewals end, about 1,000 recipients weekly will lose their job over the next two years.

A permanent end to the DACA program would not only harm the individual recipients and their families, but also have far-reaching consequences for the economy, labor market, social fabric, and overall vitality of the United States.

The economic impact would be immediate and tangible. DACA recipients contribute significantly to the U.S. economy. They are employed across diverse sectors, paying taxes, and contributing widely to consumer spending. Without the ability to work legally, they would lose their jobs, leading to a loss of productivity and tax revenue. This would undoubtedly have ripple effects throughout the entire economy, negatively impacting businesses, industries, and local communities.

The loss of DACA would also disrupt the labor market. Recipients fill essential roles in industries such as healthcare, education, technology, and agriculture. A sudden loss of these workers would inevitably result in labor shortages in key sectors, impacting the delivery of services and overall productivity.

Furthermore, DACA recipients come from diverse backgrounds and bring unique perspectives to American society. Many are pursuing higher education or are engaged in entrepreneurial ventures, contributing to innovation and cultural enrichment. Losing this diverse talent pool would hinder America's ability to remain competitive and innovative on the global stage, during the most intense period of global STEM competition we have ever experienced.

Continuing DACA and expanding the program's eligibility criteria would bring additional eligible individuals into the program, broadening its positive impact on immigrant families and the U.S. economy and innovation. Such an expansion could include those who arrived after the initial DACA cutoff, for example. By embracing a more inclusive approach, the program could encompass a wider range of deserving individuals, allowing them to contribute to American society openly and without fear.

By continuing DACA, establishing a pathway to permanent residency, and broadening eligibility criteria, we can realize the following benefits:

- Stability for Dreamers: The continuation of DACA would provide recipients with stability and protection from deportation.

Individuals who arrived in the United States as children could continue to pursue education, work, and contribute to their communities without the constant fear of removal. This stability is essential for fostering a sense of belonging and allowing Dreamers to fully integrate into American society.

- Economic Contributions: DACA recipients have become integral contributors to the U.S. economy, and the continuation of the program ensures that their economic contributions persist. These individuals actively participate in the workforce, pay taxes, and contribute to the nation's economic growth. The continuation of DACA safeguards these valuable contributors, supporting industries that rely on diverse, skilled, and motivated workers.
- Educational Opportunities: By removing barriers to education, DACA recipients can pursue their academic aspirations, further enhancing their skills and qualifications. This, in turn, benefits the nation by tapping into a pool of talented individuals who can contribute to various fields, from science and technology to arts and humanities.
- U.S. Innovation on the Global Stage: DACA recipients represent a diverse and talented pool of individuals who bring fresh perspectives, innovative ideas, and entrepreneurial spirit to the United States. By providing them with stability, educational opportunities, and pathways to permanent residency, we empower them to fully harness their potential and contribute to U.S. innovation and competitiveness on the global stage. Their contributions not only enrich American society, but also position the United States as a leader in innovation, creativity, and forward-thinking solutions to global challenges.
- Cultural Connections: DACA recipients exist in a unique set of shared circumstances. As the first generation of their families to grow up in America, they experience a cross-section of new and traditional cultures in a way that can't be taught or imitated. Their unique perspectives can help bridge cultural gaps, leading to more informed and insightful communities. Removing or marginalizing them from our national dialogue disregards this tremendous resource for societal progress.

My father's work on John Lennon's deportation case in the 1970s played a significant role in the creation of the DACA program, more than four decades later. The U.S. government sought to deport Lennon due to a prior cannabis possession conviction, but my father successfully argued that the deportation was politically motivated, leading to a legal battle that spanned several years. Ultimately, the case resulted in Lennon obtaining a green card, granting him permanent residency in the United States.

This decision set a significant legal precedent. The arguments and strategies employed highlighted the discretionary authority of immigration officials to grant relief from deportation on humanitarian grounds. This concept of Prosecutorial Discretion, which was pivotal in Lennon's case, laid the groundwork for future immigration policies, including DACA. The program relies on similar principles of Prosecutorial Discretion to grant relief to eligible individuals, allowing them to remain in the country and pursue educational and employment opportunities.

More than 50 years ago, my father knew the value of advocating for immigrants facing deportation on humanitarian grounds. Whether the immigrant in question is John Lennon, a STEM professional of extraordinary ability, or an aspiring artist from Central America, the principles of fairness and compassion in immigration law remain consistent. By successfully arguing for Lennon's right to remain in the United States, my father's work established a precedent that highlighted the importance of discretion in immigration enforcement. Through his dedication to his clients and commitment to justice, my father contributed to shaping the landscape of immigration policy for generations to come.

The Urgent Need to Bolster U.S. STEM Talent

At this point in the book, I hope you've realized at least some of the many rich benefits that immigrants bring to this country. While the economic, cultural, and professional benefits of immigration have been around forever, today's technological era is ushering in a new—and increasingly urgent—benefit: critical emerging technologies.

Competition for skilled workers in science, technology, engineering, and mathematics (STEM) fields has rapidly intensified, driving technological advancement and playing critical roles in geopolitical competition, healthcare, manufacturing, the U.S. economy, national security, and democracy.

While the United States maintains its status as the world's largest Research and Development (R&D) economy, allocating 3.5 percent of its GDP to R&D, its performance in K–12 STEM education has been lagging behind peer nations for years. Insufficient production of STEM workers poses economic and national security concerns, exacerbated by the challenges of the COVID-19 pandemic. National assessments reveal a significant decline in mathematics proficiency at both elementary and secondary levels, with average scores between 2019 and 2022 plummeting to levels last seen two decades ago.

For decades, the United States has relied on foreign talent to fill STEM positions, but the imperative now is not only to sustain this recruitment, but to enhance efforts to attract more STEM professionals globally and facilitate their entry into the country. Failure to do so risks losing top talent to competing nations.

The nation that leads in R&D will shape the future. While investing in domestic K–12 STEM education is crucial for long-term success and security, the benefits of such investments will take years to materialize. With time being of the essence, the United States cannot afford to overlook immediate solutions. Safeguarding its position as the global R&D leader necessitates an immediate focus on expanding the foreign talent pool to bolster innovation and competitiveness.

The United States must attract more highly skilled foreign talent or risk lagging behind. Our government has utilized programs like O-1A, H-1B, and employment-based visas to attract professionals, but the immigration system remains sluggish. Visa backlogs and delays continue to frustrate employers and deter talent.

Losing STEM talent to other nations poses significant risks. Countries like Canada, Australia, and parts of Europe offer streamlined immigration pathways and incentives, making them appealing alternatives for skilled professionals seeking inclusive STEM ecosystems. Though these nations aren't a direct threat in the technology game, losing talent to them dilutes the U.S. talent pool at a critical point in time.

Despite its global STEM leadership, the United States faces significant competition, particularly from China. China's growth, propelled by substantial investments in research, development, infrastructure, and education, poses a significant threat to U.S. supremacy.

While the United States has traditionally led in STEM innovation, China is narrowing the gap by harnessing its expanding pool of STEM talent and state-backed initiatives. This competition extends beyond technological capabilities to encompass geopolitical influence, economic dominance, and leadership in critical sectors.

Currently, the United States maintains its status as the largest spender on R&D, allocating $806 billion in 2021 alone. However, China closely follows as the second-largest spender, investing $668 billion in R&D during the same period.

Critical and Emerging Technologies (CETs)

In 2023, the Biden administration issued the Executive Order on the Safe, Secure, and Trustworthy Development and Use of Artificial Intelligence.[4] The goal of this order, and the subsequent establishment of the Office of Critical and Emerging Technology in December 2023, is to accelerate U.S. progress in critical and emerging technologies (CETs) like AI, biotechnology, and quantum computing.

There is no denying that U.S. leadership in STEM innovation is integral to our social and economic benefits and national security. To maintain this leadership, the executive order directs the Secretary of Homeland Security to modernize and streamline visa criteria, interviews, and reviews for highly skilled immigrants and nonimmigrants in critical areas such as AI and other CETs. The list of CETs is extensive, including everything from biotechnologies and cybersecurity to clean energy, quantum information, semiconductors, and space technologies.

While the executive order does not specifically introduce new pathways for foreign STEM professionals, it strongly emphasizes making the existing pathways easier for qualified individuals. Changes made to the National Interest Waiver (NIW) program are one such example.

Since its inception by Congress in 1990, the NIW, which allows foreign nationals to apply for an EB-2 visa without labor certification, has seen

4. Exec. Order No. 14110, *Executive Order on the Safe, Secure, and Trustworthy Development and Use of Artificial Intelligence*, Am. Presidency Project (Oct. 30, 2023), https://www.presidency.ucsb.edu/documents/executive-order-14110-safe-secure-and-trustworthy-development-and-use-artificial.

minimal changes. The NIW has traditionally been one of the more challenging immigration routes, limited to foreign nationals with exceptional abilities who can prove their presence benefits the nation. Defining "national interest" is subjective and constantly evolving, making eligibility stringent.

However, in response to concerning trends in domestic STEM talent, particularly exacerbated by the pandemic, the NIW program has undergone recent policy changes. These changes aim to prevent the United States from falling behind global competition, resulting in a significant expansion of what constitutes "national interest" and making it easier to qualify for an NIW.

In 2022, the NIW program expanded its scope to include STEM and entrepreneur applicants, alongside enhanced premium processing for EB-2 NIW petitions. The executive order emphasizes the urgency of the situation, driving home the need to leverage AI for the benefit of small businesses, workers, and entrepreneurs.

These changes represent significant progress in the U.S. immigration system, demonstrating a proactive response to evolving needs and challenges. While it's tempting to succumb to a sense of despair and perceive stagnation, the reality is far from it. But there's still much work to be done.

We must expedite progress to ensure that our immigration policies remain responsive to these constantly evolving demands. Failure to do so risks impeding our competitiveness and innovation in an increasingly interconnected world. Thus, it's imperative that we continue to push for comprehensive reforms that prioritize flexibility, inclusivity, and efficiency in our immigration processes. Only then can we truly harness the full potential of foreign talent to drive economic growth, technological advancement, and societal progress in the United States.

Consequences of Legislative Gridlock on Immigration Policies

Let's imagine a world where legislative gridlock persists, preventing significant immigration reform for decades. This shouldn't be hard to do, considering that it's not too different from the road we've been heading down for many years. Change needs to come, and it needs to come soon. If we're successful, this dark period in recent immigration history may appear as nothing more than a hiccup during an otherwise relatively direct path toward progress.

If, however, we allow partisan divisions and political challenges to prevent urgently needed changes, we must consider the implications of a status quo characterized by uncertainty and incremental policy adjustments. That is where the ship is currently being steered, and the consequences are dire. Without comprehensive reform, the United States risks perpetuating a cycle of dysfunction and inefficiency in its immigration system, undermining not only the nation's economic vitality and position as global innovation leader, but also its moral standing on the world stage.

With lawmakers unable to reach consensus on overarching immigration measures, the nation will continue to witness small-scale adjustments to existing policies. These changes will lack the coherence and depth necessary to address the systemic challenges within the immigration system, further exacerbating existing disparities and injustices. As a result, millions of undocumented immigrants will remain trapped in legal limbo, unable to fully contribute to society or achieve their full potential, and countless more will never see American soil.

Such prolonged uncertainty will further contribute to social tensions, economic inefficiencies, and challenges in community integration, all of which spell disaster—and danger—for national security. Additionally, businesses will continue to face uncertainty and barriers in accessing the talent they need to thrive, hindering innovation and economic growth.

Immigration policies also have major implications for international relations, especially with neighboring countries. Persistent gridlock will strain bilateral relations as issues such as border security, trade, and cooperation on regional challenges become entangled with the lack of progress on immigration reform. This strain will negatively impact diplomatic ties and collaborative efforts on shared concerns.

Uncertainty surrounding immigration policies will lead to labor market inefficiencies, with industries reliant on immigrant labor facing disruptions. Addressing workforce shortages and aligning labor market needs with available talent will become increasingly challenging. It will also affect innovation and entrepreneurship. We have long benefited from the contributions of immigrant entrepreneurs and skilled professionals. Stalled reforms impede the ability of talented individuals to contribute to economic growth and innovation, diminishing the nation's competitive edge on the global stage.

Furthermore, without clear guidance from comprehensive reform, enforcement practices will continue to vary from jurisdiction to jurisdiction, leading to legal challenges and debates over the constitutionality of certain measures. This inconsistency will further complicate an already challenging situation.

The imperative for collaborative, bipartisan efforts is increasingly evident, yet we continue—on both sides of the debate—to focus on linear thinking, failing to consider the concerns of the other side. Instead, we must recognize the complexity of the issue and embrace an approach that takes into account the diverse perspectives and needs of all stakeholders. This requires prioritizing the common good over partisan interests. It's time to move beyond entrenched positions and toward solutions that reflect the best of our nation's ideals and aspirations.

We must also recognize the need for solutions that balance national security and the well-being of all Americans with the principles of inclusivity and fairness. The end goal should be to create an environment where individuals can pursue citizenship through a transparent, accessible, and merit-based process, enriching the country as a whole.

The Role of Compassion in National Security

The risk of falling behind China in scientific and technological progress hinges on more than recruiting STEM talent alone. There exists a darker side to this competition, an ideological battle for the hearts and minds of individuals worldwide. Throughout this book, I have advocated for more compassionate and inclusive immigration policies for multiple reasons, not the least of which is to improve national security. But how do compassionate immigration policies strengthen national security?

When we discuss our immigration system, what we are really discussing is human lives. When we speak in terms of laws and policies and reform, it is easy to lose sight of the individuals, children, and families whose lives are on the line.

The concern over terrorism is valid, but as we've seen time and time again in the world, those who seek violence or to gain revenge over a person or group of people have almost always been victims of violence, abuse, humiliation, and extreme suffering themselves. An act of terrorism, at its core, is a means of reclaiming power. While those at the top, those orchestrating these horrific acts from the safety and comfort of their homes and offices, may have varying motivations, those acting out the orders have been victimized by their makers, and part of that victimization involves instilling in those actors a hatred for those they are acting against.

By creating an inclusive and welcoming environment that is tolerant of people from all different origins, religions, and races, we severely limit the ability of those few privileged, wealthy, powerful bastions of extremism at the top to influence and coerce their people to commit acts of terror. With compassion, we effectively cut off the head of the monster.

Eric Dai's Story

"The greatest long-term threat to our nation's information and intellectual property, and to our economic vitality, is the counterintelligence and economic espionage threat from China."

—FBI Director Christopher Wray[5]

One of the many ways that an inclusive and welcoming United States protects national security is illustrated in the case of Chinese whistleblower Eric Dai. In 2017, Dai began working with the FBI to expose Chinese Communist Party (CCP) efforts to steal semiconductor technology for military applications, among other things.

Dai, the former CEO of New York City–based Khan Funds, a billion-dollar investment firm, was once dubbed China's Warren Buffett. He played a pivotal role in aiding the FBI's efforts to combat Chinese espionage on U.S. soil, putting his safety on the line to protect this country's national security because he believed the threats made against him were also against the United States and its place in the world order. His story is one of bravery, integrity, and the considerable risks faced by those who challenge powerful entities.

In 2017, a representative of Nations Technologies, a Chinese state-owned technology enterprise, traveled to the United States to solicit Dai's cooperation in a scheme to commit industrial espionage for the benefit of the Chinese military. The man didn't give Dai a choice; it was either cooperate or pay the price. Recognizing the significant threat posed by the CCP to U.S. national security and economic interests, Dai immediately initiated contact with the FBI. His collaboration spanned three years, during which he supplied detailed insights and guidance on various espionage operations, directly supporting the FBI's counterintelligence efforts.

5. Christopher Wray, Director, FBI, The Threat Posed by the Chinese Government and the Chinese Communist Party to the Economic and National Security of the United States, Speech at Hudson Institute (Sept. 27, 2018).

During the investigation, it became clear that the scheme involved more than just Nations Technologies; the company's ties to the Chinese military were evident. The FBI now considered Dai a major asset and wanted to continue to cooperate with him, using the former investment banker as an intelligence source rather than as a witness.

It's likely that the pressure on Eric Dai to engage in industrial espionage was orchestrated by officers from The People's Liberation Army (PLA) Military Intelligence Department, a key player in conducting economic espionage. The PLA, which collects science- and technology-related information to improve China's military capabilities and defense industries, was in urgent need of advanced integrated circuits and microchips to fortify its operations.

From a counterintelligence and security perspective, there is a notable connection between the evolution of China's industrial espionage activities in 2016, the 2017 National Security Law, and the subsequent pressure on Dai in 2017. The requirement for a more advanced intelligence and warfighting operational approach under CCP Chairman Xi Jinping emphasizes the linkage between industrial espionage and the fusion of military and civilian industrial development. This strategic shift helps explain why Chinese intelligence services exerted such significant pressure to secure Dai's cooperation.

Dai's ongoing involvement with the FBI has been a true selfless effort and an unmistakable statement of his opposition to the Chinese Communist Party and his core allegiance to the United States. It should be noted that Dai and his colleagues could have easily cooperated with the CCP rather than the FBI, seeking the riches and notoriety of Chinese nationalism. Instead, each of them made the choice to stay on the side of the United States. To make this dangerous and bold of a move requires an extraordinary allegiance to the United States. It should go without saying that such an allegiance is not born of racist, exclusionary, or xenophobic immigration policies.

For Eric Dai and his circle, their experience in the United States had been a generally positive one. As a result, they were willing to put their lives on the line to protect national security and show their gratitude. This country is undeniably safer because of their actions.

The Case for Asylum for Eric

The fact that Eric Dai has provided substantial assistance to the FBI in its efforts to combat Chinese espionage on U.S. soil automatically makes him a traitor in the eyes of China. He would receive at the very least a long prison sentence if he were to be returned to China. Here, a dissident with considerable financial resources is one of the CCP's most feared type of enemies, and he will be subjected to severe political persecution if left to be judged by the hands of the CCP.

In the interviews Dai has given, he publicly made strong and direct political statements concerning his opposition to China's political system and the CCP regime, his preference for the U.S. system of freedom and democracy, and made clear that the United States is his spiritual home. These statements alone render him a political dissident in China.

Unfortunately, it is the normal practice of the Chinese authorities to criminalize by association and use family members and associates to subdue dissidents and political prisoners. Dai's decision to assist the FBI places him and his family in grave danger, particularly from Operation Fox Hunt, a Chinese government initiative ostensibly aimed at repatriating Chinese nationals accused of crimes. In reality, this program has been used to intimidate and persecute overseas Chinese, employing tactics such as threats, harassment, and even torture of family members. Dai's family in China has faced significant threats, yet another risk he took by aiding U.S. authorities.

When the CCP perceives someone as a threat, the entire state apparatus is mobilized against that individual and their associates, as seen in other cases like Bo Xilai and Zhou Yongkang, two of the most high-profile political purges in modern Chinese history.

Bo Xilai (薄熙来)

Bo Xilai was a high-ranking CCP official, serving as the Party Secretary of Chongqing, and a rising star in Chinese politics. He was known for his charismatic leadership, his "Chongqing Model" of economic and social policies, and his hardline crackdown on organized crime. His downfall began in 2012, when his police chief, Wang Lijun, attempted to seek asylum at a U.S. consulate, revealing damaging information about Bo's wife, Gu Kailai. She was later convicted of murdering British businessman Neil Heywood.

Bo was expelled from the CCP and sentenced to life in prison in 2013 for corruption, bribery, and abuse of power. Many of Bo's allies in Chongqing were investigated, demoted, or imprisoned, demonstrating how the crackdown extended beyond him.

Zhou Yongkang (周永康)

Zhou Yongkang was one of China's most powerful politicians, serving as a Politburo Standing Committee member and the head of China's vast security apparatus (Minister of Public Security). In 2014, he became the highest-ranking CCP official in history to be purged in Xi Jinping's anti-corruption campaign. His downfall was likely linked to his close ties with Bo Xilai and suspicions that he opposed Xi's leadership.

Zhou was convicted of corruption, abuse of power, and leaking state secrets, and was sentenced to life in prison in 2015. More than 300 of his family members, political allies, and business associates were investigated, arrested, or lost their positions—one of the most extensive purges in CCP history.

Both Bo Xilai and Zhou Yongkang were perceived as potential challengers to Xi Jinping's authority. These examples illustrate the extent of punishment inflicted on perceived threats, involving not only the individual, but also their family and close business associates. This pattern of collective punishment highlights the severe risks Dai and his family face due to his cooperation with the U.S. government.

Since Dai first refused to cooperate with the CCP and began working with the FBI, his life and those of his family members and colleagues have been completely upended. In 2022, two masked intruders broke into Dai's sister's house in Huntington, New York, at night. Although they stole nothing but internal surveillance cameras, they covered the house in "joss paper," traditionally used by the Chinese as burned offerings to the deceased. An obvious threat. Today, Dai refuses to swim in his Florida pool because, despite security cameras surrounding the property and the guards he employs, the location of the pool puts him at great risk of being attacked.

Given the immense risks Eric Dai has taken and the valuable support he has provided to the FBI, his case for asylum in the United States is compelling. Granting him asylum aligns with the core values of the United States: justice, integrity, and the protection of human rights. His actions not only aided in safeguarding U.S. national security, but also demonstrated a commitment to the principles of truth and justice, even in the face of significant personal peril.

Eric Dai's story is one of extraordinary courage and commitment. By granting him asylum, the United States would not only repay a debt of gratitude, but also send a powerful message in support of those who risk their lives to uphold justice and protect national security.

Steven L. Pomerantz, Assistant Director, FBI (retired), recently made the following statement about Dai's actions and bravery:

> *Mr. Dai's self-initiated contact with the FBI in 2017 and his desire and dedication in furthering the major investigations launched by the FBI based on his information is really an inspiring and important story. The individuals who solicited and coerced Mr. Dai were self-admitted significant players in the Chinese government's nefarious efforts in the United States. Mr. Dai, in the face of real and substantial threats, knowing the power of the Chinese government*

to harm him and his family, never wavered. He knew full well the power and ability of the Chinese government to destroy his business, cause him financial ruin, imprison him and cause physical harm to him and/or his family members. Nevertheless, he spent years meeting with Agents and Prosecutors providing information, identifying participants in the scheme and aiding with investigative guidance.[6]

Interview with Eric Dai

Conducted by Amy Lane Singh

Despite everything he's endured, Eric spoke to me with the optimistic, almost giddy, tone of a man embarking on a new chapter in life. He was positive and full of hope, pausing occasionally to laugh at the incredible misfortunes he has encountered since arriving in the United States. It struck me that this resilience, this extraordinary positivity in the face of adversity, must be the very quality that enabled him to build a billion-dollar company. It's clear that only with such an outlook—one that sees opportunity even in the most challenging circumstances—can someone manage the treacherous path Eric has walked.

In many ways, Eric Dai has been to hell and back, yet he speaks with the enthusiasm and idealism of a young entrepreneur on the brink of taking over the world. Our conversation was nothing short of inspiring. While I sympathize deeply with Eric's situation, I walked away from our interview with a strong conviction that he will rise above his challenges. His determination and resilience, coupled with the legal support he has, leave no doubt in my mind that he will secure the asylum he and his family so desperately need. And when he does, I am confident that he will rebuild the life he put on the line to become an American hero.

Beginning the American Journey

Eric began our interview by expressing his deep gratitude toward the entire Wildes & Weinberg law firm for handling his case with "the highest level of care and professionalism." Reflecting on his American Dream, Eric shared that his green card was initially approved due to his outstanding ability, which he believed would allow him to build a new life in the United States. Not in a million years did he expect what was to come.

Upon arriving in the United States, Eric encountered significant challenges due to his limited English proficiency and the cultural differences between China and the United States. He recalls an early incident where he was misled by a Chinese-speaking individual working at a law firm, which led to

6. Statement provided to Wildes & Weinberg.

confusion and setbacks in his immigration process. "At that time, my English was no good, and I made many mistakes because of the differences between Chinese and American culture," Eric explains. Despite these hurdles, Eric was happy to be in the United States and remained determined to establish a company here and secure the appropriate visa to do so. His belief in the American Dream propelled him forward.

After obtaining an E-2 Investor Visa, Eric successfully established his company, Khan Funds, a billion-dollar investment firm based in New York City. Over the next several years, he focused on building his business and contributing to the American economy. "I believed in the American Dream, and I worked hard to make it a reality," Eric says with pride.

Becoming a Whistleblower

In 2017, everything changed. Eric learned of the scheme orchestrated by the CCP to steal semiconductor technology from the United States, a critical component in military applications. The pressure to cooperate was immense, and Eric knew the risks involved in resisting the CCP's demands. "They didn't give me a choice. It was either cooperate or face severe consequences," Eric recalls. Despite the overwhelming pressure, Eric made the brave and difficult decision to report his knowledge to the FBI, changing from successful businessman to whistleblower overnight.

This decision was rife with challenges. Eric recounts how his lack of familiarity with American legal and cultural norms led to mistakes during the early stages of his cooperation with the FBI. "At that moment, I made a lot of mistakes . . . again, because of cultural differences and my limited English," he admits. But Eric's resolve to do the right thing never wavered.

Facing Grave Dangers

Eric's decision to cooperate with the FBI immediately placed him and his family in great danger. He remembers a terrifying experience where someone pointed a gun at his head, sending a clear message from the CCP. "They hate me," Eric says, referring to the Chinese authorities. Despite these threats, Eric continued to work with the FBI, knowing the importance of the information he possessed. "I knew that what I was doing was right, and I was willing to take the risk to protect this country," he added.

Throughout his cooperation with the FBI, Eric struggled with the feeling of being left unprotected. He expressed frustration that, despite his significant contributions, he often felt abandoned by the very system he was helping. "I do sometimes feel unhappy and angry . . . I'm fighting for this country a lot, how did I end up in this situation?" Eric asks, reflecting on the delays and lack of protection he has received. This frustration is compounded by the fact that his asylum application, which should have been straightforward given his cooperation, has been repeatedly delayed.

Legal Battles and Continued Threats

Eric's situation has become even more precarious, now that he faces legal battles on multiple fronts. He described the constant lawsuits filed against him, designed to drain his financial resources and ability to fight back. "They threaten me with constant lawsuits to, you know, kill my money, kill my energy," Eric explains, noting the overwhelming pressure of fighting these battles without the security of an approved asylum status. Despite the setbacks, Eric remains determined to fight for his rights, believing that his asylum will eventually be granted, enabling him to better defend himself against these frivolous lawsuits.

The delays in his asylum case are particularly distressing for Eric, as they have left him and his family in a state of uncertainty for years. "My mom escaped from China, came to America in 2017. . . . Now she's almost 75. . . . My daughter was 8 years old, now 16. . . . Just two years until university," Eric laments, highlighting the long wait and the impact this experience has had on his family.

One of the most frustrating aspects for Eric is the lack of communication and response from the immigration authorities. He shares that the FBI called the asylum office multiple times, but there was no response. "The agent told me the FBI had called the American office at least six times, but nobody responded or replied to them," Eric said, sighing. This has only emphasized the feeling of abandonment he has experienced. Despite all of this struggle, Eric remains hopeful that his case will be resolved, expressing the deep need for resolution for himself and his family: "My family needs that. My daughter especially needs that."

International Attention, RICO, and Hope for Asylum

Eric's case has attracted international attention, with media outlets investigating the broader implications of his story. He mentions a news story from France's Intelligence Online, which discussed his case in the context of a larger investigation involving a private investigator and connections to Chinese intelligence.

Eric speculates about the possibility of "fighting in the RICO," referencing the Racketeer Influenced and Corrupt Organizations Act, a U.S. federal law enacted in 1970 to combat organized crime. RICO is a powerful tool because it allows for the prosecution of individuals and organizations involved in a pattern of criminal activity as part of a larger enterprise. Importantly, it permits leaders of a criminal enterprise to be held accountable for the crimes they ordered or facilitated, even if they did not directly commit the illegal acts themselves.

Under RICO, Eric would not bring an asylum claim, but could potentially pursue legal action against those who have targeted him, especially if their actions involved crimes such as extortion, fraud, or threats—offenses that are often included under RICO's purview. For instance, if Eric can demonstrate that a coordinated network of individuals or organizations systematically targeted him to suppress his whistleblowing efforts, and these actions meet the criteria of a criminal enterprise, he could seek both criminal and civil remedies under RICO. In a civil RICO case, Eric could file a lawsuit himself, potentially securing treble damages (triple the actual damages sustained) if he prevails.

The potential for RICO to address international actors lies in its reach. While it is a U.S. law, RICO can apply to individuals or entities outside the United States if their criminal activities have a significant impact on U.S. commerce or involve actions directed at individuals within the United States. In Eric's case, if he can provide evidence that his targeting was orchestrated by an international network with ties to organized crime or foreign intelligence, RICO could serve as a mechanism to hold these actors accountable in U.S. courts.

All that being said, pursuing a RICO case is an extremely daunting process. It requires demonstrating a "pattern of racketeering activity" involving at least two predicate criminal acts within a ten-year period and proving that these acts are connected as part of an overarching criminal enterprise. The law's stringent requirements mean that RICO cases are challenging to build, particularly when they involve international actors with sophisticated methods of concealment.

While RICO may address the injustices Eric has faced, it is separate from his efforts to seek asylum. RICO could hold those targeting Eric accountable, but asylum would offer him safety and the opportunity to rebuild his life in the United States.

Despite everything, Eric remains determined to continue his fight, not just for himself but for his family. He hopes that the U.S. government will recognize the sacrifices he has made and provide the protection he desperately needs. "I still hold out hope for asylum," he says, holding on to his belief that justice will ultimately prevail.

What Exactly Is Asylum and How Will It Help Eric?

Eric's path to asylum has been difficult, but his determination and continued legal support will almost certainly lead him to his destination. He remains committed to fighting for the protection and recognition he deserves, hoping that his story will inspire others to stand up for what is right, no matter the cost. But what exactly is asylum and how will it help Eric?

Asylum is a form of protection granted to foreign nationals who have fled their home country due to persecution or a well-founded fear of persecution on account of race, religion, nationality, membership in a particular social group, or political opinion. It is a critical component of international human rights law, designed to provide a safe haven for individuals who face threats to their life and liberty. In the United States, asylum is a legal status that allows individuals to remain in the country and eventually apply for permanent residency after one year of asylum status.

For Eric, obtaining asylum is not just a legal formality—it is a matter of life and death. As a whistleblower who exposed Chinese government efforts to conduct espionage on U.S. soil, Eric is considered a traitor by the CCP. If forced to return to China, he would likely face severe punishment, including imprisonment, torture, or even execution. The Chinese government has a long history of persecuting political dissidents and those who challenge its authority, and Eric's high-profile case makes him an even more significant target.

Asylum will offer Eric protection from deportation to China, ensuring that he and his family are kept as far as possible from the CCP's reach. Beyond physical safety, asylum will also grant Eric the right to work in the United States, allowing him to rebuild his life and continue contributing to the economy. This legal status will provide him with the stability and security he needs to recover from the years of fear, uncertainty, and financial loss that have plagued his life since he became a whistleblower.

Furthermore, asylum will enable Eric to apply for a green card after one year, paving the way for him to become a lawful permanent resident of the United States. This is a critical step toward eventual U.S. citizenship, which will fully integrate Eric into American society and afford him all the rights and protections that come with being a citizen. For someone who has risked everything to protect U.S. national security, this is a fitting reward for his courage and commitment.

Asylum will also have a profound impact on Eric's family. His daughter, who has grown up in the United States, will be able to continue her education and pursue her own dreams without the constant fear of being uprooted and sent back to a country where her family is in danger. Eric's wife and mother, who have also faced the stress and uncertainty of their precarious immigration status, will finally be able to live without the looming threat of deportation. The grant of asylum will provide them with the peace of mind they desperately need after years of living in fear.

Beyond personal safety and legal stability, asylum will allow Eric to continue advocating for human rights and exposing the truth about the CCP's activities. His case has already drawn international attention, and with the protection of asylum, he will be able to speak out more freely without fear of retribution. As a symbol of resistance against authoritarianism, Eric's story has the potential to inspire others who find themselves in similar situations, encouraging them to stand up for justice despite the risks.

Ultimately, asylum is a lifeline that will allow Eric to continue his fight for freedom, justice, and human dignity. It is the recognition that his actions have made a significant contribution to U.S. national security and that he deserves the protection and support of the country he has risked so much to defend. By granting him asylum, the United States will affirm its commitment to protecting those who stand up against tyranny and injustice.

Eric Dai's story sheds light on the challenges faced by individuals who choose to expose wrongdoing, particularly when dealing with different cultures and legal systems. With the support of Wildes & Weinberg, Eric continues to pursue his American Dream, all while ensuring that the critical information he provided helps protect the nation he now calls home.

CHAPTER 5

Empowering Advocates and Future Lawyers

Immigration law is a unique terrain where legal expertise intertwines with human connection and understanding. Unlike many other legal fields, the role of an immigration lawyer extends far beyond mere advocacy to include empathy, cultural sensitivity, and profound interpersonal relationships. Just as a psychiatrist explores the depths of their patient's psyche or an orthopedic surgeon meticulously tends to physical ailments, an immigration attorney is tasked with deciphering the complexities of their clients' lives, hopes, and aspirations.

In the examples of the psychiatrist and orthopedic surgeon, both are medical doctors. But you certainly wouldn't let a psychiatrist perform your back surgery, nor share your deepest, darkest secrets with your orthopedic surgeon. A psychiatrist needs to understand their patient in a different way than would a surgeon. There is an intimacy about such a relationship that must transcend the world of medicine in order to be successful—just as the relationship between an immigration attorney and their client must transcend the practical application of law.

Attorneys who practice other areas of law may disagree, but I wholeheartedly believe that immigration law is the most holistic and intimate area of law in existence, at least in the United States. Immigration law encompasses every other area of law, under the giant umbrella that is the American Dream. As an immigration attorney, to truly know your client is to know them as a friend. In some cases, it is to know them as family. Certainly, it is to revere them and treat them as such.

We have invited countless clients to our family table, from Yoko Ono and Sinead O'Connor to those we've represented pro bono. It is through these more casual interactions that we are best able to know them. Understanding an individual's hopes, fears, and aspirations allows us to handle their case with empathy and precision. In doing so, we not only advocate for their legal rights, but also become stewards of their dreams. This level of intimacy and trust is what sets immigration law apart. It's not just about legal procedures; it's about building relationships, fostering understanding, and empowering the human spirit.

If there is one lesson I would like aspiring immigration lawyers and advocates to walk away from this book with, it is this: Never underestimate the power of empathy and human connection in your practice. Always remember that your role extends beyond the courtroom. You are a confidant, a symbol of hope, and sometimes even a lifeline. Strive to understand your clients not just as cases, but as individuals with unique stories and dreams. In doing so, you will not only become a more successful immigration lawyer, but also create meaningful relationships that uplift the human spirit and shape the future of individuals and families, and of the world as a whole.

The Advocate's Guide to Success

Whether you are an immigration law student, a new lawyer, or simply an advocate for a more compassionate and inclusive immigration system, the guidance that follows can help you enhance your skills, make meaningful contributions to your community, and ultimately help create a better world.

Find a Mentor

One of the most important factors in the success of your career is to find a mentor. This is true of any field, but particularly so in navigating the complexity of the immigration system. A mentor provides guidance, support, and valuable insights that helps their mentee anticipate and handle the challenges of their profession. A good mentor will openly share their experiences, help you avoid common pitfalls, and encourage your professional development. Their mentorship can be instrumental in building your confidence and shaping your career path.

While finding a mentor organically is ideal, it's not always possible, at least not early in the process. Most of us will find a mentor organically at some point in our career. In the meantime, you can utilize formal mentorship programs, such as the American Immigration Lawyers Association (AILA) or local bar associations.

The AILA offers structured mentorship programs that connect new lawyers with experienced immigration attorneys, and many local bar associations have mentorship programs specifically tailored for new lawyers. These programs often include one-on-one mentorship, group mentoring sessions, and professional development workshops. Law school programs are also a great resource. Check if your school offers alumni mentorship programs or clinics where you can work under the guidance of seasoned practitioners.

If, however, you have your heart set on finding a mentor organically, you don't have to just sit back and wait for the stars to align. Improve your kismet by attending conferences, seminars, workshops, and networking events related to immigration law. Engage with speakers, panelists, and attendees who are experienced in the field. Express genuine interest in their work and ask thoughtful questions to establish a connection.

Join organizations such the National Immigration Project or local immigrant rights groups. Participate actively in their events and committees to meet potential mentors. Volunteer at immigration clinics, non-profits, or pro bono projects. Working alongside experienced attorneys in these settings can naturally lead to mentorship opportunities.

When you do find a potential mentor, it's important to approach them in a manner that's both respectful and professional. Do thorough research on their background, areas of expertise, and contributions to the field of immigration law. This shows respect for their time and demonstrates your genuine interest.

If you meet someone at an event or through mutual connections, start with a casual conversation. Express your admiration for their work and share your own aspirations and interests. After establishing an initial connection, ask if they would be willing to meet for coffee or a brief call to discuss their career and seek advice. Be respectful of their time and be clear about your goals and why you are seeking their mentorship. Specificity will help your potential mentor understand how they can assist you.

If the initial meeting goes well, express your interest in a more formal mentorship arrangement. You could say something like, "I've really appreciated your insights and guidance. Would you be open to mentoring me?" It's important to understand that experienced professionals have busy schedules. If they need time to consider your request, be patient. And be respectful if they decline. Thank them for their time and ask if they can recommend someone else who might be available. If, however, they agree to mentor you, follow up with a thank-you email and suggest setting up regular meetings or check-ins. Keep them updated on your progress and be proactive in seeking their advice. Be sure to respect their time and their boundaries, and establish parameters that both you and they are comfortable with.

Don't be dissuaded if they decline the initial request or if the mentorship relationship doesn't go as planned. All relationships are inherently complicated, including those between a mentor and mentee. Just as you aren't likely to have married your first boyfriend or girlfriend, you may strike out with your first mentor. But all relationships help us grow, and failure is an important part of the growth process. As long as you proceed with honesty, authenticity, and respect, even a failed mentor–mentee relationship can be very valuable.

Engage in Pro Bono Opportunities

Volunteering with pro bono organizations is an excellent way to gain hands-on experience, make meaningful contributions to the community, and develop your skills as an immigration lawyer or advocate. Below are just a few of the many organizations focused on immigrant and refugee rights.

Immigration Advocates Network (IAN)

- Volunteer to conduct legal research and draft briefs, memos, or other legal documents for cases involving asylum seekers, undocumented immigrants, and others in need of legal assistance.
- Participate in community outreach programs to educate immigrants about their rights and available legal resources. This might include conducting workshops, seminars, or informational sessions.
- Offer your time to answer questions and provide guidance through IAN's legal hotline, helping immigrants navigate complex legal processes.

Kids in Need of Defense (KIND)

- Volunteer to represent unaccompanied minors in immigration proceedings. This can involve preparing asylum applications, representing children in court, and advocating for their best interests.
- Mentor law students or new lawyers who are also volunteering with KIND, providing them with guidance and support as they work on cases.

- If you are bilingual, assist with translating documents or interpreting during client interviews to ensure clear communication.

International Refugee Assistance Project (IRAP)

- Volunteer to manage cases for refugees and displaced persons seeking resettlement or asylum. This includes gathering evidence, preparing applications, and coordinating with other legal and support services.
- Engage in policy advocacy work by drafting policy papers, participating in advocacy campaigns, and meeting with legislators to push for changes that benefit refugees and asylum seekers.
- Provide remote legal assistance to clients who are located in different parts of the world, utilizing technology to communicate and collaborate on their cases.

American Immigration Council (AIC)

- Get involved in impact litigation cases that challenge unjust immigration laws and policies. Work on high-profile cases that aim to create systemic change.
- Contribute to research projects and publications that highlight important issues in immigration law, helping to inform and shape public policy.

Pro Bono Resource Centers

- Volunteer at local legal clinics that offer free legal services to immigrants. Assist with screening clients, providing legal advice, and helping with form preparation.
- Conduct training sessions and workshops for other volunteers or community members on various aspects of immigration law and practice.

Asylum Seeker Advocacy Project (ASAP)

- Represent asylum seekers in their legal proceedings, including preparing asylum applications, representing them in court, and providing ongoing legal support.
- Join emergency response teams that provide immediate legal assistance to asylum seekers at borders or detention centers.

Local Non-Profits and Community Organizations

- Partner with local non-profits that serve immigrant communities to provide legal advice and support. This might include helping with visa applications, DACA renewals, or family reunification processes.
- Work with organizations that offer holistic services, including legal aid, social services, and mental health support, to provide comprehensive assistance to immigrant families.

Develop Language Skills

Improving proficiency in languages commonly spoken by immigrants is an invaluable asset for an immigration lawyer. Being able to communicate with clients in their own language not only facilitates clearer understanding and more effective representation, but also builds trust and rapport. Obviously, it's impossible to learn every language spoken by potential clients, but learning to speak at least one other language fluently, and even a few words in other common languages, can be immensely rewarding.

Understanding that they cannot reasonably rely on a single lawyer to speak the majority of languages spoken by clients, most immigration law firms will hire attorneys and support staff that can speak different languages. That way, there is always someone available who can communicate with clients in their native language.

And the benefits of learning another language go much deeper than professional success. Personal benefits include expanded social networks and travel opportunities, and improved memory, problem-solving skills, and creativity. If you decide to become bilingual (or trilingual), the following are among the most common languages spoken by immigration law clients. Determining which languages might be most beneficial to you can vary based on factors such as your geographic location or specific client bases that might have higher concentrations of particular immigrant communities.

Spanish

Spanish is the second-most spoken language in the United States. A significant portion of immigrants, particularly from Latin American countries such as Mexico, El Salvador, Guatemala, and Honduras, are Spanish speakers. Proficiency in Spanish allows you to communicate directly with a large number of clients, reducing reliance on interpreters and ensuring accurate understanding of their needs and circumstances.

Mandarin and Cantonese

Many immigrants from China and Taiwan speak Mandarin or Cantonese. These languages are among the most spoken languages globally. Speaking Mandarin or Cantonese can help you serve the Chinese-speaking immigrant community more effectively, understanding their cultural nuances and specific legal concerns.

Arabic

Arabic-speaking immigrants come from various countries in the Middle East and North Africa, including Syria, Iraq, Egypt, and Sudan. Knowledge of Arabic can help you address the needs of refugees and asylum seekers from conflict-affected regions, providing comfort and clarity during stressful legal processes.

Vietnamese

Vietnamese is commonly spoken among immigrants from Vietnam, many of whom have settled in the United States due to historical and political circumstances. Communicating in Vietnamese can enhance your ability to assist clients with unique immigration issues related to their specific background.

Korean

Korean-speaking communities are well-established in various parts of the United States, including major metropolitan areas. Understanding Korean can help you engage with this community, offering tailored legal advice and services.

Hindi and Urdu

These languages are widely spoken by immigrants from India and Pakistan. Proficiency in Hindi or Urdu can help you connect with South Asian clients, addressing their immigration needs with cultural sensitivity.

French and Creole

French is spoken by immigrants from countries such as Haiti, Senegal, and other parts of West Africa. Haitian Creole is particularly important for Haitian immigrants. Speaking French or Creole enables you to communicate with and better understand the unique challenges faced by these communities.

Why Language Skills Are So Helpful

Effective Communication

- Direct communication in the client's language ensures that legal advice and instructions are clearly understood, minimizing misunderstandings.
- Clients are more likely to share detailed and accurate information about their cases when they can express themselves comfortably in their native language.

Building Trust

- Speaking a client's language fosters trust and rapport, making them feel respected and valued.
- Clients often feel more at ease and confident when they can communicate without language barriers, especially during stressful legal proceedings.

Cultural Sensitivity

- Language skills often come with a better understanding of cultural nuances, which is crucial for providing culturally competent legal representation.
- Demonstrating effort to learn and use a client's language shows respect for their cultural background, which can greatly enhance the lawyer–client relationship.

Efficiency

- Reducing reliance on interpreters speeds up the legal process and ensures that no nuances are lost in translation.
- It can also reduce costs for both the client and the attorney by eliminating the need for translation services.

Broader Client Base

- Language skills allow you to serve a broader range of clients, expanding your practice and making your services more accessible to diverse communities.

- Being known as a multilingual attorney can enhance your reputation and attract more clients seeking language-specific legal services.

Engage in Advocacy and Policy Work

Advocacy and policy engagement are essential for affecting systemic change and promoting a more just and humane immigration system. Here are some practical examples of how you can contribute to these efforts.

Write Articles and Op-Eds

- Identify relevant newspapers, magazines, and online publications that cover immigration issues.
- Pitch articles or op-eds highlighting key immigration policy issues, sharing personal experiences or providing analysis and recommendations.
- Use your expertise and unique perspective to contribute valuable insights to public discourse.
- Start a blog or contribute to existing blogs focused on immigration law and policy.
- Share articles, analyses, and updates on social media platforms to reach a broader audience and spark discussions.
- Engage with readers and respond to comments to deepen understanding and promote dialogue.

Participate in Campaigns

- Identify advocacy organizations and grassroots movements focused on immigration reform.
- Volunteer your time and expertise to support their campaigns, events, and initiatives.
- Get involved in advocacy efforts such as rallies, marches, and lobbying efforts targeting policymakers.
- Sign and share online petitions advocating for specific policy changes or legislative reforms related to immigration.
- Participate in letter-writing campaigns urging elected officials to take action on pressing immigration issues.

- Encourage friends, family, and colleagues to join these efforts to amplify their impact.

Stay Informed and Participate in Discussions

- Stay informed about immigration policy changes, legal developments, and current events by following reputable news sources, academic journals, and policy briefings.
- Attend webinars, seminars, and conferences focused on immigration law and policy to deepen your understanding and stay updated on emerging issues.
- Participate in public forums, town hall meetings, and community discussions on immigration issues.
- Share your expertise, insights, and perspectives with policymakers, community leaders, and stakeholders to inform decision-making processes.
- Offer testimony at legislative hearings, providing evidence-based arguments and personal stories to advocate for policy reforms.

Collaborate with Other Advocates

- Collaborate with other advocates, lawyers, community organizers, and grassroots activists to amplify your advocacy efforts.
- Join or establish coalitions and working groups focused on specific immigration issues or policy priorities.
- Pool resources, share expertise, and coordinate advocacy strategies to maximize impact and drive meaningful change.
- Build relationships with policymakers, government officials, and key stakeholders involved in immigration policy.
- Foster partnerships with organizations and individuals who share your advocacy goals and can offer complementary expertise or resources.
- Leverage collective influence and support to advance shared policy objectives and advocate for the rights and dignity of immigrants.

Get Involved in the Community

Volunteering with local immigrant communities is not only a meaningful way to give back, but also a necessary step in becoming a more effective advocate for immigrant rights. Here are some of the many reasons why volunteering in immigrant communities is so important.

Understanding Their Challenges

- Volunteering allows you to directly interact with immigrants and refugees, gaining firsthand insight into their experiences, challenges, and needs.
- By listening to their stories and learning about their journeys, you develop a deeper understanding of the complexities of the immigration system and the barriers they face.

Becoming Culturally Competent

- Immigrant communities often have unique cultural norms, traditions, and communication styles.
- Volunteering provides an opportunity to immerse yourself in these cultural contexts, building cultural competence and sensitivity into your approach to legal assistance.

Providing Legal Assistance

- Many immigrants lack access to affordable legal representation due to financial constraints or language barriers.
- By volunteering your legal expertise, you help bridge this gap and ensure that vulnerable individuals have access to justice and fair treatment under the law.

Empowering Individuals and Families

- Offering free informational sessions and workshops empowers immigrants by equipping them with knowledge about their rights, legal options, and available resources.
- Empowered individuals are better equipped to navigate the complexities of the immigration system and make informed decisions about their future.

Building Trust and Relationships

- Volunteering builds trust and rapport with immigrant communities, demonstrating your commitment to serving their needs and advocating for their rights.

- Trust is essential for effective communication, collaboration, and partnership building in advocacy efforts.

Developing Long-Term Relationships

- Volunteering creates opportunities for long-term relationships with immigrant communities, fostering ongoing collaboration and support.
- As you build relationships based on trust and mutual respect, you become a trusted ally and resource for the community, enhancing your effectiveness as an advocate.

Strengthening the Community

- Volunteering contributes to the empowerment and resilience of immigrant communities by providing them with tangible support and resources.
- As immigrants become more informed and empowered, they can advocate for their own rights and contribute to building stronger, more cohesive communities.

Encouraging Collective Action

- Volunteering creates a sense of solidarity and collective action within immigrant communities, encouraging collaboration and mutual support.
- Through collective efforts, communities can amplify their voices, advocate for systemic change, and address common challenges more effectively.

Utilize a Client-Centered Approach

A client-centered approach is essential for providing effective legal representation in immigration law. It prioritizes the needs, concerns, and well-being of the client above all else, recognizing that each individual seeking immigration assistance brings with them unique circumstances, experiences, and aspirations.

Ultimately, a client-centered approach not only leads to more successful outcomes in individual cases, but also ensures that clients feel empowered, respected, and supported throughout the process. To successfully utilize a client-centered approach, one must begin with the following.

Developing Strong Interpersonal Skills

- Practice clear and concise communication with clients, using language that is accessible and easy to understand.
- Develop the ability to explain complex legal concepts in simple terms, ensuring that clients are fully informed about their rights and options.

Building Trust and Rapport

- Establish a welcoming and non-judgmental atmosphere in your interactions with clients, fostering trust and rapport from the outset.
- Take the time to get to know clients on a personal level, showing genuine interest in their stories, backgrounds, and aspirations.

Practicing Active Listening and Empathy

- Practice active listening by giving clients your full attention, maintaining eye contact, and nodding or using verbal cues to indicate understanding.
- Avoid interrupting or rushing clients during consultations, allowing them ample time to express their concerns and share their experiences.

Engaging with Empathy

- Cultivate empathy by putting yourself in the client's shoes and seeking to understand their perspectives, emotions, and motivations.
- Acknowledge and validate clients' feelings, demonstrating empathy and compassion in your interactions.

Responding with Reflection

- Use reflective listening techniques to clarify and validate clients' feelings and concerns.
- Reflect back what you have heard to ensure mutual understanding and show clients that you are actively engaged and empathetic to their needs.

Continuously Improving Skills

- Solicit feedback from clients, colleagues, and supervisors to identify areas for improvement and refine your client-centered approach.

- Actively listen to feedback with an open mind and willingness to learn and grow.

Participating in Professional Development

- Attend workshops, training programs, and seminars focused on interpersonal skills, communication techniques, and cultural competence.
- Stay informed about best practices in client-centered lawyering and incorporate new strategies and insights into your practice.

Engaging in Self-Reflection

- Utilize regular self-reflection to assess your strengths and weaknesses in client communication and empathy.
- Identify opportunities for growth and set specific goals for enhancing your client-centered skills.

Performing Role-Playing Exercises

- Engage in role-playing exercises with colleagues or mentors to practice active listening, empathy, and communication skills in simulated client interactions.
- Use feedback from these exercises to refine your approach and build confidence in your ability to effectively engage with clients.

Prioritize Self-Care and Resilience

There is no way around it—the field of immigration law can be quite demanding. Practicing self-care and cultivating resilience are essential for maintaining emotional and mental well-being. Taking care of yourself is not selfish; it's required for sustaining your passion and commitment to advocating for the rights and well-being of immigrants and refugees. Here are a few useful tools to help you prioritize self-care.

Look After Your Physical Well-Being

- Prioritize regular exercise, healthy eating habits, and sufficient sleep to support your physical health.
- Take breaks throughout the day to stretch, move your body, and recharge your energy.

Use Mindfulness and Relaxation Techniques

- Incorporate mindfulness practices such as meditation, deep breathing exercises, or yoga into your daily routine to reduce stress and promote mental clarity.
- Engage in activities that bring you joy and relaxation, whether it's reading, spending time in nature, or pursuing hobbies.

Set Boundaries

- Establish clear boundaries between work and personal life to prevent burnout and maintain a healthy work–life balance.
- Learn to say no to excessive work demands or commitments that may compromise your well-being.

Seek Social Support

- Lean on the support of peers, mentors, and trusted colleagues who understand the challenges of immigration law.
- Participate in support groups or professional networks where you can share experiences, seek advice, and receive encouragement.

Engage in Positive Self-Talk and Perspective

- Practice self-compassion and positive self-talk, acknowledging your efforts and strengths even in the face of setbacks or challenges.
- Cultivate a resilient mindset by reframing obstacles as opportunities for learning and growth, and maintaining a hopeful outlook for the future.

Seek Therapeutic Support

- Don't hesitate to seek professional counseling or therapy if you're struggling with persistent stress, anxiety, or other mental health concerns.
- A therapist can provide valuable support, guidance, and coping strategies to help you navigate the emotional demands of immigration law.

Self-Reflect

- Take time to reflect on your experiences, emotions, and coping mechanisms regularly.

- Identify triggers of stress or burnout and develop strategies to address them proactively.

Be Flexible and Adaptable

- Cultivate flexibility and adaptability in your approach to work and life, recognizing that challenges and setbacks are inevitable.
- Embrace change as an opportunity for growth and resilience building, rather than as a source of stress or uncertainty.

The Importance of Community Involvement

In addition to being an immigration lawyer, I am also the mayor of Englewood, New Jersey, where I also previously served on the City Council. While such a level of community involvement is not a prerequisite for success in immigration law, it has certainly benefited my career. There is frequent overlap between these two distinct roles because, as I mentioned earlier, immigration law encompasses nearly every aspect of the human experience. For instance, the letter in this section was addressed to me as Mayor Wildes, not Attorney Wildes, although I could have responded in either capacity.

Letters like the one that follows are common. Clients, community members, advocates, and concerned citizens frequently write to me seeking assistance with immigration matters, dispute resolution, human rights violations, advocacy for improved legislation, or community issues. I strive to respond to each inquiry with the same level of consideration and empathy. To be successful in both roles—as an immigration lawyer and as mayor—my clients, constituents, and community members must be like family to me. This perspective was instilled in me by my father, and it has been an invaluable lesson.

Viewing everyone as family has not only contributed to my professional success, but also enriched my personal relationships and overall sense of well-being. Growing up with my father's example has truly helped me see humanity as one interconnected whole. I don't merely imagine that my clients and constituents are family; I genuinely believe it.

Hi Mayor Wildes,

Thank you again for your time today and attention to the threat I received in our community. Before getting into the incident, I want to note that Dana and I have the privilege to live anywhere in the US—and we choose Englewood, NJ for a few reasons—the most important was the strong sense of community here. We first went to services in July at Ahavath Torah and we were impressed with how warm the community was, welcoming us with open arms, and Rabbi Poupko's wife dropped fresh challah off at our door on our first Shabbat here. We loved the community so much that we made a permanent move here 3 months ago. As you know, it's a strong, beautiful, connected and united community. We knew this was going to be our home and where we could raise proud, Jewish Israeli children. As mentioned, I signed a 20 year lease in downtown Englewood and will be opening a kosher pizza restaurant in the next few months. We're not going anywhere.

However, we received a violent, shocking, and hate-filled threat yesterday, in our home, and I won't tolerate it. Our community shouldn't tolerate it. I'm speaking up and taking action with the police because no one in our community should feel scared to walk around wearing a yarmulke, or dressed modestly, or shopping at a kosher store.

My wife and I will not tolerate threats based on our religious beliefs, nor should anyone in our community (Jewish or not).

Below is a summary of what occurred, if you would like any further information or detail, we will and can provide.

Best,

Shalev & Dana

Summary of Events—

On the afternoon of October 26th, Shalev was sitting on the back terrace of his apartment, reading the news on his phone. Suddenly, a resident from a unit on the 5th floor opened their window and asked Shalev if he was Jewish. Shalev, who wears a yarmulke, said "Yes" and the individual began shouting threats and anti-Semitic obscenities, including "Kill the Jews," "F*** the Jews," and "F*** Israel."

> Disturbed by the commotion, Shalev's wife, Dana, rushed onto the balcony. At this point, a second man appeared at the window, joining in with further obscenities and making obscene gestures towards them.
>
> Reacting quickly, Dana ran to the lobby of their apartment building to inform the management of the threats being made. Simultaneously, Shalev contacted the police. Later that day, both Dana and Shalev provided sworn statements to Detective Maciej Mlynaryk of the Englewood Police Department, detailing the incident. The management of the apartment building, along with its parent company, took the incident seriously and immediately addressed the situation.

I am deeply saddened to hear about the distressing incident my clients experienced in our tightly knit and wonderfully diverse community. The hateful threats and violence they endured are not only unacceptable, but also antithetical to the values of compassion, inclusivity, and respect that we hold dear.

As the mayor of Englewood, a fellow member of the Jewish community, and an immigration attorney, I stand with my clients in condemning all forms of hatred and bigotry. Their courage in speaking up and taking action sends a powerful message that such acts have no place in our community or anywhere else in this great nation. Furthermore, these events and the letter also point out, quite beautifully I might add, that despite the hateful actions of a few, the love and support of the larger community is immense.

While I am proud of my Jewish heritage, I am equally committed to upholding the principles of justice and kindness that define us as Americans and as humans. Regardless of our backgrounds or beliefs, we must unite against hate in all its forms and strive to create a world where everyone can live without fear of persecution or discrimination.

As my clients rightly pointed out, the strength of our community lies in our unity and support for one another. I commend them for their resilience and determination to stand up for what is right, even in the face of adversity.

In times of darkness, it is our collective resolve and compassion that will light the way forward. Let us continue to stand together, support one another, and uphold the values that define us as a community. We are, and always have been, one big family. When humanity awakens to this truth, the world will finally find peace.

Eugene Gasana's Story

Since the genocide of 1994, which claimed over half a million lives and left a painful and open wound on Rwanda's history, the nation has made remarkable progress in rebuilding its infrastructure and developing its economy. Despite these advancements, civil and political rights remain severely restricted, and freedom of expression is tightly controlled. Criticism of government policy or President Paul Kagame can lead to severe repercussions, not only within Rwanda, but also for those who have sought refuge abroad.

In October 2023, Human Rights Watch (HRW) released a report detailing how the Rwandan government continues to monitor and suppress dissidents beyond its borders. This extraterritorial repression includes a range of tactics, from threats and intimidation to more severe actions such as killings, beatings, kidnappings, and manipulated extradition requests. The findings highlight a disturbing pattern of international reach in Rwanda's efforts to silence opposition, raising significant concerns about the global implications of these severe violations of human rights.

The HRW investigation revealed the extensive reach of the Rwandan government's oppressive tactics against dissidents living abroad. These tactics include online harassment, physical abuse, the misuse of law enforcement, and threats against family members. This orchestrated campaign has created a pervasive environment of fear, leading many Rwandans abroad to practice self-censorship and live in constant fear of attacks against them or their relatives in Rwanda. These findings highlight the chilling impact on those who, despite being thousands of miles away, cannot escape the long arm of repression.

My law office became intimately familiar with the Rwandan government's abuse of power when we were approached by one of its most prominent dissidents, Eugene Gasana, the former Rwandan permanent representative to the United Nations in New York City. Gasana, who was once part of President Kagame's close entourage, faced severe repercussions after he spoke out against Kagame's decision to amend the constitution and run for a third term in the 2017 election. His outspoken stance led to his removal as ambassador, after which he was summoned back to Rwanda. Refusing to comply, Gasana came to Wildes & Weinberg and applied for U.S. lawful permanent resident status, which was granted in 2018.

Gasana's refusal to return to Rwanda triggered a series of personal, professional, and financial attacks against him and his family still in Rwanda. Authorities swiftly seized his bank accounts and land in Rwanda. Compounding his troubles, a few months later, he faced allegations of rape and sexual harassment from a former employee, Benita Uruhisho, who claimed that Gasana assaulted her in 2014 while she worked at the U.N. mission. During the investigation into these allegations, conducted by the New York County District Attorney's Office Sex Crimes Unit, the involvement of senior Rwandan government authorities quickly became evident. The case was closed and no criminal charges were filed against Gasana.

But the Rwandan government was just getting started. In 2019, Benita Uruhisho filed a civil complaint against Gasana, seeking punitive damages. Then, in 2020, Rwanda's prosecutor general issued an international arrest warrant for Gasana that temporarily led to the issuance of an Interpol Red Notice. However, after further review, the Interpol commission determined that Gasana's files should be deleted from Interpol's database, saying, "[t]here is a predominant political dimension to this case and that the retention of the data would not be compliant with Article 3 of INTERPOL's Constitution."[1]

Following the publication of the HRW report, Uruhisho's attorneys were ordered to produce the invoices for her legal fees. Not surprisingly, they were signed by the Rwandan government. But just in case there is still any question as to the benefactor of her ongoing accusations against Gasana, the following is a statement made by Uruhisho's counsel during a 2023 court hearing:

> *I can tell you that our invoices are sent via e-mail to our client and as the affidavit says, the invoices are sent to the Witness Services Victim Unit of the National Prosecution Authority as it said in the affidavit. [. . .] At any rate, Your Honor, we're representing to you that the payments are coming from Rwanda, the National Prosecution Authority of Rwanda. Our payments are when—when we receive our payment is from the Republic of Rwanda, so the issue about who is paying the fees, it is the Republic of Rwanda. We are not hiding that.*[2]

In 2017, I was approached at a private event by Brigadier General Patrick Karuretwa, who served as Kagame's personal principal private secretary until 2021. Since then, this man has been head of the Rwanda Defense Force's International Military Cooperation—so, an important player in Rwanda's military and diplomatic circles.

Karuretwa was in attendance at a dinner arranged by one of my friends. He approached me and said that Gasana was involved in abuse in Congo and that he was "bad news" and I should be careful in representing him. He went

---

1. John Holmes, "Join Us Or Die": Rwanda's Extraterritorial Repression, Human Rights Watch (Oct. 10, 2023), https://www.hrw.org/report/2023/10/10/join-us-or-die/rwandas-extraterritorial-repression?utm_source=chatgpt.com.

2. Testimony of Lewis Mudge, *Transnational Repression by Rwanda* (Feb. 15, 2024), https://www.hrw.org/news/2024/02/15/transnational-repression-rwanda?utm_source=chatgpt.com.

on to say that Gasana would not face criminal charges if he returned quietly to Rwanda, and that Kagame is understanding and forgiving and a good president. The entire incident was unnerving and felt more like the trailer to a Hollywood thriller. But it was real life.

While Karuretwa's words were obviously meant to intimidate me into dropping Gasana's case, I stood firm in my decision to represent him. Seeing firsthand the lengths to which the Rwandan government would go to silence its critics only reinforced my resolve to defend Gasana, and others who make the courageous decision to stand up against tyranny.

Also in 2017, Gasana's siblings in Rwanda were detained for several weeks and later accused of fraud and transferred to a Kigali prison. No evidence was presented against them and no judicial process occurred. They were simply held without due process, as the Rwandan government willingly exploited the legal system. Although Gasana's siblings were released two months later, several of his relatives' passports have been confiscated, making it impossible for them to leave Rwanda. So they remain trapped there, essentially hostages, waiting for the next major disruption to their lives. They live in a state of constant uncertainty and fear, knowing that their basic rights and freedoms will likely be violated again, without recourse.

There is no doubt in my mind that the world would be a better place if more people chose to confront injustice and defend the fundamental rights of fellow humans, no matter the personal cost, like Eugene Gasana. I also understand that the decision to take a stand is often at the expense of not only personal safety, but also the safety and well-being of loved ones. I do not look down upon those who choose to comply with oppressive regimes out of fear for their families. Instead, I aim to provide support and amplify the voices of those who speak out. By standing in solidarity with these brave individuals, we may give others the will to follow suit.

Gasana's case illustrates how far the Rwandan government is willing to go to destroy its opponents. To fulfill their mission, they will work tirelessly and relentlessly to diminish their target's professional prospects, drain their finances, and turn them into a social pariah. They will keep going and going until the target is worn down and can no longer fight or even speak out. And their resources seem infinite.

If Gasana was the only such case, it would be bad enough. But he is one of many. By speaking out, he exposes the systemic abuse and persecution faced by countless others who have dared to oppose the regime. His courage galvanizes international support for those who continue to suffer in silence.

Despite the many challenges he has endured and continues to face, Eugene Gasana remains a key figure in the fight against the Rwandan government's repressive tactics. His case is the perfect example of how the practice of immigration law often goes much deeper than the individual or family we represent; sometimes, a single case becomes a fight for human rights on a global scale. A single case could dramatically alter the actions of oppressive regimes, saving lives and livelihoods, and literally changing the course of history.

Interview with Eugene Gasana

Conducted by Amy Lane Singh

(A) Tell me about your experience working with Mike.

(E) I was actually lucky to find Mike. I went somewhere else first, spent two or three months going in circles with another lawyer. Then Danny Ayalon, the former Israeli ambassador, said, you should go see Mike.

Mike immediately received me, and it was like this family relationship from the start.

I mean, where else do you see an immigration lawyer invite you to his son's wedding?

He integrated us into his family, and he was so protective, so friendly.

(A) Did Mike do anything that really just blew your mind?

(E) Yes, so many things. It was a very complicated case; Mike was getting a lot of pressure from the government of Rwanda to drop my case. He could have easily decided not to represent me, and I think most lawyers would have. You know, even friends will betray you for easy money or because they're being threatened. But not Mike. He refused.

The craziest thing is, he never even told me this was happening! For six years, he was being pressured by Kagame, and I only found out when I read about it in the Human Rights Watch article! Mike never mentioned it, that's the kind of guy he is. He stood firm, and I owe him. Big time.

He was always very professional, but also like a brother. One of the very few people who was there for me through all of this.

Mike also seemed to be able to work miracles. My oldest son was about to turn 21, and we didn't have his green card yet. His birthday was on October 5th, and would you believe, Mike got that green card on October 4th. I don't know how he did it. It was a miracle.

(A) What can other immigration lawyers and law students learn from Mike?

(E) What makes Mike unique is that while he is extremely professional, he is also human. So very human. You don't see a lawyer in front of you, not at all. You see a human being like you. But the whole time he says things like, no worries, we will get it.

You know you are in good hands, professional hands. But you also feel like you're there with a friend. Like he's your brother. And this is very important, especially for someone dealing with immigrants. They are not just clients looking for a professional to say 1 + 1 = 2. They are there to be rescued. You are their rescuer.

Immigration lawyers and law students should know this—your clients need to see your humanity first, and they need to trust you, completely. Everything else comes second. When I first met Mike, he didn't ask me about money. He asked about my kids.

I liked and trusted Mike from the beginning.

EPILOGUE
A LIFE WELL LIVED

Remembering My Father, Attorney Leon Wildes

As I sit down to write these words, my heart weighs heavy with both sorrow and immense pride. In the winter of early 2024, we bade farewell to a beloved father and grandfather, mentor, and true guardian of justice—my father, Attorney Leon Wildes.

Leon Wildes at Benjamin N. Cardozo School of Law. *(Photo courtesy of the Wildes family archive.)*

Growing up, I witnessed firsthand the incredible dedication and passion with which my father approached his work. His commitment to justice was not just a profession but a calling—a calling that would manifest itself in one of the most pivotal moments of his career: the case of John Lennon.

In the world of immigration law, my father's name will forever be synonymous with the landmark case that prevented the unjust deportation of the iconic musician. Faced with insurmountable odds and political pressures, my dad fought fearlessly and advocated tirelessly for Lennon's right to remain in the country he loved.

But my father's legacy extends far beyond this singular victory. Throughout his career, he dedicated himself to defending the rights of immigrants from all walks of life. His firm became a sanctuary for those seeking refuge and protection in a world often fraught with uncertainty and prejudice.

Impressive as the countless legal victories and accolades may be, it is not my father's professional achievements that I will remember most dearly. It is the love, compassion, and integrity with which he lived his life that leaves an eternal mark on my soul. Today, this is my greatest comfort.

To me, my father was more than just an accomplished attorney—he was my guiding light, my confidant, and my hero. His love and support shaped me into the person and the lawyer I am today, instilling in me values of empathy, compassion, and hard work that will guide me for the rest of my days.

As I mourn the loss of my father, I take solace in knowing that his legacy will endure through the countless lives he touched and the principles he so passionately defended. Though the world may mourn the loss of such a great man, I will forever cherish the memories of a loving father whose kindness, wisdom, and spirit will continue to inspire me and countless others for generations to come.

The excerpt below, written by my father, Leon Wildes, provides a glimpse into his early life and the formative experiences that shaped his remarkable journey. My grandfather's entrepreneurial spirit and pride in being an "American by choice" deeply influenced my dad's worldview. Despite being the only Jewish child in his class, his upbringing instilled in him a profound appreciation for the values of middle America and the ideals of his adopted country. This experience undoubtedly taught my father the importance of a welcoming community.

From humble beginnings in a small town, and then a small office, my father embodied the quintessential American success story. His advocacy for immigrants' rights and his instrumental role in some of the most important cases of modern times have not only shaped the course of individual lives, but have also contributed to the very fabric of American society. Through his work, my father has not only defended the dreams of his clients but has also championed the fundamental principles upon which the American Dream is built.

> I was born and raised in a small coal-mining town in Pennsylvania. Olyphant had no more than a population of 10,000 in its heyday, mainly Polish and Ukrainian miners and their industrious families. I was the only Jewish kid in my class.
>
> My father referred to himself on official forms as a "merchant." But he prided himself on being a "peddler," taking his wares door to door in the more remote, even smaller towns that surrounded Olyphant. He always referred to himself as an "American by choice" compared to his children, who being born in this country, were merely "American by chance." My father cherished his adopted country and all that it stood for.

I was raised with the values of middle America, in an atmosphere where almost every high school graduate enlisted in the Armed Forces, where Franklin D. Roosevelt was a virtual deity, and the United States government could do no wrong. In the clothing store where I was practically raised, a large portrait of FDR held the place of honor. For twelve years, in Olyphant's public schools, I pledged allegiance to a flag which we all deeply respected.

As young children during World War II, we did knitting for an afghan which was to be sent to an army base, collected flattened tin cans for the war effort, and put all the money we could scrape together into United States Savings Bonds. I wrote daily airmail letters to a cousin serving in the Pacific and followed with close attention how the Allies, the forces of good in the world, battled the forces of evil. Just like the cowboy movies we watched, we knew who wore the white hats.

My father early on told my brother and myself that his little business held no future for us, and that he would pay for all the education we needed to find something better for ourselves. My brother attended St. Thomas Aquinas University in nearby Scranton and went off to medical school in Chicago. When I expressed an interest in studying religious subjects at Yeshiva University in New York, I had my family's highest blessings.

But when I started considering law school instead of the rabbinate, only my father supported that notion. According to my mother, "lawyers starved three times a day from hunger." No one in our family had ever gone into that profession. But, believing in the great American adventure, its system of justice, my dad urged me on despite a lack of funds.

I recall telling him that a tuition scholarship to the New York University School of Law had decided me on attending there. My dad called, knowing that I had been admitted to more prestigious law schools. "I know that you would prefer to go to Harvard, and I don't want you to be concerned about the money. We have plenty of money, and you don't need to look for a scholarship." In actuality, he was still paying back a loan to his brother-in-law for my college education.

Studying at Yeshiva University broadened my horizons considerably yet reinforced Olyphant's values. Despite the fact that among young New Yorkers, I considered myself less than sophisticated, the university was dedicated to proving that traditional religious and moral values were very much at home in the American environment. It's no coincidence that most of the nation's Jewish Army Chaplains came from my alma mater.

As I approached graduation from college, the question of what I wanted to do with my life became much more real and poignant. I discussed the scholarship and my father's offer to pay for Harvard Law School with my student adviser, Professor Linn, and he advised me to accept the NYU scholarship. The professor thought that I needed the toughening and sophisticating atmosphere of a competitive New York school. He was probably right.

Law school further deepened my appreciation of Olyphant's homely values, helping me gain the tools to become part of the most wonderful system of civil justice in the world. I dormed with scholarship students from other parts of the country, all of them destined to join the top echelon of America's legal community.

As I neared graduation from Law School, I considered taking a position with a federal agency such as the FBI, The Department of State, or a similar government job. My dad, of course, encouraged all of my plans. But those jobs were basically in Washington, DC, and my hope was to live in a religious Jewish community in the New York area, so I opted for a job in private practice. But after a year or so, I went back for a degree in corporate law at the NYU Graduate School of Law's evening program.

At the time, Professor Elmer Fried taught the only available course on immigration law—not just at NYU, but in the whole country. No other law school had such a class. The course description fascinated me. Some of the people who needed the help of an immigration lawyer were the most disadvantaged in society, and such a lawyer's assistance came at the very moment of their greatest need.

Professor Fried brought a genuine insight to the course, and I found his lectures fascinating. So, when I noticed an index card on the bulletin board advertising a possible job in the field, I went to discuss it with him.

The job was with HIAS, the Hebrew Immigrant Aid Society. I knew the organization not only helped Jewish people to migrate but also taught these newcomers the American way. The notice sought an attorney with fluency in either Yiddish or Hebrew.

I asked Professor Fried if this was a good opportunity for a young attorney to learn more about immigration law. He warned that the experience might be frustrating—HIAS, like many of the voluntary agencies doing pro bono immigration work, does not generally challenge the government, sue in federal court when aliens' rights were abrogated, or take forceful positions against government action.

However, he certainly confirmed that it was a place where I would learn a lot about immigration law.

I applied for the job and got it immediately. HIAS gave me the opportunity to spend a full year studying and working with immigration law exclusively. The caseload assigned to me hardly took a quarter of my daily work time, and I was free to study and research any and all of the issues raised in my cases.

I also used my time at home to draft an article which I intended to publish in The New York Law Journal, which accepted my handwritten manuscript. It dealt with a subject that had perplexed me. U.S. immigration law established that the Secretary of State could review all the work of his department's Consular Officers—except for granting or denying of U.S. visas. This left an area of decision with no review.

The courts, rather than provide the review themselves as suggested by other federal legislation, took the position that since the Secretary of State had no review authority, they should certainly not review consular visa denials. I disagreed completely with that analysis, discussing the remedies available for persons whose visas had been denied. The article apparently filled an important need in the legal community and made some valid suggestions for the Immigration Bar.

I received a call from Edith Lowenstein, the editor of Interpreter Releases, the most important publication in the immigration field, asking for permission to republish the article. I readily agreed. Officials of the State Department must have seen the republished article, and I later understood that it was being used as a text for a six-week course given to future visa officers.

I learned a lot and accomplished some good during my year at HIAS, but Professor Fried's admonition was well-taken—I became increasingly disappointed with the fact that HIAS would not pursue its clients' claims in court, always maintaining a high level of cooperation with the U.S. government. I decided to call my old professor and explore the possibilities of a job in private immigration practice.

Fried was an adjunct professor, meaning that he was in active practice while teaching a course in his field during the evening. He was very well regarded in the field and knew all the potential offices where I might apply for a position. Generously, he introduced me to three of the very few lawyers who both practiced privately in the immigration field and had enough work to employ another attorney. All three granted me interviews, but no job offers followed.

When I discussed this with the professor, he assured me that all the lawyers were impressed with my qualifications, but they feared that I might end up leaving them to open my own office—and they'd lose both my services and their clientele.

Fried suggested that I open my own office. I had the guts to do so, and I had accumulated $5,000 in a bank directly across the street from HIAS. I've never quite figured out how I managed to live during my year at HIAS and still have practically my full salary at the end of it. I guess the answer lies in teaching bar-mitzva lessons and the occasional legal work I got from friends and acquaintances, drafting a will here and there, handling a contract, a real estate closing, or some other business which sustained me during that crucial period.

My first clients in private practice gave me the opportunity for something I had long desired—a visit to Israel. During the summer of 1960, I was retained by the parents of two young men who had lost their American citizenship while abroad. They had gone to help establish a Jewish homeland when the State of Israel was founded. When they failed to respond to notices sent by their American draft boards in the early 1950s, they were considered to be delinquents. In fact, they were eventually served with notices by the United States Embassy in Tel Aviv that they had lost their American citizenship on the ground of having remained abroad to evade service in the United States military.

This created a special difficulty. Persons who lost citizenship under that provision of the immigration law could not come back to the United States, even though their parents were American citizens who could ordinarily sponsor their return.

I traveled to Israel for an eight-week journey with the two young men whose parents had retained me. They served as my guides and companions. In an old jalopy, which one of them was qualified to repair as a mechanic, we wandered across the entire country, and I succeeded in touring Israel in a way which surpassed all subsequent visits. During our travels, they explained that they had served in Israel's War of Independence upon first arriving in 1948.

The research that I had done in anticipation of the trip really paid off. The Nationality Act of 1940 had been interpreted to hold that when a person commits an act of expatriation, the loss of his citizenship is automatic and does not require the confirmation of the U.S. government. Well, the young men's service in the Israeli army was also an automatic ground for loss of U.S. citizenship. Since that took place several years before the draft notices arrived, they had already lost their citizenship and could not be punished for draft evasion. I explained to them that I might be able to resolve their situation if I could prove that their service in the Israeli army was actual and voluntary.

We then proceeded to try and get that proof. The Israeli Army had a distinct aversion to confirming in writing that these boys had served, as they believed that could hurt them in their dealings with the United States government. After an extensive discussion of the law with an Israeli official who was a Ph.D., I convinced him that it was in their interests and in the interests of their families that his government actually confirm their service.

After my wonderful tour with my two young friends, I returned to the United States armed with proof of the fact that they had lost their citizenship before the grounds claimed by the State Department occurred, so they could now be sponsored by their families to arrive as aliens.

My brief to the Board of Passport Review of the U.S. Department of State was truly a brief one. When I appeared before the Board, I awaited the acknowledgment of the elderly chairman of the panel before I began my argument. Each of the nine members had a copy of my brief with the official Israeli confirmation of my clients' service in the Israel Army.

Finally, the chairman of the board looked up and said, "We have considered your presentation. It is indeed highly unusual for an attorney to appear before us wishing to prove that his client actually lost American citizenship. Your argument is accepted by us. This board finds that your clients lost their American citizenship by serving in the armed forces of Israel in 1948."

The chairman continued, "I trust that you are now going to go across the hall at this time." I had already noticed the location of the Department of State's Visa Office and took the comment to mean that the chairman expected me to start the process of bringing my clients to the United States through the petition of their American citizen parents. Accordingly, I responded, "Yes, I believe that I will."

Upon leaving the board, I entered the visa office waiting room, where the receptionist said, "You are expected by Mr. Auerbach across the hall." That puzzled me. I had heard of Dr. Frank Auerbach, an immigration scholar who had published the first and only textbook in existence at that time on Immigration Law. I knew that he was a former

HIAS employee as well, but I was totally surprised that not only was so important a personality in my field aware that I was in Washington but also expected to meet with me.

Frank Auerbach, an impressive gray-haired gentleman, rose from behind his desk to greet me. "I have been anxious to meet you since I first read your article in Interpreter Releases. You know, we have made good use of that article in training our Consular Officers in visa work.

"I also was quite impressed with your approach to the citizenship cases which, I trust, you have just argued before the Passport Review Board. Would you be interested in becoming an attorney with our staff at the State Department? I think we would have a position available for you."

I was dumbfounded. I practiced with HIAS for a year and perhaps an additional year on my own, and now the Director of the Visa Office of the U.S. Department of State himself, this distinguished scholar and government official, actually offered me a job!

"I'm more than flattered," I responded, "but I would have to give your kind offer some consideration and get back to you, if that would be okay." He agreed, explaining that he would be delighted to have me on board and that I should feel free to call him if I had any further questions.

I returned to New York on a cloud to think over this offer. More likely, I was in a state of shock.

In the end, I stuck with private practice, and in a few short years, I managed to save enough money to afford a real office. I took a beautiful large room in a suite at 355 Lexington Avenue, had it carpeted professionally, and moved in. My rental was $350 a month, but this was partially paid by a dear friend, Bill Volin, who was counsel to a butcher's union which allowed him a private practice as well. He covered $100 of the rent each month, but only came in once or twice a week to meet with a private client in the office. I devised a method to permit the room to look like it was his on a full-time basis. Whenever he called to inform me that he was bringing in a client, I would replace the name on my door with a plate showing Bill's and take my diplomas from over the desk and transfer his. Then, when he arrived, I would hand him some mail as though I was his law clerk, explain that his clients were all under control and that if he needed me, I would be in the library. The system worked perfectly to keep my overhead under control to such an extent that I felt that I could risk marrying Ruth.

I built up a small reputation with diligent work and successful outcomes for my clients. My article on visa denials also resulted in a good number of referrals from other attorneys, who gave me their "impossible" cases. Through extraordinary effort, I was uniformly successful in the cases given me, and my clients in turn referred relatives and friends who needed help.

When Elmer Fried, my former Immigration Law professor, told me that he was looking for office space and asked whether I would be interested in joining him, I hastened to do so, and called upon another dear friend, David Fund, who was both an accountant and an attorney, to sign a lease at 515 Madison Avenue, where I have now maintained my offices for over four decades.

Having access to Elmer Fried, whose knowledge in the immigration field was extraordinary, and to David Fund, whose experience in corporate and business matters was unsurpassed, I was taking my practice to a new level in top-notch company.

While at this point in my career I was still accepting cases in almost any field of law, I felt that the privilege of handling immigration matters for clients, their relatives, employers, friends, and acquaintances, was the most gratifying of all my legal efforts. Assisting a person to regularize his immigration status and get started on life in a new country is the most rewarding kind of work one can imagine. Many of my clients became employers themselves, and in turn sponsored other non-citizens. Corporations, banks, and industrial concerns sought out our services based upon their favorable experience in sponsoring one of our clients.

I began to hire young attorneys, paralegals, and other staff, always with some trepidation when it involved increasing the costs of running the office, but always seeking out the best and brightest people that I could find to assist me in my work. In 1960, I formed a partnership with Steven Weinberg, a talented immigration lawyer, and we have practiced together ever since as Wildes & Weinberg. My son Michael joined us in 1993 and became a partner in 1996.

Following the example of Elmer Fried, I happily accepted the invitation of the Benjamin N. Cardozo School of Law to teach Immigration Law, lecturing on the subject for thirty-three years. In 1970 I was elected national president of the American Immigration Lawyers Association, the bar association in my field. In fact, it was shortly after completing my term in office that I got the call to consult with John Lennon and Yoko Ono about their immigration problem.

> I think I can say that my career pretty well fit the daydream of an All-American success story for a kid from Olyphant. With this case, though, I found myself defending not just John and Yoko's personal dreams, but the foundation of the American Dream itself.

In honoring the life and legacy of my father, Attorney Leon Wildes, let us not only celebrate his remarkable achievements, but also strive to carry forward his vision of a world where justice, compassion, and equality prevail. In doing so, we honor not only his memory, but the timeless values he held dear.

Leon and John Lennon leaving court.
(Photo courtesy of the Wildes family archive.)

Rest in peace, dear father, knowing that your legacy will forever shine as a light of hope and inspiration in a world that sorely needs it. Your light lives on in the hearts of all who had the privilege of knowing you. Until we meet again, may your spirit soar free, knowing that your life was indeed a life well lived.

INDEX